MAXINE HONG KINGSTON

Maxine Hong Kingston. Photo by Jane Scherr. Courtesy of Jane Scherr and University of California, Berkeley.

MAXINE HONG KINGSTON

A Critical Companion

E. D. Huntley

CRITICAL COMPANIONS TO POPULAR CONTEMPORARY WRITERS
Kathleen Gregory Klein, Series Adviser

Greenwood Press
Westport, Connecticut • London

Library of Congress Cataloging-in-Publication Data

Huntley, E. D.
    Maxine Hong Kingston : a critical companion / by E.D. Huntley.
      p. cm.—(Critical companions to popular contemporary writers, ISSN 1082–4979)
    Includes bibliographical references and index.
    ISBN 0–313–30877–2 (alk. paper)
    1. Kingston, Maxine Hong—Criticism and interpretation. 2. Women and
literature—United States—History—20th century. 3. Chinese American women in
literature. 4. Chinese Americans in literature. I. Title. II. Series.
PS3561.I52Z695 2001
813'.54—dc21   00–034113

British Library Cataloguing in Publication Data is available.

Library of Congress Catalog Card Number: 00–034113
ISBN: 0–313–30877–2
ISSN: 1082–4979

First published in 2001

Greenwood Press, 88 Post Road West, Westport, CT 06881
An imprint of Greenwood Publishing Group, Inc.
www.greenwood.com

Printed in the United States of America

The paper used in this book complies with the
Permanent Paper Standard issued by the National
Information Standards Organization (Z39.48–1984).

10 9 8 7 6 5 4 3 2 1

For all of the Women Warriors whom I have encountered along the way—Sarah Brabant, Betty Brown, Joan Brown, Judith Domer, Charmazel Dudt, Mary Dunlap, Lisabel Huntley, Janet Lembke, Joyce Lawrence, Elisa Manalaysay, and Jane Solem—*Thank You* for inspiring, mentoring, supporting, and believing in me.

And for Aisha Nicole Ahmad and Alyssa Noelle Ahmad, who will be Women Warriors one day.

Contents

Series Foreword

The authors who appear in the series Critical Companions to Popular Contemporary Writers are all best-selling writers. They do not simply have one successful novel, but a string of them. Fans, critics, and specialist readers eagerly anticipate their next book. For some, high cash advances and breakthrough sales figures are automatic; movie deals often follow. Some writers become household names, recognized by almost everyone.

But their novels are read one by one. Each reader chooses to start and, more importantly, to finish a book because of what she or he finds there. The real test of a novel is in the satisfaction its readers experience. This series acknowledges the extraordinary involvement of readers and writers in creating a best-seller.

The authors included in this series were chosen by an Advisory Board composed of high school English teachers and high school and public librarians. They ranked a list of best-selling writers according to their popularity among different groups of readers. For the first series, writers in the top-ranked group who had received no book-length, academic, literary analysis (or none in at least the past ten years) were chosen. Because of this selection method, Critical Companions to Popular Contemporary Writers meets a need that is being addressed nowhere else. The success of these volumes as reported by reviewers, librarians, and teachers led to an expansion of the series mandate to include some writers with wide critical attention—Toni Morrison, John Irving, and Maya Angelou, for example—to extend the usefulness of the series.

The volumes in the series are written by scholars with particular expertise in analyzing popular fiction. These specialists add an academic focus to the popular success that these writers already enjoy.

The series is designed to appeal to a wide range of readers. The general reading public will find explanations for the appeal of these well-known writers. Fans will find biographical and fictional questions answered. Students will find literary analysis, discussions of fictional genres, carefully organized introductions to new ways of reading the novels, and bibliographies for additional research. Whether browsing through the book for pleasure or using it for an assignment, readers will find that the most recent novels of the authors are included.

Each volume begins with a biographical chapter drawing on published information, autobiographies or memoirs, prior interviews, and, in some cases, interviews given especially for this series. A chapter on literary history and genres describes how the author's work fits into a larger literary context. The following chapters analyze the writer's most important, most popular, and most recent novels in detail. Each chapter focuses on one or more novels. This approach, suggested by the Advisory Board as the most useful to student research, allows for an in-depth analysis of the writer's fiction. Close and careful readings with numerous examples show readers exactly how the novels work. These chapters are organized around three central elements: plot development (how the story line moves forward), character development (what the reader knows of the important figures), and theme (the significant ideas of the novel). Chapters may also include sections on generic conventions (how the novel is similar to or different from others in its same category of science fiction, fantasy, thriller, etc.), narrative point of view (who tells the story and how), symbols and literary language, and historical or social context. Each chapter ends with an "alternative reading" of the novel. The volume concludes with a primary and secondary bibliography, including reviews.

The alternative readings are a unique feature of this series. By demonstrating a particular way of reading each novel, they provide a clear example of how a specific perspective can reveal important aspects of the book. In the alternative reading sections, one contemporary literary theory—way of reading, such as feminist criticism, Marxism, new historicism, deconstruction, or Jungian psychological critique—is defined in brief, easily comprehensible language. That definition is then applied to the novel to highlight specific features that might go unnoticed or be understood differently in a more general reading. Each volume defines two or three specific theories, making them part of the reader's understanding of how diverse meanings may be constructed from a single novel.

Taken collectively, the volumes in the Critical Companions to Popular Contemporary Writers series provide a wide-ranging investigation of the complexities of current best-selling fiction. By treating these novels seriously as both literary works and publishing successes, the series demonstrates the potential of popular literature in contemporary culture.

Kathleen Gregory Klein
Southern Connecticut State University

Acknowledgments

My intense gratitude goes to a great many individuals.

Maxine Hong Kingston, for writing *The Woman Warrior* just when I needed to read such a memoir.

Georgia Rhoades, T.J. Arant, and Nancy Origer, for friendship.

Michele Croteau, Laurie Lyda, and Laurin Blanks, for invaluable research assistance. Laurie, again, for proofreading and the index.

Candace Brennan, Cara Ernst, Maria Richardson, Deanna Shelor, Toni Caicedo, Ellen Perry, and Ruskin Storrs, for insights, discussions, ideas, and debates about dual identities and discovering a genuine voice.

Margaret Kilgore, for keeping my schedule from getting too tangled.

Kathleen Gregory Klein, for getting me involved in this project.

Lynn Malloy, for astute reading, editorial guidance, diplomacy, and all-around much-needed help with the final manuscript.

And always, David Huntley, for everything! And Beowulf and Thurber, for everything else.

The Life of Maxine Hong Kingston

Maxine Hong Kingston was born Maxine Ting Ting Hong on October 27, 1940, the Year of the Dragon, in Stockton, California. Named "Maxine" after a blonde gambler who was always remarkably lucky, and "Ting Ting" from a Chinese poem, she was the third child of Chinese immigrants Ying Lan Chew and Tom Hong, and the first of their six American-born children. Much of the available published information about Kingston's parents and her own childhood is embedded in her first two books, *The Woman Warrior* (1976) and *China Men* (1980). Additional facts—including records of Kingston's education and early career—have emerged in the numerous interviews that she has graciously granted to scholars and admirers over the last two decades, as well as in *Hawai'i One Summer, 1978* (1987) and *Through the Black Curtain* (1987).

Tom Hong, Maxine's father, who had undergone a rigorous education in his native China for a career as a professional scholar, was a teacher in his home village of Sun Woi (New Society Village) near Canton (Guangzhou) before he, like thousands of other Chinese men in search of a better life, emigrated to the United States in 1925. America in the early twentieth century had little use for an educated immigrant whose years of extensive training in the ancient Chinese classics had honed his expertise in and passion for traditional Chinese philosophy, poetry, and calligraphy. Hong—who had, by this point, christened himself with the English name of "Tom" in honor of Thomas Edison—was forced to settle for earning a living by engaging in considerably less intellectual employment. By working as a window washer and saving his earnings, he amassed sufficient capital to invest in a laundry in New York's Chinatown, as one of four business partners, all young Chinese immigrants. For several years, he and his partners enjoyed the semblance of a carefree bachelor life. Spending a considerable portion of their incomes on expensive clothes, restaurant meals, dance-hall women, motorcycles, and flying lessons, they sent home to China photographs of themselves in zoot suits and spats, standing beside rented airplanes, or posing beside the stone lions on the steps of the New York Public Library. That freewheeling, pleasurable life was curtailed somewhat when Tom sent for his wife. On her arrival from China, she instituted order in the bachelor chaos of the shared apartment, cooking regular meals and preparing their lunches. Tom's life took an even more drastic turn not much later, when his partners in the laundry cheated him out of his share in the business by drawing up legal partnership documents that excluded him. Tom and Ying Lan, who was pregnant by that point, left New York and crossed the continent to settle on the West Coast in Stockton, California's small Chinatown.

Maxine's mother, Chew Ying Lan (Brave Orchid in *The Woman Warrior*), had married Tom Hong in China and the couple had two children who died very young. When Tom left for America, the couple was separated for fifteen years, during which time Tom sent money to Ying Lan. She first trained in medicine and midwifery at To Keung School of Midwifery in Canton, and subsequently embarked on a successful medical practice as a Western-style physician. Later, when the Japanese invaded Canton during the Second World War, Ying Lan put her medical skills to good use by superintending a field hospital concealed in a cave. Despite her extensive medical training and experience, however, Ying Lan discovered on her arrival in America—as had her husband before her—that her hard-won education in China was not marketable in the economy of her new country.

In a speech at a 1988 conference in China, Maxine Hong Kingston provided additional information about her family's history, revealing that she is the descendant of several sojourners. She told her audience that in her father's family, men traditionally sojourned in North America three or four times before returning permanently to China. The men in her mother's family were also sojourners, but Chew Ying Lan was the first woman in the family to emigrate to the United States. She bribed her way onto a ship to San Francisco in 1939, apparently managing to get out of China just before the Second World War escalated into the terrible conflict that it would become.

In the first century of Asian immigration to America, the term "sojourner" was employed in China to describe those men who left their families to live and work in the United States for several years. Sending most of their earnings home to China—where the money often supported large extended families in the ancestral villages—these men returned home every few years or so to deal with family matters and to father children before returning to America for another temporary working sojourn. Tom Hong, Kingston's father, was somewhat unusual in that after he departed from his village, he never returned to China, but instead managed to send for his wife to join him in the United States where they settled and raised their children.

Kingston never deliberately interviewed her parents about their histories, preferring instead to wait until they decided to speak about themselves; and for most of her life, she believed that her mother first set foot on American soil at Ellis Island because all of the family stories began with the New York period. She also imagined her father's story to be fairly straightforward. Not until Maxine Hong Kingston was an adult and an internationally renowned author did her mother elaborate on the family's immigration saga. According to Ying Lan Hong, Tom Hong came to the United States through Cuba, stowing away on a Cuba-to-New York ship, getting caught, jailed, and deported—three times! This story may explain the family fear of deportation that Kingston remembers from her childhood. Ying Lan herself arrived in California and spent three weeks at the Immigration Station on Angel Island before she was allowed to enter the continental United States. From California, she traveled by train to New York to meet her husband. Clearly, well into her old age, Ying Lan was continuing to exercise the storytellers' ancient right to modify stories, setting the family records straight, providing her storytelling daughter with additional information about the family history.

CHILDHOOD AND EDUCATION

Tom and Ying Lan took up residence in Stockton, California, where Tom had been offered a position as manager of an illegal gambling house owned by a wealthy Chinese immigrant. In Stockton, at age forty-five, Ying Lan gave birth to their first American child, Maxine. The Hongs would have five more children. Facing the reality of her new life in the United States, and realizing that the American medical establishment was not receptive to the idea of a Chinese-trained doctor, Ying Lan was forced to do menial labor as a tomato picker, cannery worker, and house-cleaner. Tom's position at the gambling house required him not only to oversee its operation and supervise its staff, but also occasionally to be arrested during almost predictably regular police raids. He was canny about his arrests, never giving his real name and—because he apparently sensed that quite a few people thought that all Chinese looked alike—inventing a different name for each arrest. Consequently, he never acquired a police record in his own name. When World War II put the gambling house out of business, Tom Hong started the New Port Laundry on El Dorado Street in Stockton, and Ying Lan, in addition to raising their children and juggling her multitudinous jobs outside the home, began helping her husband in the family laundry. Like other immigrant children, Kingston and her siblings were put to work in the family business as soon as they were old enough to be of help. Years later, she recalls inventing games to ease the drudgery of her tasks: "If I did ten T-shirts I'd allow myself to take a break" (Brownmiller 210).

Growing up on Hazleton Avenue in Stockton and surrounded by Chinese immigrants who had made their homes there, Maxine spoke Chinese at home and around her parents' friends. Her first language was Say Yup, the dialect of Cantonese that was spoken by nearly everyone in their community, an enclave which was composed largely of people who had emigrated from the same village—Sun Woi—in China. Although Stockton's Chinatown—not much more than a block of small businesses and houses—was demolished when a freeway was routed through the area, Kingston emphasizes that even when every trace of the geographical entity, the physical Chinatown had vanished, the community that was Chinatown continued to flourish in the rituals, celebrations, memories, and communal activities of its inhabitants. Kingston's childhood neighborhood on the south side of Stockton was working-class and racially diverse. She remembers that "the people next door were Black, and there were Mexicans and Filipinos" (Seshachari 21), and that the neighborhood, close to the less desirable sections of the city, was rough, with the ethnic groups tending to keep to themselves. It was there that Kingston experienced very early the shame of being called "Chinaman," in addition to learning to dodge attacks from bicycle-riding bullies; and as a Chinese child, she associated only with other Chinese and spoke only the Chinese language. Until she was five and the Hongs put her in school, she had no English-speaking acquaintances or play-mates.

Maxine Hong Kingston also remembers the more joyful aspects of her childhood. Available in Stockton were variety shows to raise money for the China Relief fund, Chinese opera on stage and on the screen, American movies on Saturdays, and films imported from Hong Kong on Sunday afternoons. She recalls "parades with a red flag, street-wide for the bystanders to throw money into" (*Black Curtain* 6). Everyday life was punctuated by traditional Chinese theatre and staged performances in all of their many forms. Chinese theatre was alive and well in California, in contrast to what was happening in the old country. From relatives still in China came letters telling the Hongs that Chinese theatres had gone dark, or had turned Communist, featuring only shows that met the approval of the party.

The Chinatown of Kingston's childhood still exists in spirit in the San Joaquin Valley, among the immigrant families whose older members have chosen to remain there instead of moving to other locations. Until their deaths, Kingston's parents continued to live in Stockton, refusing to relocate to a safer neighborhood, and finally allowing Kingston and her siblings to install an alarm system as well as enclose the house and yard within a security fence. Comparing her childhood neighborhood with San Francisco's much larger and more famous Chinatown, Kingston describes the Chinese community in the Valley as an enclave in which people speak the peasant Chinese dialects, and know one another so well that any gossip instantly affects an individual's reputation—a fact that Brave Orchid stresses to her daughter with the story of No-Name Woman in *The Woman Warrior*. Perhaps the primary distinguishing characteristics of Kingston's childhood community is the fact that it was and continues to be a place where neighbors from the same village maintain the same connections and attempt to create the same sense of community that they remember from life before they emigrated. As a child, Kingston experienced this neighborliness daily because the New Port Laundry served as the informal community center for Stockton's Chinese population. Customers and neighbors congregated at the laundry not only to do business, but also to catch up on the news of the day, to disseminate stories and neighborhood gossip, and—most important for Kingston—to reminisce about the life they left behind in China. This communal "talk-story" provided Kingston with a fund of stories—legends, myths, historical accounts, family tales, and revisions of familiar narratives—from which she would later draw the raw material that shaped her memoirs and fiction.

Maxine Hong Kingston has referred to the early years of her education as the "silent years" because during that period, she found speaking up difficult, possibly because she was a Chinese speaker in an English-speaking environment. When she entered school she was not yet completely fluent in English, and her silence, combined with her unfamiliarity with English and the American school system, may have been responsible for her failure to pass kindergarten that year. While in the first grade, she managed to earn a score of zero on an intelligence test when she colored the examination page black—an act that foreshadowed later developments in her school career. A section of *The Woman Warrior* describes the three years of Kingston's most profound silence, a period during which she consistently produced her "black curtain" art, much to the consternation of her teachers and her parents, all of whom misinterpreted what the child was attempting to portray. Although like her classmates, Kingston produced drawings of the usual flowers and houses, she then proceeded to obliterate the pictures with thick layers of black paint. Her teachers saw only the black paint and concluded that she was a troubled child, asking her parents to come in for a serious conference about their daughter. But Kingston says that for her, the black paint was a positive image representing a stage curtain at the precise moment before the curtain rose to reveal the set on which a play would be enacted.

> Before I could read or write or even speak much, an idea came to me of black curtains that hang over something wonderful—some amazing show about to open. All my life, I've looked for those black curtains; I want to part them, and to see what is on the other side. . . . As a kid I loved black crayons and black paint and ink and blackboards, through which I could see glorious light and hear voices and music. (*Black Curtain* 5)

Kingston surmises that her association of the color black with curtains had its origins in the thirty-two blackout curtains that her parents installed in their windows during the years of World War II. To the family, already besieged with letters from China full of dreadful news about the war, those curtains were comfortable symbols of safety and protection:

"We were safe from the street, the city, strangers, World War II" (*Black Curtain* 5). For the child, Maxine, with a mind brimming with stories and mythical images but without the linguistic facility to render those stories into written text, the blackened pictures may have symbolized her awareness that she was the keeper of something precious and significant—her stories—that for the moment she could neither reveal nor express, not having the vocabulary with which to release those creations of her imagination.

Of course, once Kingston became fluent in English, she was released from her linguistic and artistic silence. "When I learned English," she says, "I wrote that the black curtains rose or swung apart" (*Black Curtain* 5). The English language was a delight to her, and she reveled in the facility with which its twenty-six letters allowed her to represent her thoughts, not only in English, but also in Chinese. Mastering English also expanded her world by making a considerable body of literature accessible to her, and she embraced reading as an escape from the realities of life in Stockton. Two books, in particular, had a significant impact on Kingston. Reading a novel by Louisa May Alcott and—like thousands of little girls—identifying with the March sisters, she was abruptly reminded that she was different from those young women when the book introduced "this funny-looking little Chinaman" and Kingston realized that in the eyes of readers, she was more like the "little Chinaman" than the March sisters (Hoy 62). During the years of Kingston's childhood, Asian American girls were not the heroines of novels. For Kingston, the second important book, Jade Snow Wong's *Fifth Chinese Daughter*, had the opposite effect. If Alcott's novel excluded Kingston and others like her, Wong's memoir afforded her the rare and beautiful experience of finding someone much like herself portrayed in literature, proving to her that the Chinese did not always have to be represented in books as eccentric servants or peculiar foreigners with laughable accents.

Her early educational setbacks notwithstanding, Kingston eventually did well in school, especially at Edison High School in Stockton, developing into a straight-A student and publishing her first essay, "I Am an American" in *American Girl* (1955) while she was still a high school student. In her senior year, she wrote an article describing Chinese New Year for a Stockton newspaper, and was awarded a journalism scholarship to the University of California at Berkeley, an institution that she had long dreamed of attending.

Kingston entered the University of California as an engineering student with eleven scholarships; but college proved initially to be a major culture shock for the young woman who had no experience with the university community. Kingston remembers that she began the semester and then was ill for two weeks, in part, she believes, because she "didn't understand what anything was" (Robertson 26). Her grades suffered, as a result. Lacking any real interest in engineering (which was on her parents' short list of desirable careers), she thought about changing her major to journalism, and worked for the Berkeley student newspaper, *The Daily Californian*, but journalism proved as incompatible as engineering. On the night shift at the student paper, Kingston was unable to keep from falling asleep. Worse yet, she disliked journalistic writing. Although she had been writing since her childhood, she was not interested in straightforward factual reportorial writing, preferring instead to write creatively from her imagination. English became the logical choice as a major, but Kingston did not make the transition easily. She had always loved to read and write, and she had difficulty adjusting to the idea of earning a university degree in a field she enjoyed, feeling that there was something wrong with any individual who chose to do something that was enjoyable and came easily. To the poet Marilyn Chin, Kingston revealed that she felt as though she had abdicated her responsibilities to her family by pursuing a degree that was fun. In the interview with Chin, Kingston explained that her upbringing had instilled in her the notion that anything valuable was, by definition, also difficult to attain (Marilyn Chin 69).

Once she adjusted to university life, Kingston participated enthusiastically in the culture that was Berkeley in the 1960s, aligning herself with the Free Speech movement, joining in protests against the war in Vietnam, and directing her energies toward activism through which she and other like-minded students hoped to make a difference. Like thousands of young people in that freewheeling decade, she also experimented with drugs, "[and they] messed with our minds and time and space [and] our perceptions of events were changed and expanded" (Vitale). Her experiences within the drug culture inspired and shaped her third book, *Tripmaster Monkey*. During her college years, Kingston frequently played the role of tripmaster, an individual whom she describes as a kind of tour guide for those under the influence of psychedelic drugs, someone who invoked imagery and described fantasy geographies. As tripmaster, Kingston eschewed drugs, concentrating instead on guiding her friends on their psychedelic travels, ensuring their journeys to pastoral landscapes (Seshachari 18).

In 1962, Kingston graduated with a B.A. in English from Berkeley, and later that year, married Earll Kingston, an actor who was also a graduate of Berkeley and whom she had met during a production of Bertolt Brecht's *Galileo*. Their only son, Joseph Lawrence Chung Mei, was born in 1963. The next year, she returned to the University of California to complete course work that would earn her a teaching certificate. For five years, she taught English and mathematics at Sunset High School in Hayward, California, while Earll taught at Berkeley High School. At the same time, they both continued to be active in anti-Vietnam war protests and in the Free Speech movement. In 1967, the Kingstons with their young son left California to get away from the disturbingly burgeoning drug culture and the increasingly violent antiwar movement. They had become disillusioned with the protest culture and discouraged about the unstoppable escalation of the war; moreover, their friends were also leaving Berkeley, "retreating from the barricades . . . [and] starting communes in the northern California woods" (*Hawai'i* 15).

En route to the Far East—which was their original destination—the Kingstons stopped off in Hawai'i, and remained there for seventeen years, eventually purchasing their first house in Manoa Valley in Honolulu. Initially, they did their best to live according to their pacifist ideals, refusing, for example, to engage in any employment or activity that might be interpreted as supportive of the war or to collude—however peripherally—in anything that enhanced the war-driven economy. Living in inexpensive lodgings, furnished with castoffs, above a grocery store, they "discovered that a human being could live out of the dumpsters behind the supermarket" (*Hawai'i* 15), and they supplemented their diet with fruit and nuts picked from nearby trees. Not surprisingly, they also immersed themselves in projects that opposed or subverted the war effort; and they became involved, through the Church of the Crossroads, with a sanctuary for military men who were absent without leave (AWOL). The experience proved unexpectedly enlightening. Kingston discovered that contrary to her assumptions, soldiers who were AWOL did not share her political views on the war. Most of them—"mere kids"—could see nothing wrong with the war, and had, in fact, escaped the military life for surprisingly mundane or practical reasons: they hated military food, didn't get along with superior officers, or wanted a vacation from the army or the navy. Even more disturbing, Kingston found that some of the soldiers she met actually took pleasure in violence, relishing the experience of decimating enemy troops with assault weapons.

The Kingstons found that despite Hawai'i's distance from the mainland United States, the island state was not free from reminders of the Vietnam War. On the contrary, Hawai'i was a participant in the official war effort. Kingston says: "We should have thought of it—hardware and soldiers were sent to Hawai'i, which funneled everything to Vietnam. Tanks and jeeps in convoy maneuvered around the rim. Khaki soldiers drove khaki vehicles, camouflage that did not match the bright foliage" (*Hawai'i* 16). In fact, Hawai'i was a way station for troops and supplies en route to the battlefields of Southeast Asia, as well as for the dead on their way home to the mainland. Military activity was noticeably present, with "soldiers shooting at target practice up in those beautiful mountains, doing their war games" (Robertson 90). It became clear to the Kingstons that not only had they not avoided the war, but they had landed "in the very midst of it, as close as you could get and remain in the United States" (*Hawai'i* 16). Predictably, the activist lifestyle, which was already difficult for the Kingstons to maintain, began to seem futile, and they returned to the workforce—Maxine to teaching, Earll to acting. She taught English, language arts, and English as a second language at several high schools as well as at Honolulu Business College and Mid-Pacific Institute. Her husband joined a Shakespearean theatre troupe.

For two and a half years, Kingston worked on the manuscript that would become *The Woman Warrior* before she sent fifty polished manuscript pages to three agents, hoping that one of them might be able to help her to find a small press that would be interested in what she had written. Aware that the manuscript she had produced was nothing like most of the books that she had encountered either in her university studies or in her leisure reading, she nevertheless hoped for at least a small printing. One of the three, the literary agent John Shaffner agreed to represent her, and sent her partial manuscript to Norton and Little, Brown, both of which rejected it. Kingston withdrew that manuscript from circulation and completed the book, whereupon Shaffner resubmitted it, this time to Knopf, which accepted it despite editors' uncertainty about how to market the book. *The Woman Warrior* was published by Knopf in 1976, and immediately attracted the praise of the respected critic John Leonard, who announced in the *New York Times* that a stunning first book by an unknown author was "one of the best I've read for years" (Leonard, "Defiance" 21).

With the publication of *The Woman Warrior* in 1976, Kingston's career as a high school English teacher ended, and a new career as an important American writer was launched. Although Maxine Hong Kingston has definitely not abandoned teaching, her classrooms now tend to be on college and university campuses where she holds appointments as a visiting lecturer or distinguished professor. In 1990, she was named a Chancellor's Distinguished Professor at her alma mater, the University of California at Berkeley, and although she put in brief stints on other campuses and took a leave of absence from Berkeley in 1993, she returned to that campus in 1997. In addition to her formal university teaching, Kingston is in great demand as a conference speaker and reader, and most recently as a writing workshop leader for Vietnam War veterans.

In 1984, Maxine Hong Kingston, who had never been to China although she had appropriated and reworked its cultural myths in two books, finally traveled to the country of her parents' birth, a country that had been a dominant geographical presence in her imagination since she was a child, a country that had shaped her stories and her voice. The visit, which was sponsored jointly by the University of California at Los Angeles and the Chinese Writers Association, included—in addition to Kingston—the American writers William Gass, Allen Ginsberg, Francine du Plessix Gray, William Least Heat Moon, Toni Morrison, Harrison Salisbury, Leslie Marmon Silko, and Gary Snyder.

Kingston did not undertake her first Chinese journey lightly. For years, she had resisted visiting the country from whence her parents' stories had come, describing her hesitation as the product of a crisis of sorts. Aware that Chinese immigrants invent and reinvent a China about which they tell stories, and having seen "memory villages" (miniature replicas of home villages, complete with houses, trees, and fields, or tremendously detailed dioramas of remembered Chinese landscapes), Kingston had chosen to re-create the China of reconstructed memory—what she describes as "the mythic China"—in her books of memoirs. Years before her first visit, she wrote in *Ms.* about her fear that China "may not be there at all, I having made it up" ("Reservations" 67). Not surprisingly, she feared that the real China might be so unrecognizably different as to render her books geographically and culturally inaccurate: "What if China invalidated everything that I was thinking and writing?" (Rabinowitz 181). Kingston was not alone in her misgivings about the planned trip to China. Her mother feared political repercussions, afraid that because Kingston had criticized the Chinese patriarchy and had described some of the tortures inflicted by the Communist regime, she would be in danger while she was in the country. In fact, so concerned was Ying Lan about her daughter's well-being that she begged Kingston to retract some of her criticism of China.

Neither woman should have worried—the China that Kingston encountered closely resembled both the country of her imagination and the setting of Ying Lan's stories. In China, she felt affirmed in her belief that through talk-story, her ancestors and her mother had bestowed on her a centuries-old tradition that remains completely accessible (Skenazy, "University" 134). For Kingston, reality validated the geography of her imagined China: "One of the great thrills was to see how well I had imagined it. Many of the colors, and the smells, the people, the faces, the incidents, were much as I imagined" (Rabinowitz 181). Ying Lan Hong's fears also proved completely unfounded. Her daughter was a celebrity in China, especially in the province of Guangdong, from which the family had emigrated decades earlier. Harrison Salisbury, one of the writers in the traveling group, recalls that nearly every inhabitant of the Hongs' ancestral village claimed to be related to Maxine Hong Kong Kingston. Local writers made every effort to ensure that she was feted lavishly and housed in the best corner room in the newest hotel in town.

While she was in China, Kingston had the opportunity to visit her family's home village and her mother's medical college, places that she had described in her books although she knew them only from her mother's talk-story. The visit was an eye-opener: Kingston saw for herself the well in which No-Name Woman had drowned herself, entered the Hong family temple, and discovered the building in which Brave Orchid had attended medical school and faced down the Sitting Ghost. But Kingston also was made aware of at least one small but important detail about which her mother's stories had not been specific—in the ancestral village, the narrow lanes, tightly clustered houses, and small, cramped interiors were forceful reminders that an individual transgression reverberates quickly through a community that is forced to live in such close proximity. Kingston saw for herself how the disturbing and unwelcome news of No-Name Aunt's pregnancy had inevitably become public property, affecting everyone, not only in the family, but also in the village. Specific details aside, however, Kingston was amazed as well as pleased that the China she encountered was so strongly reminiscent of the China in her imagination and in her books. She was gratified when she realized that the landscape she encountered was the one that she had described so often in her prose, and the familiarity of the Chinese geography gave her the feeling of coming home. Moreover, she came to understand completely that talk-story is indeed a strategy for transmitting culture from one generation to another (Bonetti 43). Four years later, on a return journey to China to attend the Fourth Sino-American Writers Conference at Leshan, Sichuan Province, Kingston explained why, years earlier, she had at first consciously decided not to travel to China before she began to narrate the stories of her forebears—in her books, she wanted to be able to recreate her imagined China, the China of memory, as the setting for her retellings of traditional stories. On her first encountering China at last, she was "relieved and happy to find that my imagination is true. As we travel about, China is confirming for me that the strong imagination can know reality" ("Garland" 42).

During the intervening four years between visits, Kingston's work had become even more popular with Chinese readers, thanks to pirated editions and translations from Taiwan and Hong Kong that made the books more readily available, even to non-English speakers. Again, Kingston found that Chinese writers were eager to discuss her work, but to her astonishment, she also realized that they claimed her as one of their own, as a writer who had helped to preserve some of the traditional genres that the Cultural Revolution had successfully all but obliterated. For these Chinese writers and literary scholars, Kingston represented a link with their cultural roots, with a literary tradition that they had feared was extinct. Kingston realized that she symbolizes artistic continuity to these writers. Despite the fact that she is an American who writes in English, her Chinese colleagues consider her work to reside within the Chinese literary canon, and they look to her for inspiration and direction (Marilyn Chin 65).

CRITICAL RECEPTION

Kingston was overwhelmed with the kind of reception that *The Woman Warrior* received, about which most writers only fantasize. An almost instant popular and critical success, the book won some of the top national awards in the literary world, as well as a place on best-seller lists. That popularity continued for years—a decade later, in 1989, *The Woman Warrior* was still on the list of best-selling trade paperbacks. In their introduction to a collection of interviews with Maxine Hong Kingston, Paul Skenazy and Tera Martin summarize the popular impact of Kingston's first book:

> It is estimated that [Kingston's] work is the most anthologized of any living American writer, and that she is read by more American college students than any other living author. Students, particularly Asian American women, look to her as a

model, find themselves in her tales, seek her out with syco-
phantic regularity. (Skenazy vii)

Early reviews attest to the power with which Kingston's work immediately engaged readers. Writing in the *Washington Post Book World*,
William McPherson describes *The Woman Warrior* as "a strange, sometimes savagely terrifying and, in the literal sense, wonderful story of
growing up caught between two highly sophisticated and utterly alien
cultures, both vivid, often menacing and equally mysterious" (McPherson E1). For Jane Kramer, another reviewer, *The Woman Warrior* is "a
brilliant memoir. . . . an investigaton of soul, not landscape. Its sources
are dream and memory, myth and desire. Its crises are the crises of a
heart in exile from roots that bind and terrorize it" (Kramer 1). Reviewers
cited the poetry of Kingston's prose, as well as the seamless blending of
fantasy, myth, and history into the powerful narrative that is *The Woman
Warrior*. Kramer describes Kingston's narrative voice as "clear as the
voice of Ts'ai Yen [the poet whose story is told in the last chapter of the
book] who sang her sad angry songs of China to the barbarians. . . . as
fierce as a warrior's voice, and as eloquent as any artist's" (Kramer 1).
Publisher's Weekly praised Kingston's prose for "exhibiting the delicacy
and precision of porcelain" (*Publisher's Weekly* 72). Other reviewers focused on Kingston's portrayal of the struggles undertaken by marginalized individuals who seek to create a stable identity. Describing *The
Woman Warrior* as an important book, Elizabeth Fifer, of the *International
Fiction Review*, writes that Kingston has produced "a poetic, thoughtful,
wonderfully subtle reclamation of self" (Fifer 69); and Sara Blackburn,
writing for *Ms.*, suggests that the book "illuminates the experience of
everyone who has ever felt the terror of being an emotional outsider"
(Blackburn 39).

Proof of the enduring power of *The Warrior Woman* is the fact that the
book has been translated into several languages, and published in dozens
of official and pirated editions. It has also been the subject of hundreds
of book reports, term papers and research projects, countless theses—
both honors and master's degree—and doctoral dissertations. In the
years since its publication, scholars not only in the United States but also
in Asia and Europe have read and reread, interpreted and reinterpreted,
debated, analyzed, deconstructed, and most of all, appreciated and been
profoundly moved by Kingston's narratives. More significant is the
book's continuing crossover appeal to all audiences—readers of all ages,
genders, ethnic and national backgrounds have been inspired, provoked,

and entertained for more than two decades since *The Woman Warrior* was published.

Published in 1980, four years after *The Woman Warrior*, Kingston's second book, *China Men*—like its predecessor—garnered lavish praise from readers and reviewers. Again critic John Leonard was enthusiastic, describing, in the *New York Times*, the impact of the book as "sheer magic: poetry, parable, nightmare, the terror and exhilaration of physical labor, the songs of survival, the voices of the dead, the feel of wood and blood, the smell of flowers and wounds. History meets sensuality" (Leonard, "Books" C9). In the *New York Times Book Review*, novelist Mary Gordon notes that Kingston's "success at depicting the world of men without women must be the envy of any woman writer who has tried to capture this foreign territory. Her understanding of the lacerations of crushing physical work and the consolations of community is expressed in nearly perfect prose" (Gordon, "Mythic" 24–25).

Readers recognized in the second book the beguiling narrative voice that had drawn them into the world of *The Woman Warrior*. Like others captivated by Kingston's entrancing and provocative prose, one writer, Anne Collins, found herself responding emotionally and creatively: "Her fermentations of myths and dreams and nervy sideways dances at the possible truths of family history are so intoxicating that the next logical step after their reading must be to tear all the pages out, roll them up and smoke them" (Collins 48). Paul Gray, writing for *Time*, labeled *China Men* "a fitting companion" to *The Woman Warrior*, noting that Kingston, with this volume, enables her male ancestors finally to win the respect that they deserve (Gray 26). Frances Taliaferro of *Harper's* suggested that in *China Men*, Kingston is "all of her Chinese ancestors as well as her American self" (Taliaferro 77). This last assessment is particularly appropriate in light of Kingston's insistence that she is first of all an American, and only secondarily a person of Chinese ancestry—a definitive that San Francisco reviewer Tamar Jacoby clearly understands when she praises the clarity of Kingston's "plain American voice" (Jacoby 11).

Enthralled by Kingston's panoramic narratives of the histories of men in her family, by the courage and tenacity displayed by the thousands of sojourners whose stories are embedded in *China Men*, readers embraced Kingston's second effort as they had *The Woman Warrior*. "It tells of emigration, persecution, work, endurance, ritual, change, loss and the eternal invention of the new," wrote Jean Strouse in *Newsweek*, neatly cataloging the themes that inform and shape *China Men* (Strouse 88). And although *China Men* has not achieved *The Woman Warrior*'s iconographic

status, it is nonetheless a landmark American memoir, an appropriate
sequel both to Kingston's first book and to William Carlos Williams's *In
the American Grain*, a historical narrative that Kingston credits with directly inspiring the narrative shape of *China Men*.

In 1987, Kingston published two limited-edition books: *Hawai'i One
Summer, 1978*, a hard-bound collection of eleven prose pieces illustrated
with original woodblock prints by artist Den Ming-Dao—son of Jade
Snow Wong—and released in an edition of 200 copies; and *Through the
Black Curtain*, published by the Friends of the Bancroft Library in Berkeley, California. All but one of the pieces in *Hawai'i* were written in the
summer of 1978 and published originally in the *New York Times*. In these
essays, Kingston reflects on a variety of subjects representing some of
the most significant elements of her life in Hawai'i—the Vietnam War,
the Kingstons' first house in Oahu, high school reunions, dishwashing,
a small island called "Chinaman's Hat," a writers' conference. One essay,
about the California poet Lew Welch, was rejected by the *Times*; nonetheless, Kingston included it in the collection as her tribute to a poet
whom she admires so much that she kept an inspirational quote from
him in front of her at her writing desk: "When I write, my only concern
is accuracy. I try to write accurately from the poise of mind which lets
us see that things are exactly what they seem. I never worry about
beauty, if it is accurate there is always beauty. I never worry about form,
if it is accurate there is always form" (quoted in *Hawai'i* 65). *Through the
Black Curtain*, comprised of excerpts from *The Woman Warrior* and *China
Men*, as well as short sections from the then-unpublished *Tripmaster Monkey*, also includes Kingston's exploration of the significance of black
curtains in her imagination and her writing. Equally interesting is Kingston's commentary on the role of theatre in the Chinese American experience, as well as her identification of the theatre as a significant
influence on her own books.

The publication of *Tripmaster Monkey: His Fake Book* in 1989 took some
of Kingston's most devoted readers by surprise when the book turned
out not to be a talk-story mixed-genre memoir in the vein of *The Woman
Warrior* and *China Men*, but a rollicking and unmistakably postmodern
American novel with would be poet Wittman Ah Sing at its center. Anne
Tyler, writing in the *New Republic*, praises the work: "That Wittman is
Chinese gives his story depth and particularity. That he's American lends
his narrative style a certain slangy insouciance. That he's Chinese-
American, with the self-perceived outsiders edgy angle of vision, makes
for a novel of satisfying complexity and bite and verve" (Tyler, "Manic"

46). Critic Herbert Gold places *Tripmaster Monkey* in a literary tradition generally associated with another culture, suggesting that in the novel, Kingston "blends the kind of magic realism familiar to readers of Latin American fiction with the hard-edged black humor of flower-epoch comic writers and performers—a little bit of Lenny Bruce and a whole lot of Gabriel Garcia Marquez. Kingston's energy, talent and unique perspective make an odd dish work, like some sort of hefty Chinese *nouvelle maxi-cuisine* stew" (Gold 1).

Maxine Hong Kingston has garnered an impressive collection of awards for her three major prose works. In its publication year, *The Woman Warrior* won the National Book Critics Circle Award for nonfiction, followed the next year with a National Education Association Award and the *Mademoiselle* Magazine Award. Two years later, in 1979, *Time* rated *The Woman Warrior* as one of the ten most important nonfiction works of the 1970s. *China Men* has done equally well. On its release in 1980, it was immediately named to the American Library Association's Notable Books List, and won the National Book Award for nonfiction. The years following brought the American Book Award, nomination for the National Book Critics Circle Award, and the distinction of being named runner-up for the Pulitzer Prize. *Tripmaster Monkey*, published in 1989, won the P.E.N. USA West Award for fiction that year, and almost a decade later, the John Dos Passos Prize for Literature in 1998, also the year in which Kingston became the recipient of the Fred Cody Lifetime Achievement Award, presented by the Bay Area Book Reviewers Association.

Kingston has herself been honored repeatedly over the years, first for her writing, but also for her activism. A number of colleges and universities—including Eastern Michigan University, Colby College, Brandeis University, and the University of Massachusetts—have conferred on her the honorary doctorate. In addition, she has held distinguished lectureships and endowed professorial positions on campuses across the United States. She has been the recipient of countless literary and arts awards, Guggenheim and National Endowment for the Arts fellowships, the Lila Wallace Reader's Digest Award, and, in 1997, the National Humanities Medal, awarded by the president of the United States.

The most unusual and culturally significant award that has been bestowed on Maxine Hong Kingston is her designation as "Living Treasure of Hawaii," a title inspired by and similar to the "Living Treasure of Japan." Kingston was honored as a "Living Treasure" by a Honolulu Buddhist sect in a formal ceremony, with its traditional Sanskrit chants and incense, held at the Hoopa Hongwanji Temple on the Pali in 1980. Kingston was the first Chinese American to be so honored. At the time of the award, she was one of the youngest ever to receive the designation (the Japanese require that individuals so honored be at least eighty years old)—for *The Woman Warrior*, and especially for introducing the world to the immigrant experience, thereby making that experience a part of the American story. Significantly, the tradition of naming an important person a "Living Treasure," which originated in ancient China and flourishes to this day in Japan, has now become an American ritual, thanks to the immigrant community in Hawai'i which has translated an ancient Asian distinction into the American idiom.

Although her fame as a writer rests largely on the three award-winning works that comprise her major oeuvre, Kingston is a fairly prolific writer and has produced other prose pieces—as well as some poetry. Her essays on writing have been anthologized in widely circulated collections. Other essays—on her life and career, on China, on language, and on other writers—have been published in national periodicals, including *The New York Times, Mother Jones, American Heritage, Ms., North American Review*, and *Amerasia Journal*.

After *Tripmaster Monkey*, Kingston began to focus on her plans for another book, which she intended to call *The Fourth Book of Peace*. She told interviewer Donna Perry in May 1993 that the book, which would continue the story of Wittman Ah Sing's erratic odyssey into adulthood and maturity, would somehow incorporate both fiction and nonfiction. She said that it would be a novel, as well as an account of her creative process, a book in which the fictional section would portray Wittman Ah Sing growing into full maturity, while the nonfiction part would trace Kingston's own creative process (Perry 180).

Less than half a year after that interview with Perry, two tragedies changed Maxine Hong Kingston's life. Her father died that September. And a month after his death, in October, the Kingstons lost all of their possessions in a major fire that swept through Oakland, California, and raged through their Rockridge neighborhood. Both events had a profound effect on Kingston's life and writing career, significantly altering at least one major project—the novel that she had intended to publish as a sequel to *Tripmaster Monkey*— and leading Kingston to reflect on her relationship with her silent and seemingly distant father.

A decade before he died, Tom Hong had finally, tentatively, emerged from behind the wall of silence that he had erected to protect his memories and the stories of his past. Persuaded to read a pirated Chinese translation of *China Men* from Hong Kong, he had finally, obliquely, revealed more of his life and thoughts in response, Kingston believes, to a sentence in *China Men* that challenges him to speak up if his daughter's multiple versions of his life story are incorrect or inadequate. In elegant calligraphic Chinese penmanship, Tom Hong carefully inscribed his own poetry in the margins of the pirated translation, also adding his responses, including additions and corrections, to what Kingston had conjectured and written about his life. Unlike his wife, Ying Lan, who had chanted and talked story, using her physical voice to reveal her life and the family history to her daughter, Tom Hong relied on the written word, employing the artistry of the brush strokes that he had perfected in another life, long before his daughter had begun her writing career. The door to communication between father and daughter had opened, albeit only slightly, but for Kingston that opening was more than enough. At the time, Kingston speculated that this written conversation might be the only genuine avenue for serious communication between her father and herself—after all, they were both writers. She has commented that such written exchanges are very much a part of Chinese literary tradition. In old China, a poet would create a poem, another poet would respond or add a section to that poem, and a third poet would finish the work. It was also customary for writers to produce elaborate commentary on their colleagues' work (Skenazy, "University" 155). Kingston's assessment of her literary "conversation" with her father is very much in keeping with her acute awareness of and allegiance to her ancestral culture and its literary traditions, and her acknowledgment of the influence of those traditions on her life and art. By the time of her father's death, Kingston had achieved a rapprochement with him, making her loss more profound; and coming so soon after her bereavement, the fire that consumed her home dealt a severe psychological blow to Kingston, who was still in mourning.

Neither Maxine Hong Kingston nor her husband was at home when the Oakland fire first started. Earll Kingston was in Virginia performing a role in a Chekhov play, and she was in Stockton, participating in the ritual ceremonies commemorating the one-month anniversary of her father's death. She heard about the fire on the car radio as she was driving home to Oakland, and by the time she arrived close to her street, police roadblocks prevented her from getting to her house. Twice attempting to get to her home by evading the police, Kingston ultimately was forced to retreat, when she got within a block of her house and saw that the entire neighborhood had been destroyed.

Gone was not only their house, but with it their family photographs, keepsakes, and works of art by friends. Also destroyed was two years of work—Kingston's 156-page manuscript for her fourth book, a manuscript that she describes as finished pages of good prose that she had already subjected to her own rigorous revision process (Joan Smith 190). Also lost in the conflagration were Kingston's collection of material for the new book, notes about the three legendary books of peace mentioned in Chinese mythology, and other information that she had amassed about the mythical Chinese cities of refuge, safe places in which fugitives could find sanctuary during wars and times of persecution (Joan Smith B4).

That work-in-progress was to have become *The Fourth Book of Peace*, a title that alludes to the three Chinese books of peace that Kingston suspects might have been lost when a fire swept through one of China's great libraries. Always alert to parallels, she notes that her attempt to re-create the ancient books of peace was also destroyed by fire. The co-incidence was so striking that she told herself, *"you're really onto something here"* (Mandelbaum 46). Although her manuscript was irretrievably gone, Kingston was imbued with the determination to reconstruct the lost book somehow, and she appealed for help with the gargantuan task in an address to the delegates at the 1991 Modern Language Association meeting. Her wish list was a revelation of the extraordinary range of influences on allusions in what was to have been Kingston's new work. She requested copies of photographs of Anais Nin, Hemingway's manuscripts, stories from World War II and Vietnam (Seshachari 14). Clearly, as she had done with her first three books, Kingston was breaking ground with the planned book. The response to her appeal stunned and overwhelmed her. In an interview at Weber State University, Kingston told Neila Seshachari that while many people showered her with the usual, and very welcome, offerings of clothes, shoes, household items, and even teddy bears, others offered audiotapes and videotapes of Kingston reading portions of the now lost novel-in-progress—invaluable contributions that would allow Kingston to reconstruct from those recordings some portions of the text of her lost manuscript. In fact, she notes that one woman presented her with an Epson QX10, a computer exactly like the one that the flames had devoured!

For some time after the fire, Kingston was unable to write (she and her husband also found themselves unable to read!), but slowly, by concentrating on writing in her journal only about her own feelings, she reacquired her ability to tell stories and create fictional narratives. Seeking inspiration from her childhood attempts to write stories, she began by using words to describe her emotions and her thoughts, writing only about herself at first, and paying little attention to grammar or style—focusing all of her energy on the elemental process of expressing pain and loss (Mandelbaum 52). Hoping to discover a way to reconstruct her lost manuscript, Kingston agreed to undergo hypnosis. While in the hypnotic state, she imagined herself sprinkling special water from a vial onto her writing materials, including her computer. The water transformed the surfaces that it touched into shining gold, at which point she says she called on the fictional characters from the novel that had burned, and they all materialized in her imagination. According to Kingston, these fictional characters "agreed to come to her aid in the event that she became stuck or lost" (Mandelbaum 47).

The painstaking process that ultimately enabled Kingston to reacquaint herself with the pleasure of creating with words will become part of the planned fifth book, a work which she describes as structurally complicated, incorporating as it does a substantial chunk of her confessional writing about the loss of her father and her manuscript. She has decided to incorporate a considerable amount of her writing about the creative process as a lengthy prologue to the continuation of Wittman Ah Sing's story, the portion on which she was working when the fire destroyed her manuscript (Schroeder 90). Adding that she has not yet seen another book that resembles her new work-in-progress, tentatively titled *The Fifth Book of Peace*, Kingston labels her latest project a "nonfiction fiction nonfiction sandwich" (Schroeder 91).

It is obvious from Kingston's comments about *The Fifth Book of Peace* that the author's enthusiasm for experimenting with genre has not waned. Announcing that the new book will incorporate a nonfiction section, she adds that she is also working on another section that continues the story of Wittman and Taña (from *Tripmaster Monkey*) in a form that she describes as innovative—"I don't know how critics will categorize it" (Skandera-Trombley 22). Kingston intends to incorporate into the book several endings omitted from her earlier works; in addition, she wants to be able to demonstrate through the book how a soldier can return home after a war and evolve into a nonviolent, peace-loving human being.

Kingston struggled for some time with the task of structuring what, by 1996, had grown into 1,800 pages of text for her new book. A meditation-induced childhood memory of the game, "Rock, Scissors, Paper," provided the inspiration that she sought: *The Fifth Book of Peace* will be organized into four sections—Fire, Paper, Water, and Earth. The section entitled "Fire" will open the book with Kingston's memoirs of her losses in 1991; and following will be "Paper" which incorporates material about moving from factual writing to fiction. In "Water"—the section destroyed in the fire—Kingston plans to chronicle the further adventures of Wittman Ah Sing from *Tripmaster Monkey*, as he and his friends devote their efforts to establishing a utopian community of Vietnam War draft-dodgers in Hawai'i. She says that the incessantly talkative Wittman will finally learn to be silent and to listen in the new book. The concluding section, "Earth," will focus on a journey that Kingston undertook with a group of Vietnam veterans to an international Buddhist community in France, where the veterans had the opportunity to meet with—among others—several expatriate Vietnamese nuns and monks. Kingston remembers that the community, comprised of individuals from several continents and a variety of religious faiths, was centered on one ideal: to discover a way to live in peace (Mandelbaum 53).

Ying Lan Hong, Kingston's intrepid mother, lived into her nineties, dying in 1997, six years after her husband. Age did not slow her down or silence her—the Brave Orchid of *The Woman Warrior* continued to dominate her daughter's world, continued to talk-story, to inform the world around her of her opinions. At one point, announcing to Kingston that she had just recorded a tape of herself chanting a tale of adventure, the elderly Ying Lan suggested that her taped story was "better than the woman warrior story," which she dismissed as not very good. "This is the one you should have written" (Mandelbaum 49).

Refusing to confine her energies to writing and university teaching, Maxine Hong Kingston has been conducting an ongoing series of writing workshops for "veterans of all wars" (Schroeder 93). After attending a retreat conducted by Thick Nhat Hanh for war veterans, Kingston, funded by a fellowship from the Lila Wallace Fund, initiated her workshop sessions partly as a strategy to help herself to develop a deeper understanding of both peace and war. The day-long retreats and workshops incorporate a combination of Buddhist meditations and pacifist techniques (Kingston is a practicing Buddhist) with writing instruction and practice. To the veterans, she says, "Let's make an art out of this war that we were all in" (Schroeder 94). Kingston eagerly points out how much she has learned much from the experience, especially from the activities in which workshop participants engage. With a group of veterans from her workshops, Kingston visited a Buddhist commune that sheltered a large contingent of Vietnamese, and the veterans were forced to learn how to interact peaceably with people once considered their enemies. Kingston also engineered conversations between peace activists and supporters of the war, between American veterans and veterans from North and South Vietnam (Skandera-Trombley 46). As a result of the workshops, Kingston also traveled to Vietnam, meeting with both war veterans and writers, listening, observing, amassing ideas and stories, storing up images and motifs for her work-in-progress, which will focus on peace.

In addition to her work on *The Fifth Book of Peace*, Kingston is compiling an anthology of writing by war veterans from the workshops that she has been conducting. For her, the anthology is a logical extension of a narrative that she began years ago; it is a continuation of the last chapter of *China Men*, in which she tells the story of her brother who survived the Vietnam War. Kingston describes the workshop participants as compelling writers who not only have provocative stories to share with the world, but also possess a powerful desire to give voice to those stories. Clearly, their drive to disseminate their stories parallels Kingston's own compulsion to share the narratives that emerge from and occupy her imagination.

Maxine Hong Kingston believes that part of her mission as a writer involves experimentation with literary form by pushing the boundaries of genre, even as she struggles to invent what she imagines as "a beautiful, human, artistic language of peace" (Perry 169). She describes the conventional structure of the novel and the short story as "violent" because both forms require conflict, crisis, "a denouement where things explode." She dreams of rediscovering or somehow reconstructing the three legendary Chinese books of peace, now—according to traditional mythology—lost for centuries (Perry 169).

In "The Novel's Next Step," an article published in *Mother Jones* shortly after the publication of *Tripmaster Monkey*, Kingston shared her thoughts on the direction in which her writing is going. She wants to write what she calls a "global novel," with the United States as its setting because this country continues to be the destination of individual journeys from every corner of the earth ("Novel" 39). Naming Salman Rushdie's *The Satanic Verses* (1988) as a pioneer global novel "for which the author has risked his life and art" (39), Kingston continues with a description of the new genre that she envisions: "The danger is that the Global novel has to imitate chaos: loaded guns, bombs, leaking boats, broken-down civilizations, a hole in the sky, broken English, people who refuse connections with others" (39–40). She wonders how writers can manage to

stretch the novel to represent contemporary life with its lack of guar-
antees of any kind of order without the genre falling apart. And she
ponders how the novel can portray the surreal in society and its inhabitants. Clearly, whatever that next book will be like, it will represent
Kingston's ongoing work toward reimagining and restructuring the
novel, a genre which has from its beginnings been an experimental form
of writing. In pushing the boundaries of the genre, she is following in
the literary footsteps of writers like Laurence Sterne, Ann Radcliffe, Virginia Woolf, Jorge Luis Borges, and Julio Cortazar, among others.

Kingston's quest to redefine genre, to discover and create innovative
narrative forms, and to construct a linguistic structure appropriate to
new forms of storytelling, goes well beyond a desire simply to reconfigure
generic boundaries. She hopes that she can redefine larger categories—
fiction and nonfiction—that she also finds confining and limiting. She
imagines a very wide border between fiction and nonfiction, envisioning
fiction as a narrow place on one side of that border, while nonfiction is
a narrow place on the other side. In that vast border in the center exists
real life, and fantasies, dreams, and visions (Schroeder 84). Although she
finds the label "fiction" to be useful as a positive term that encompasses
narrative text produced by the imagination, she contends that as descriptive literary terminology, the word "nonfiction" has dubious value, and
she argues that the word is indistinct, and can be applied to nearly any
genre (Schroeder 84).

Kingston did not choose to label her work as "nonfiction"—the decision about the label was made by her publisher, Knopf, and her editor,
Charles Elliot. The publisher needed to define a category for *The Woman
Warrior*, and suggested that nonfiction was more marketable. Kingston
believes that too many publishers think that American readers are uni-
maginative, that memoirists are easier to market on talk shows because
television producers want writers who embody their books (Mandelbaum 49). Kingston was not convinced of the appropriateness of the
nonfiction designation for her work; however, when Elliot pointed out
that poetry is also classified as nonfiction, she finally agreed. Paul Mandelbaum notes that the decision to market *The Woman Warrior* as nonfiction paved the way for the creative memoir, a genre that he identifies as
one of the most marketable genres in contemporary publishing (Mandelbaum 50). Ironically, the question of genre has sparked criticism of
Kingston from those who insist that *The Woman Warrior* is pure fiction
and should have been labeled as such. Kingston herself points out that

the book is one woman's memoir of growing up Chinese American in California.

MAXINE HONG KINGSTON AS A WRITER

Attempts to describe Kingston's work frequently turn into lists of the narrative forms that the author employs as she combines legend, myth, history, memoir, folktale, anecdote, and autobiography into a genre of her own invention. Perhaps because Kingston's prose style is unusual— circular, recursive, disjointed, episodic, unlike the familiar linear narratives in traditional western texts—and because it is so different from other literary works that readers and critics have previously encountered, Maxine Hong Kingston is frequently asked to respond to questions about herself as a writer, as well as to queries about her sources, her language, her images and allusions, and about her writing process.

Kingston always wanted to be a writer, and as a child she dreamed of writing for a living the way that other little girls in her community fantasized about careers as nurses or teachers or mothers. But she also claims not to know of any specific influence that might have nurtured in her the desire to write. Indeed, she feels that she is a born writer, telling interviewer Kay Bonetti, "While I've had problems speaking, I've always been a writer" (Bonetti 34).

When she was a child, Kingston kept her writing a secret from her family, although in many interviews she implies that writing was—for her—a compulsion, a need. "My writing is an ongoing function, like breathing or eating," she told Arturo Islas, adding that she started writing as a child by scribbling words about anything and everything (Islas 22). In answer to questions posed by Donna Perry, Kingston describes her early attempts at writing as secretive. She hid her work and pretended to be doing something else, meanwhile making sure to write "all the things that were forbidden to say" (Perry 181). Kingston's compulsion to articulate what she should not, to shape unspoken stories, to write about taboo subjects, is reflected in the opening sentence of *The Woman Warrior*. Young Maxine quotes her mother's strictures on recounting the story of No Name Woman, the aunt whose illegitimate pregnancy disgraced an entire family, making its members vulnerable to the scorn of their village, and forever obliterating the aunt's name from all family history.

Kingston clearly remembers her first piece of creative writing, an effort that resulted from a flash of inspiration. She was a nine-year-old fourth grader at the time, when "all of a sudden this poem started coming out of me. On and on I went, oblivious to everything" (Robertson 26). When she finally stopped, she had written thirty verses. Once she discovered writing, she refused to stop, and eventually she cleared a space for herself in the family pantry, giving herself a private room not only in which to write, but also a place in which to store her writing materials, notes, and a typewriter. She has never lost that need to write, an activity essential to her very existence: "I breathe, I eat, I sleep, I write. I also write to communicate with my fellow beings. Creating myself as an American and Chinese American and American culture and Chinese American culture as beneficial by-products" (Alderson et al.).

Kingston describes herself as essentially a solitary writer, a description borne out by her childhood habit of concealing her writing, as well as by her appropriation of the hidden corner of the pantry as a writing space. During the early years after she had become an acclaimed writer, she wrote in an attic in which the ceiling was a scant two inches above her head when she stood. Although the workshops with which she has been involved have introduced her to collaborative efforts and communal writing, she remains a private writer; nonetheless, she does admit that the community process has become important to her, especially after the loss of her manuscript in the 1991 fire, and the overwhelming response of readers and fans to her requests for help with the reconstruction of the lost book. She admits that by appealing to her readers, she was, in essence, telling them that they were members of her community and that she needed their assistance: "I'm not going to write your book all by myself! Will you help me write it? You help me with the research and just send me all this material" (Seshachari 14). In another acknowledgment of her need to belong to a community, Kingston reflects on her realization that writing does not have to be solitary, that "talk-story"—her own narrative strategy—is communal. Concluding that modern American writing depresses and alienates because it is the product of solitary action, she hopes that by transforming writing into a communal act, she can create prose that radiates hope and human connections (Joan Smith B4).

The actual writing process is, for Kingston, a painstaking labor-intensive experience, a process of both creating and re-creating, crafting and revising. When *The Woman Warrior* and, later, *China Men* were published, Kingston gave credit to her lifetime passion for writing and rewriting until she has absorbed and is able to express the beauty and wisdom of her thoughts (Perry 181). Stories that she had heard and subsequently written down during her childhood became the nucleus of her two volumes of memoirs in which she recounted the saga of her extended family. Because the early childish stories revolved around the very same issues that inform her published work, Kingston enjoys saying that she worked on her books for forty years, although at the beginning "I didn't have the vocabulary yet" (Perry 181). Kingston says that she actually worked on *The Woman Warrior* and *China Men* over several decades, gradually developing the facility with words and language that would enable her to articulate her memories with vividness, clarity, and grace. For Kingston, writing is clearly a lengthy and reflective process that entails far more than simply putting pen to paper; as she describes it, writing has its origins "in the living that you do before" (Seshachari 12). Writing is the product of experience and thoughtful recollection of that experience.

On a typical writing day, Kingston arises early in the morning with the intention of writing for at least five hours before she stops for the day. "If everything goes well I can quit at noon or one," she notes in an interview conducted for and published in *Contemporary Authors*. "But usually things don't go right, so I keep at it until I get about five hours in" (206). Identifying discipline as one of the main problems for her as a writer, Kingston describes writing as a painful act, an activity that she sometimes unconsciously puts off. In fact, early in her career, she revealed that although she tried to begin her daily writing sessions as early as possible, she occasionally procrastinated by doing other tasks such as washing dishes or sharpening pencils.

Kingston does not write from an outline; instead, she conjures up visual images that she afterwards "translates" into her luminous prose. She had once wanted to have a career as an artist, and she still frequently begins the creative process by drawing and sketching ideas, producing visual representations of her thoughts. Once she does begin to write, however, she often finds it difficult to stop. Frequently she has no idea how her writing will develop, and she sometimes begins by sketching: "I draw a blob and then I have a little arrow and it goes to this other blob . . . it's like a doodle" (Ross 292). When the drawings become words, those words reveal stories and scenes about which Kingston was unaware; in fact, she notes that she often does not recognize a pattern until well into the writing process. On occasion, she confesses, the ending comes as a surprise. Kingston has made similar comments to others who have asked similar questions about the process that leads to her books. A believer in the idea that writers tap into an internal creative source, she observed early in her career that at times, she produces prose about ideas that she has not consciously acknowledged, "stuff I didn't even know I knew. . . . It's not like I've decided what I'm going to write" (Kubota 27).

Not long after the publication of *China Men* in 1980, Kingston elaborated on what she describes as her two strategies for producing text. One, which she describes as bearing some resemblance to "having a fit," involves what appears to be a variety of automatic writing, the onset of which she cannot control. She admits that what she refers to as "a fit" can happen to her almost anywhere, and that when she is thus inspired, she finds herself doing what she picturesquely describes as "writing all over the floor or up the walls," utterly unconscious of what she is doing (Pfaff 26). Her second method of producing text—according to her, a far less efficient kind of writing—focuses on generating words in a process akin to free writing, an experience that sends her into a word-inspired odyssey, as she writes feverishly, setting down on the page a vision created and shaped by the words as they emanate from her pen. The experience is short-lived but intense, as images rush from Kingston's imagination to the paper. She notes wryly that while this method generates a great deal of text, much of it is not very good writing (Pfaff 26). The material produced in that inspired rush always needs rewriting, a process over which Kingston labors intensively. *China Men* is an interesting example of the care with which Kingston creates her prose. She produced at least eight complete drafts of the manuscript, and she actually revised the book one more time at the galley proof stage—editing her own work so drastically that the entire book had to be typeset afresh, costing her a thousand dollars.

Kingston's Audience

Given the popularity of *The Woman Warrior* as an assigned high school or college text in a variety of disciplines across the curriculum, as well as the favorable critical attention that has focused on Kingston's other work, Kingston is often asked for whom she writes, who she believes her audience is. In response, she has made statements both in print and in interviews about the nature and identity of the audience for whom she creates her stories. Her first audience is herself. "When I write most deeply, fly the highest, reach the furthest, I write like a diarist—that is, my audience is myself," she writes in one of her most widely circulated essays, "Cultural Mis-readings" (64). Yet, she has often said, as well, that she writes for everybody, believing as she does that the creative productions of the individual imagination are both timeless and universal. Kingston identifies her third and very distinct audience in the closing paragraph of her essay, "Cultural Mis-readings," in which she notes that at the beginning and end of *The Woman Warrior*, she has deliberately embedded questions that can only be answered by Chinese American readers; and she has included cultural references that only that group will recognize instantly. By writing for herself, Kingston legitimizes her stories to herself. By writing for the general audience, she ensures the dissemination of the stories that she wants to include in the American narrative. And, finally, by writing for her fellow Chinese Americans, she introduces to that group one voice that she hopes will inspire others to speak out.

For Kingston, the most crucial audience for her work appears to be the general public. In a 1986 interview conducted by Jody Hoy, Kingston reiterated her intention to write for everyone, even for readers who have not even been born, pointing out that before she knew her work would find a market, she had decided that if she never found a publisher, she would photocopy her stories for others to read. She says that she writes for everyone, including future generations of readers, encompassing all nations and continents. In many interviews, Kingston has described her audience as "very wide" or "the universe," adding that she has always tried to be as inclusive as she can through her interrogation of familiar concerns and issues, the tensions of both belonging and being an outsider, of being alone as well as a member of a community. Kingston writes about the constant struggle to shed isolating thoughts and actions, and to communicate with others (Skenazy, "University" 143).

Kingston's desire to write for present and future audiences, for all readers—"for the common reader" as well as for the high school and university audiences that have so avidly embraced her work—seems at odds with the extraordinary array of allusions, literary and cultural references, and unfamiliar symbols at play in *Tripmaster Monkey*. She admits that she was surprised when reviews of her third book made much of the book's supposed impenetrability to the average reader. During a week as Regent's Lecturer at the University of California at Santa Cruz, she attempted to reconcile her intentions with the text that appears so difficult: "An educated audience would get more out of it [and] would have the fun of puzzling the allusions out" (Skenazy, "University" 143). She added the hope that readers who are not English majors will also enjoy the novel, relating perhaps to the essence of the narrative even though they might miss some of the more unusual allusions.

Kingston and the Writer's Responsibility

Maxine Hong Kingston takes very seriously the career that she has carved out for herself as a writer, a chronicler of human experience, a teller of stories. She clearly believes that writers have a responsibility to the reading public, and she states that one purpose of her writing is to "take people's preconceptions and break them apart," and to "take them to a point where they would experience enlightenment and they could do it by reading my words" (Hoy 54).

Kingston is amused by occasional criticism that her writing is didactic or preachy, or even pedagogical. That criticism has been most noticeable in reviews of *China Men*, especially in reference to its embedded chapter describing anti-immigration legislation aimed at Chinese in the United States. Revealing that her mother must bear at least part of the responsibility for the didactical elements, Kingston says that she experiences a recurring dream in which her mother—"big, middle-aged, at her strongest"—demands to know what Kingston has done to enlighten American readers. In that dream, Ying Lan Hong asks her daughter, "Have you educated America yet?" At times, the question has global implications, as Ying Lan demands to know how her eldest American child plans to educate the world (Schroeder 93).

Kingston's desire to effect social change through her writing is evident in the way that she conducts her writing workshops for Vietnam veterans. The participants in these workshops are creative individuals whose experiences during the Vietnam War left them with stories that they need to tell. Kingston encourages them to write from the heart, and to publish what they have written, for only by reaching readers can writer hope to change the market, and by extension, to change the canon (Skandera-Trombley 45). One interesting feature of Kingston's workshops is her incorporation of meditation at the beginning and conclusion of each day, as well as her invocation of Kuan Yin, goddess of mercy, "the Bodhisattva of compassionate listening" (Schroeder 94).

Early in her career, Kingston had refused to be labeled "political," fearing that the word with its connotations and cultural baggage was a limiting descriptor. Because her writing has always emerged from "personal emotions" and peculiar circumstances, Kingston resisted having her work defined by external standards, and she retreated from what she described as "aesthetic standards and socially relevant standards" imposed on her by others (Perry 173). Over time, however, Kingston's attitude toward the political label has altered. The enthusiastic reception that her books have earned proves that her prose stands on its own merits, that her writing needs no validation based on traditional aesthetic standards. More to the point, her early activism and involvement in the peace movement has regained a central position in her career, and she is now able to describe herself as a political writer in the sense that she writes to "affect politics" through working toward the goal of changing the world "through artistic pacifist means." Kingston believes that artists and writers have both the power and the responsibility to redirect public consciousness one reader or viewer at a time. As a pacifist, she is committed to discovering a way to prevent wars, to turn the world toward peace through the medium of her art.

Maxine Hong Kingston's political stance is evident not only in her writing, but also in interviews, speeches, and public presentations. Always alert to opportunities for educating her audience, Kingston speaks out on the major issues with which Asian Americans grapple daily. One such opportunity came during the 1990 television series, *World of Ideas*, when host Bill Moyers remarked, "So much of what you write about, your own childhood, your ancestors, sounds so exotic to mainstream Americans that it's another world, and I wonder what they take away from that world" (Perry 172). Kingston, who has always considered herself an American writer, voiced her hope that readers would ultimately learn not to think of her characters as "exotic" any longer, but would realize that she writes about Americans, as well as about the nature of humanity. The points she makes—that there are different versions of the American experience, and that we should not exoticize what we do not understand—are a central concern in all of her books.

Since the publication of *China Men*, many have taken note of Kingston's assertion in that book that the term "Asian American" (without the hyphen) is the most accurate designation for any individual whose ancestry can be traced to one of the Asian countries. She contends that using the word "Asian" as an adjective—the usage inherent in eliminating the hyphen—privileges the word "American" (correctly) as the designator for anyone whose citizenship is American and whose ancestry is Asian. Although *China Men* was published in the mid-1980s, Kingston continues to be concerned and outspoken about the dominant culture's unconscious tendency to label non-African American people of color as foreigners, speaking out in correction whenever she has the opportunity. In a comment about editorial practice in California newspapers, she describes the pervasiveness of the problem, complaining that they'll say "'Asian laundering Democratic party funds' on the front page . . . and they are actually writing about Asian Americans, but they leave American out. . . . Every day I pick up the paper and they are writing about a Chinese or Asian and it is really about Americans" (Skandera-Trombley 44).

In keeping with her pacifism and her attempts to understand war, Kingston has spent considerable time and emotional energy with her writing workshops for veterans of the Vietnam War, against which she protested during her student days. Inspired by the prompting of these survivors of a conflict that divided America, she has learned to redefine the word "veteran." She includes in the word's embrace a multitude of individuals who also suffered through and ultimately survived that war: internees in prison camps; people who witnessed the deaths of family members and close friends; the men, women, and children who never wore military uniforms, but who nevertheless were forced to become unwilling participants; and the parents of men who served in the armed forces. Kingston and the writers' group have also identified others whom they call "peace veterans": rioters who protested the United States' involvement in the war; "people who were in the streets" (Schroeder 94); demonstrators; and people who were jailed for resisting the draft. Her work with the veterans' groups is itself a profoundly political act, a public manifestation of her quest for a process that will lead the world to peace.

Maxine Hong Kingston: Storyteller

Storytelling is one of the dominant tropes (image or figurative expression) in Kingston's work, perhaps the most important one. *Woman Warrior* and *China Men* are both collections of related stories; *Tripmaster Monkey* has at its core a protagonist who seeks to construct his identity through storytelling; and Kingston's own narrative style is a Chinese folk genre called "talk-story." In Tom and Ying Lan Hong's China, so many people were illiterate that storytelling was the only viable strategy for the transmission of culture from one generation to the next, and Chinese immigrants carried the storytelling tradition with them to the new world. As a child in Stockton's Chinese community, Kingston listened to her parents and relatives talk-story some of the myths and history that had crossed the Pacific Ocean with them. She absorbed from those sessions the cultural narratives, legends, and snippets of Chinese history that formed the framework of the books she would write as an adult. Raised in that storytelling culture, Kingston, not surprisingly, developed into a raconteur herself: "As far back as I can remember I was a storyteller, and before I could write, I was inventing stories" (Skenazy, "University" 122).

Because Kingston's parents were educated, they passed on to their daughter not only traditional Chinese narratives like the tale of Fa Mu Lan or the historical account of General Yue Fei (1103–41), but also classical Chinese literature. Kingston recalls that her parents read the works of Tu Fu and Li Po, and that in the evenings, her mother read T'ang Dynasty poetry aloud while her father listened (Marilyn Chin 69). Kingston adds that stray fragments of European culture crept into the storytelling sessions of her childhood, commenting that she was in college before she realized that the story of Robinson Crusoe came from an English novel rather than from Chinese folklore. The Chinese tale that Kingston remembers hearing during her childhood as "The Adventures of Lo Bun Sun"—a tale that she eventually discovered to be a retelling of Daniel Defoe's novel—later became a chapter in *China Men*, functioning as a parallel narrative to the stories of Chinese men who were forced to create or piece together various strategies for survival in Hawai'ian sugar cane fields or on the transcontinental railroad.

The principal storyteller in the Hong household was Ying Lan, Kingston's mother, who employed the narrative form as a strategy for transmitting traditional Chinese culture and moral lessons to her six American-born children. In her essay, "A Chinese Garland," Kingston describes her mother's narrative dexterity: "She constantly tells stories—family history, Chinese folk tales, epics and legends, including the chant of Fa Mu Lan, the Woman Warrior" ("Garland" 42). Inspired by her mother's example, Kingston as a child naturally gravitated toward the story form, and she recalls that "the first stories [she] made up were oral and in Chinese." Not until she learned English in school, at around age eight, did she begin to write poetry and fiction that she had kept in her imagination. Kingston says that "The English language and written stories came to [her] simultaneously" ("Garland" 42).

Because her earliest writing focused entirely on re-creating the tales she had heard all her life, Kingston continued to rely on the narrative form for all writing assignments while she was in school. Even as a high school student, she cast her class work in story form. She remembers a class assignment that required her to write about California's agricultural products. Instead of the expected essay, she created a story about hitchhiking hoboes who visited localities that grew different crops. Clearly, she was more fascinated by the hoboes, by humans instead of economics (Kubota 27). Years later, she wryly admitted that at the time she did not understand what a term paper was or what such an assignment entailed, claiming that she did not understand the essay form until she was a university senior. She told Gary Kubota that she "got some really bad grades during the transition" (Kubota 27).

Perhaps because her childhood and her imagination were shaped by stories, Maxine Hong Kingston very early felt the compulsion to recount her own stories, in particular, her versions or retellings of tales her mother and aunts had told her about the family and about ancestors in China. As a child, she lacked the vocabulary and style to make her stories compelling, but over the years, she wrote and rewrote her stories, and with each revision, she developed her facility with language and imagery, gradually honing her skill until she became the artist that she is today.

As a storyteller, Kingston simultaneously employs and perpetuates a traditional Chinese cultural practice that has found its twentieth-century expression in both high and low culture: in significant works of fiction and poetry, in Chinese opera, in retellings of myth and legend, and in the performances of itinerant professional raconteurs who construct and reconstruct stories. She notes, for example, the practice of storytelling-for-hire in certain Asian cities, in which professional storytellers enter restaurants to narrate stories for customers at their tables. Just before the climax, these storytellers stop, refusing to conclude a story without payment—the larger the payment, the better the ending (Islas 32).

Because the storytelling tradition allows for a fluid narrative, one that can be revised and reshaped to speak to specific audiences, Kingston works in that tradition, manipulating, reworking, and modifying the stories that she absorbed as a child in order to use them to explain and to come to terms with her multiple landscapes—China, America, a Cantonese village, a neighborhood in Stockton, and ultimately the world.

Kingston's technique derives from the ancient right of storytellers to change a story with each retelling to fit the circumstances of that telling and the audience that is listening. Her mother and her mother's friends told and retold their several versions of how they came to America, each time revising the stories to fit the occasion, the listeners, the context of the telling. As she listened, young Maxine was profoundly impressed not only with the effectiveness and malleability of stories, but also with the capacity for a single story to become relevant to a variety of contexts and audiences. Emphasizing that the oral tradition is very much alive, she points out that stories influence action by changing with the demands of each context, "according to the needs of the listeners, according to the needs of the day, according to the interests of that time" (Islas 31). Consequently, any story can differ from day to day.

As she worked on *China Men* and struggled to shape her father's story, Kingston employed the narrative strategies that she learned in childhood, and created several possible versions of her father's journey to America, incorporating all of those retellings into the finished work that also introduced the stories of Kingston's grandfathers and uncles. A crucial influence on those stories was her consciousness that she had become one of her family's storytellers, charged with the responsibility of adapting the stories of her male ancestors into forms that could be shared with a general audience and ultimately incorporated into the American narrative.

One of Kingston's recollections about her childhood illustrates her early attempts to find the right voice with which to tell the stories that she created in her imagination. At first, she used Greek mythology as the template for her stories. More familiar with the tales of Jason and the Argonauts, Kingston attempted to force the Chinese stories into the epic form. Not surprisingly, she was unsuccessful—the Chinese tales required a narrative structure of their own, one that re-created the oral versions by employing talk-story as the narrative (Bonetti 34).

Because she is aware that the source of her stories is the Chinese oral tradition—both the cultural coded narratives and the talk-story that transmitted those narratives from one generation to the next—Kingston has consciously worked to craft a prose style that replicates as closely as possible the speech of the storytellers to whom she listened as a child. She credits the influence of American author Gertrude Stein who, in her works, re-created distinctive ways of speaking by relying on the creative use of syntax and rhythm. "One of my goals as a writer is to capture Chinese American speech," she says, "and to do so without having to invent an unreadable orthography" (*Black Curtain* 6). Because she feels this responsibility to represent as accurately as possible the way that her characters might speak, Kingston listens carefully to the individual speech patterns manifested by storytellers, to the rhythms and cadences of people who talk-story. She is working toward discovering a linguistic rhythm that will allow her to transcribe and translate Chinese dialect and accents. She writes in English about people who speak Chinese, and she feels that she must find the most appropriate rhythms to represent Chinese speech (Ross 292). Kingston refuses to employ what she derides as "strange misspellings that make people sound stupid" (292), a reference to literary attempts to recreate linguistic accents or dialects through phonetic spellings that are intended as reproductions of unfamiliar syllables, often to the detriment of the speech that is recorded.

A singular and tremendously significant consequence of Kingston's visit to China was her discovery that she has, indeed, managed to convey through English words and sentences the rhythms and cadences of the Chinese spoken by the people about whom she writes. She learned that Chinese scholars, well-versed in both the official English versions of her books and the pirated Chinese translations, had concluded that the pirated editions—generally in Mandarin—were inaccurate. It apparently was evident to these scholars, who based their opinions on the original English editions, that Kingston's characters in *The Woman Warrior* and *China Men* speak a dialect of Cantonese; consequently, new official translations into Cantonese have been commissioned in China.

In an increasingly global culture, Maxine Hong Kingston is a bridge between China and the United States. Not only has her work been embraced in China as an important link between classical Chinese literature and contemporary efforts to create a new literary culture in China, but her books now exist officially in both English and Chinese. Equally important is Kingston's role as a strong voice for Asian Americans in a multicultural United States. This is a country in which diverse ethnicities, identities, cultures, and faiths coexist, sometimes uncomfortably, occasionally painfully, but always aware of the existence of an America that encompasses and embraces—albeit sometimes reluctantly—a tremendous range of cultural practices and origins.

Kingston stresses the fact that her work is American rather than Chinese, noting that she has always imagined her characters as American despite their memories of China. Her wish is for readers to realize that her ancestors—the people whose stories she tells—belong with the tremendous variety of individuals who make up the population of the United States. Those stories, she says, are appropriately the province of American literature.

In a letter to Asian American literary scholar David Leiwei Li in 1988,

Maxine Hong Kingston articulates her mission and her place in American literature:

> I am in the tradition of American writers who consciously set out to create the literature of a new culture. Mark Twain, Walt Whitman, Gertrude Stein, the Beats all developed ears for dialect, street language, and experimented with how to make written language sound like spoken language. The content of that language is the ever-changing mythology. I am writing American mythology in American language. (Li, "China Men" 496)

2

Maxine Hong Kingston and the Asian American Literary Tradition

With the publication of Maxine Hong Kingston's *The Woman Warrior* in 1976, writing produced by Asian Americans entered the mainstream of twentieth-century American literature, achieving—with one book—both popular acclaim and a solid position in the canon of American literature. *The Woman Warrior* has inspired intense discussion among readers, reviewers, and academic critics because it so clearly resists categorization within specific genres and traditional textual geographies. The book is obviously not a novel, although pieces of fiction are embedded in the text. It is not biography, not history, not poetry, despite the strong resemblance between Kingston's prose and some of Walt Whitman's and Allen Ginsberg's poetry. *The Woman Warrior* has been labelled both fiction and nonfiction, and because the work resembles neither traditional autobiography nor conventional novel, the literary debates over its genre have resulted in no clear consensus.

The publishers of Kingston's third book, *Tripmaster Monkey*, were quick to label the work a novel and thus Kingston's "first work of fiction." *Tripmaster*, like *The Woman Warrior* and *China Men*, belongs to a much more elusive and slippery category of writing, sometimes described as "indigenous ethnography"—a phrase that also inspires a variety of conflicting definitions. "Indigenous ethnography" is also used to describe a number of significant Native and African American texts, placing Kingston squarely in the company of writers like Gloria Anzaldua, Toni Morrison, and Leslie Marmon Silko. These writers' experimentation with genre in combination with their appropriation of a variety of oral narrative forms is creating a new American literary aesthetic and sensibility. In fact, Kingston is still somewhat more frequently discussed in the context of African American, Latina, and Native writers rather than in comparison with Asian American writers. Nevertheless, Kingston is unarguably a product of the Asian American community. At the center of her books is the experience of Asian immigrants and their descendants; her materials include Chinese folklore, history, and literature; and her narrative strategy most closely follows the unwritten conventions of Chinese talk-story. Moreover, and equally important, Kingston's texts occupy an increasingly significant cultural space, inhabiting the invisible borderlands between China and America, the geography of the immigrant nation, the country of diasporaic people who have lost a homeland and yet have not fully gained a new country of the heart. Kingston's literary universe is Asian America.

The reading public as well as mainstream literary reviewers and critics enthusiastically hailed the publication of *The Warrior Woman* as a signal event in American literary history. However, the book was not received so warmly by a significant and vocal—if somewhat limited—number of Asian American writers and critics, as well as a few academic sinologists or scholars whose research focuses on China and its history, culture, and politics. The resulting heated discussion (much of which exists in print) about Kingston's work has informed and shaped the character and direction of Asian American literature—and to a certain extent, Asian American Studies—since the late 1970s. Central to the discussion is the argument about who are and are not Asian Americans, and what is and is not Asian American literature. In order to contextualize not only Kingston's work, but also the positions espoused by the author's defenders and critics, it is helpful for the reader to become familiar with the history of Asian immigration to the United States.

ASIANS IN AMERICA

No specific date is available for the arrival of the first Asians in North America, but available records reveal that Chinese travelers reached Mexico at least as early as the seventeenth century. History also records the presence of the so-called "Manilamen" in Louisiana in the 1760s. These were men from the Philippines, crewmen who escaped involuntary servitude in the Spanish galleon trade between Acapulco and Manila by jumping ship off the coast of southeastern Louisiana. Although a few Chinese sailors came ashore at Boston and Philadelphia in the eighteenth century, not until just before the nineteenth century did large numbers of Chinese begin to arrive in California. Fleeing from economic difficulties and the ravages of the Taiping Rebellion and Opium Wars, most of the earliest Chinese immigrants to the United States came from one small area: Guangdong Province on the coast of southern China. The majority of these immigrants were men traveling in search of work and a better life on the other side of the Pacific Ocean.

With the discovery of gold in the foothills of California's Sierra Nevada Mountains in 1849, the wave of immigrants swelled to flood stage as thousands of Chinese men, as well as a surprising number of women, embarked on the expensive and arduous journey by crowded ship to the new land that they optimistically christened *gum sun* or "the Gold Mountain" in the Toishan dialect spoken by many immigrants. On their arrival in America, large numbers of immigrants were hired to work in the mines and on the transcontinental railroad, while others found employment as domestics, agricultural laborers, odd-job handymen, cooks, and fishermen. A fortunate few managed to acquire sufficient capital to establish small businesses such as laundries, restaurants catering to other Chinese, and shops that sold sundries as well as items that were impossible to get in non-Asian stores.

Between the 1840s and 1870s, the absence of any formal immigration policy meant that thousands of able-bodied and willing Asians—mainly Chinese—joined the labor force in Hawai'i and mainland United States. These immigrants redressed a crucial labor shortage through their willingness to take on menial jobs scorned by white Americans who had come from the East Coast with dreams of instant riches from the gold mines. Many of these new arrivals from China were sojourners—men whose immigration journeys had been funded by the combined resources of their families. These men were expected to amass comfortable sums of money—enough to send money orders to China each month, while still accruing savings that would allow them eventually to return home to a comfortable family life cushioned by money in the bank. During the boom years of the American West, Asian workers were welcome, but when mining slowed, the railroad was completed, and cheap labor was no longer a necessity, these workers became undesirable aliens. Surprisingly, however, the first piece of legislation directed against Asians was not enacted against laborers despite the fact that their services had ceased to be a desirable commodity. That first law targeted women. While the earliest female immigrants included a few wives and daughters, a number of Asian women who also came to the United States with the earliest immigrant groups were prostitutes, an institutionalized but unacknowledged presence in the predominantly Asian sections of the mining and railroad camps, and in the Asian community at large. In the early years, these women were virtually invisible to the mainstream culture, but as the numbers of immigrants increased, the women's presence become more noticeable.

Although the majority of Chinese immigrants were unaccompanied men who hoped to find lucrative work in the mines and later on the transcontinental railroad, approximately 5,000 Chinese women also arrived in America before 1870. Afong Moy, reputed to be the first Chinese woman to arrive in the continental United States, was brought to New York City in 1834 by the American Museum, which put her on display to show Americans what a Chinese woman looked like (Fessler 6). Billed as "a Chinese lady in native costume," Afong Moy was the first of several women from China who were made the objects of public curiosity in venues like P. T. Barnum's Chinese Museum, where a woman identified only as Pwan-Yekoo was described as "strange" and "wonderful," and where much was made of her exoticism and difference from "New York bells" (Huping Ling 3). In addition to displaying Chinese fashions, these women treated the crowds to the sounds of a few spoken phrases in Chinese, as well as to demonstrations of the use of chopsticks and performances of Chinese music. These women were not, strictly speaking, immigrants—rather, they were visitors who entered the United States almost as though they were featured guest performers.

Possibly the first Chinese woman to emigrate to California was Marie Seise, a servant who came to America in 1848 as a member of the household staff of the Charles V. Gillespie family (Yung 14). While some of the early immigrant Asian women were servants like Marie Seise, others were sex workers, not unlike some of the white women from the East Coast who came to California to share in the gold-driven economic boom. Sketchy records reveal that the majority of Chinese prostitutes were, in fact, little more than slaves or indentured servants who had been kidnapped from remote villages in rural China and sold to brokers and brothel owners. They were then shipped like human cargo to the camps and temporary villages that were established close to mining operations and railroad construction sites. Controlled by the *tongs*, powerful secret Chinese organizations, the white slave traffic flourished in the predominantly male Asian communities in the United States.

Only a handful of women eventually managed to escape their servitude and enforced poverty; among those few who did, the most famous was Ah-Choi or Ah Toy, "the girl in the green silk pantaloons" (Yung 14). Arriving in San Francisco from Hong Kong in 1848 or 1849, Ah-Choi was not only a desirable courtesan, but also an astute businesswoman. She managed within two years of her arrival in California to establish her own business, a successful brothel on what is now Waverly Place in San Francisco. Patrons at Ah Toy's establishment paid one ounce of gold (sixteen dollars in mid–nineteenth-century currency) for the privilege of "[gazing] upon the countenance of the charming Ah Toy" (Gentry 52). Unlike many of her fellow Chinese immigrants, Ah Toy/Ah-Choi was fascinated by, rather than fearful of, the American judicial system, and she regularly appeared in court to sue clients who tried to cheat her. She also made it a point to speak publicly in defense of her profession during the frequent investigations of prostitution in California. The presence of increasing numbers of Chinese prostitutes eventually became public knowledge, fueling anti-Asian sentiment, and ultimately giving rise to and perpetuating the myth of the Asian woman as a predominantly erotic, sexually subservient, essentially immoral female. Consequently, 1870 saw the passage of the "Act to Prevent the Kidnapping and Importation of Mongolian, Chinese, and Japanese Females for Criminal and Demoralizing Purposes." The passage of that law drastically limited the number of Asian women who entered the United States legally during the years that followed.

The first *inclusive* discriminatory legislative act directed at a specific ethnic group—the 1882 Policy of Exclusion—banned further immigration of Chinese laborers, and permitted only limited entry of those who could prove that they were students, diplomats, businessmen, or temporary visitors. In addition, the act prohibited the return of more than 22,000 Chinese laborers who had traveled to China to visit the families that they had left behind. Coming a mere twelve years after the 1870 Act, the effects of the 1882 Policy were immediate and long-lasting: Chinese families were practically legislated out of existence in the United States, and a "bachelor" culture, comprised of men in their middle years or older, came to represent Chinatowns on both coasts. This predominantly male culture forms the background of events in Kingston's *China Men*.

Until the middle of the twentieth century, large numbers of the earliest Chinese immigrants were men who were forced by circumstance to live out most of their adult lives in the bachelor communities of the various Chinatowns all over the American West. Before the Second World War, Asian men were considered in terms of cheap temporary labor, not humanized as husbands or fathers, and legislation prevented the entry of all but a very few Chinese women into the United States. Consequently, an entire generation of Chinese men was unable to father a new American generation. Unable to procreate in America, they were aware that as long as they remained in the country, they would have no children to succor their old age or tend their graves. Hundreds of these men therefore became courtesy uncles to the handful of children who were born in Chinatowns in the early years of the twentieth century. So rare was the presence of such children, however, that when Ah Goong in *China Men* travels from community to community after the Driving Out, he is compelled to remark on the wonderful novelty of meeting entire immigrant families, "miraculous China men who had produced families out of nowhere," men who have wives and children who call Ah Goong "Uncle," creating in him a yearning to remain with them to be the uncle of the family (*China Men* 147).

For almost a century, legalized discrimination limited the numbers of Asians who could enter the United States, even while immigration from European countries caused a rapid increase in the white populations of the East Coast and the Midwestern states. Exclusion legislation also produced an aging male Asian population in the Western states, and inspired in China a thriving black-market industry in fraudulent immigration documents. Maxine Hong Kingston also explores this practice in *China Men*, providing historical context through a long section detailing the history of anti-Chinese discrimination, a narrative strategy that has both enlightened and annoyed readers. When asked in an interview about the placement of that section, Kingston explained that readers would have skipped an introduction and an appendix; moreover, she felt that footnotes were inappropriate in a memoir—and because the information is essential, she made it part of the narrative.

Between 1882 and 1943, all aspiring Asian immigrants who arrived in California were detained and questioned—before 1910, in a San Francisco waterfront facility known as "the Shed"; after that year, in wooden barracks at Angel Island. Unlike New York's Ellis Island which offered European immigrants the hope-inspiring presence of the Statue of Liberty, Angel Island provided Asians only with the shadow of notorious Alcatraz prison. Angel Island became the temporary quarters—for varying lengths of time, from weeks to years—of hundreds of laborers, as well as students, merchants, and other Asian travelers who also suffered detention, occupying themselves during their incarceration by carving into the barracks walls a poetic record of their ordeal (see pages 51–52).

Paralleling the legal initiatives to control Asian immigration to the United States, and shaping public opinion well into the 1970s were portrayals of Asians in popular culture and later, the media, as "inscrutable"—incomprehensible, unknowable, unreadable. Some of the most durable stereotypes of Asian men grew out of employment conditions for Asian immigrants in the American lumber camps, mining communities, and cane and pineapple plantations of the nineteenth century. In general unskilled, unlettered, and unable to speak more than rudimentary English, many of these immigrants worked as houseboys, kitchen help, cooks, laundry employees; they performed tasks that were often associated with women in domestic spaces. Although thousands of other men engaged in heavy (masculine) labor—laying railroad tracks, felling redwood trees, clearing hillsides, loading ore carts, digging, setting dynamite charges—it was the Chinese cook and the Filipino houseboy who made an indelible impression on the writers and later, film-makers, who immortalized the American West. Other stereotypes—especially Fu Manchu, Charlie Chan, the effeminate mandarin with long fingernails and brocaded robes—might, ironically, have resulted partially from the exoticizing effect of the "literary tour guide" genre. This was popularized by Asian writers like Lin Yutang and Onoto Watanna, whose works were avidly read and often believed by readers to be the only available authentic accounts of life in China or Japan.

Widely distributed popular American journals such as *Good Housekeeping* and *Colliers* perpetuated the belief that Asians were exotic at best, frightening at worst—and terminally unassimilable. Asians were described as materialistic, politically suspect, and above all, unalterably alien thanks to their unfamiliar religions and difficult native languages. To the largely ethnocentric general public, all Asians looked alike, with the exception of the few culturally inscribed caricatures that became stereotypes. These included the dutiful houseboy and the inscrutable detective; among women, the shy China Doll and the dangerous Dragon Lady; the ancient and omniscient Oriental sage; and much later, the Second World War's bloodthirsty "Jap" and the Vietnam War's treacherous "Chink" and "Gook." The late twentieth-century invention of the

more benign stereotype of "the model minority" might appear finally to
have provided a positive antidote to the damning stereotypes of over
half a century, but it continues to perpetuate, albeit more subversively,
the idea that Asians are indelibly foreign by segregating them as a minority group within a minority population.

ASIAN AMERICANS

Until the 1960s, the term *Oriental* was employed in America and Europe to refer to the inhabitants of the Asian (and even Middle Eastern)
countries, as well as for immigrants from that part of the world and their
descendants in the Western nations. Because of the term's connotations
of exoticism and unfathomable difference, politicized members of America's Asian populations began to resist the appellation, preferring initially to identify themselves by specific national origins—as Americans
of Chinese, Japanese, or Korean ancestry. Eventually, these separate designations, with their undertones of double political allegiances, became
unwieldy, fragmenting a group that badly needed cohesiveness in order
to be taken seriously. Only if the groups' members were visible and vocal
would they be able to exercise the political clout that their numbers suggested they should possess.

The Asian American Movement, began in the 1960s, was energized by
the national struggle for civil rights, and escalated by anti-Vietnam War
activism. It gained considerable momentum after the immigration re-
forms of 1965 effected major changes in the composition and size of
America's Asian population. Although early exclusion laws had created
a situation which curtailed the ability of most Asian immigrants to form
nuclear family units, thus limiting for half a century the number of Asian
American children, the relaxing of immigration laws in the late 1940s
and the resulting establishment of families of Asian origins contributed
to a dramatic increase in the number of Asian American university
students. Central to the Asian American Movement was its identity as
a coalition of young people of college age from diverse Asian backgrounds. As a creative, articulate, and vocal group, this coalition exer-
cised its political muscle and began to interrogate the cultural practices
and institutional policies that had kept Asian immigrants and their descendants at the margins of American life for over half a century. Among
the significant and long-lasting changes effected by the Asian American
Movement was the privileging of the term "Asian American" over the

old designation, "Oriental," a word which to many second and third-generation Americans of Asian ancestry was encumbered with negative connotations of exotic otherness and marginality.

That umbrella designation, "Asian American," was coined to encourage cultural and political cohesion among immigrants from Asia and American-born citizens of Asian ancestry. At its most inclusive, the term embraces U.S. and Canadian citizens who have ancestral ties to countries within a huge geographical territory stretching from Pakistan to Japan, from Siberia to Indonesia. Embedded in that comprehensive label is an assumption that, aside from differences of national origin, ethnicity, class, education, religion, and self-definition, Asian Americans share certain common experiences that warrant naming, acknowledgement, interrogation, and ultimately resistance. Although the phrase does cause some discomfort among many citizens who are frequently identified as Asian Americans—Americans who, if they must be labelled, ironically now prefer the old and more specific designations such as "Chinese American," "Filipino American," or "Americans of Japanese Ancestry"—the phrase is useful as a unifying political statement and as an expression of solidarity among immigrant communities and ethnic groups.

ASIAN AMERICAN LITERATURE

The question of what constitutes Asian American literature has elicited a range of responses, including the very early statement by Kai-yu Hsu and Helen Palubinskas on the selection process that shaped their 1972 anthology, *Asian-American Authors*: "In this anthology every effort was made to represent the works of writers of Asian origin who have had extensive living experience in America. Those born and reared in America were considered first; then those who came to this country when very young and remained here" (Hsu and Palubinskas 1). Hsu and Palubinskas anthologize only works by authors of Chinese, Japanese, and Filipino ancestry or birth, at the same time acknowledging the existence of other "Asian-American authors whose heritages lie beyond the shores of China, Japan, and the Philippines" (1). Two years later came a more rigidly circumscribed definition embedded in the assertion by the editors of *Aiiieeeee* that their anthology is "exclusively Asian-American. That means Filipino-, Chinese-, and Japanese-Americans, American born and raised" (Frank Chin et al. vii). Like the earlier anthology, *Aiiieeeee* embraces authors from only three national backgrounds; unlike Hsu and

Palubinskas, the *Aiiieeeee* editors refused to consider including anyone who had not been born in the United States, excluding anyone "who consciously set out to become American" (Frank Chin et al. x).

Elaine Kim's seminal study of Asian American literature broadens the definition to include "published creative writings in English by Americans of Chinese, Japanese, Korean, and Filipino descent" (Kim xi). Moreover, while limiting her study to English texts, Kim emphasizes her belief that Asian American literature does include texts written by American immigrants in their first languages. Situating Asian American literature in a more universal context, Kim points out that while the literature "elucidates the social history of Asians in the United States," it also "shares with most other literature thematic concerns such as love, desire for personal freedom and acceptance, and struggles against oppression and injustice" (Kim xii–xiii). She also reminds readers to be aware that like all writers, Asian American authors "are not necessarily 'typical' or 'representative' of their nationalities or racial groups" (xiii)—a warning that has relevance for our later discussion of Maxine Hong Kingston and her work.

More recently, King-Kok Cheung has defined Asian American literature as having been produced by writers of Asian descent who were either born in or who have migrated to North America (Cheung, *Interethnic* 1). Cheung and Stan Yogi have, in fact, compiled an annotated bibliography of Asian American literature, a body of work which they describe as "works by writers of Asian descent who have made the United States or Canada their home, regardless of where they were born, when they settled in North America, and how they interpret their experiences" (Cheung and Yogi v). Increased immigration of peoples from Vietnam and Cambodia, India and Pakistan, Indonesia and Malaysia, and even Burma has significantly changed the nature and composition of the Asian American population, and literary anthologies published in the 1990s have reflected those demographic changes.

Asian American Literature: A History

In the introduction of a widely used recent (1996) anthology of Asian American writing, author and scholar Shawn Wong cautions against treating Asian American literature as a new and isolated phenomenon:

> What we need to realize is that Asian American literature has been published here since the nineteenth century, most nota-

bly the works of Sui Sin Far. The literature is not new; rather, it was neglected and forgotten. Asian American literature should be considered within the larger context of American multi-cultural literature and American literature in general. (Shawn Wong xvii)

In the context of the history of Asians—especially Chinese—in America, Wong's reminder suggests that Asian American literature, in its earliest incarnations, was more than likely produced by writers who came to the United States as adults with already established cultural and national identities. These identities, combined with a desire to fit into American culture, to belong, would significantly shape and color their literary efforts. Seeking some form of assimilation—even temporary—these writers cast themselves as cultural ambassadors who could move easily between East and West, between ethnicity and the mainstream culture.

Very few firsthand written records were left by the Chinese who emigrated to America in the nineteenth century. Except for a handful of diplomatic families and students, and still fewer highly educated exceptions like Kingston's father, the first Chinese who entered the New World were generally male, almost illiterate even in their mother tongue, untrained in any skill beyond manual labor, and single-mindedly focused on earning enough money to support their extended families who remained in Guangdong's emigrant villages. With the exception of the Angel Island poets (see pp. 51–52), the earliest Asian American writers—scholars and diplomats, for the most part—were relatively privileged and highly educated individuals who did not, could not represent the majority of Asians who lived and worked in the United States. In fact, they unconsciously sought to distance themselves from the largely working-class and uneducated immigrant community.

Shawn Wong, an Asian American writer and scholar, suggests that the earliest piece of truly Chinese American writing could quite well be a language text compiled by the anonymous "Wong Sam and Assistants" and published by the Wells Fargo Company for the linguistic education of Chinese workers in the mining camps and railroad settlements of the Western territories (Shawn Wong 6). It is more accurate to say, however, that Asian American literature probably began with the publication of essays and stories by Edith Maud Eaton.

By most accounts, Edith Maud Eaton (1865–1914) and—to a lesser extent—her sister, Winnifred Eaton (1875–1954) are the grandmothers of Asian American literature. Born to an English artist, Edward Eaton, and his Chinese wife, Grace Trefusis, the sisters and their siblings were brought to the North American continent by their parents who lived first in the United States before eventually settling in Canada. Despite the fact that neither sister looked especially Asian, both made the conscious decision to foreground their Asian heritage when they took up careers as writers.

Edith Eaton, choosing to assert their mother's Chinese identity, wrote under the Cantonese name, Sui Sin Far ("Narcissus"). She focused her creative energy on exposing and protesting the oppression under which Asian women suffered, on defending the value and legitimacy of her Chinese heritage, and on speaking out on women's issues. A Eurasian herself, and consequently the living personification of a dual heritage, she attempted—through her writing—to bridge the chasm between the two cultures of her ancestry. She announced: "I give my right hand to the Occidentals and my left to the Orientals, hoping that between them they will not utterly destroy the insignificant 'connecting link' " (Sui 132). Sui Sin Far's 1912 collection of stories, *Mrs. Spring Fragrance*, portrays Chinese and Eurasian characters realistically and sympathetically as human beings who have emotions and ambitions and needs, rather than as caricatures or stereotypes.

Winnifred Eaton adopted a Japanese identity, calling herself Onoto Watanna and claiming that her mother was a Japanese noblewoman from Nagasaki. Unlike Sui Sin Far, whose work contested the popular assumptions that undergirded anti-Asian prejudice, Onoto Watanna appropriated the current popular taste for the exotic, writing formulaic romances portraying beautiful maidens in bright kimonos against the backdrop of a Japan of cherry blossoms, tea houses, bamboo groves, and delicate furnishings in traditional shoji-screened homes. In this overtly "Oriental" setting, a fragile, childlike woman and an influential and successful man meet and fall in love. Circumstances drive them apart, but after a succession of heartrending separations and setbacks, the lovers are reunited. Because Watanna's novels reproduced widely accepted stereotypes—exotic Japan, helpless and adoring Oriental women, powerful and masterly white men—and reinforced widely held beliefs that feminine Asia needed the help of masculine America, the novels were immensely popular, going through multiple printings, and in the case of *A Japanese Nightingale* (1901), even being adapted for the Broadway stage.

Edith and Winnifred Eaton were certainly the most famous and successful of the earliest Asian American writers, but they were by no means the only immigrant writers who attempted to explain Asian culture to the general American reader. Unlike the Eatons who wrote fiction, however, other writers of Asian origins tended to favor ethnographic writing—nonfiction expository works that allowed readers to become armchair travelers, journeying vicariously not only into immigrant neighborhoods and communities, but also to China, Korea, and Japan.

From the late nineteenth to the early twentieth century, a handful of Asian students and visitors wrote travelogs, either books that illuminated the customs and folkways in the writers' native countries, or memoirs written in the personae of curious outsiders and revealing, often in humorous self-deprecating language, their reactions to the United States. Among the pseudotravelogs was a series of volumes commissioned by the D. Lathrop Publishing Company; the series started with the publication of Lee Yan Phou's *When I Was a Boy in China* (1887) and ended four decades later with New Il-Han's *When I Was a Boy in Korea* (1928). These volumes were very nearly anthropological in their focus on the commonplaces of everyday life and on cultural practices in countries considered by many readers to be not only foreign, but heathen. Eventually, with the arrival of more Asians in the United States, the travelogs became domesticated, focusing on Asians in American communities rather than abroad, and the books were transformed into literary tourist guides to Chinatowns, little Japans, and other ethnic enclaves. Lin Yutang's novel, *Chinatown Family* (1948), a classic example of the genre, is ostensibly a kind of Chinese Horatio Alger story, charting the struggles of an immigrant family that rises to affluence through the unstinting efforts of industrious parents and obedient children. Punctuating the plot are a number of obligatory set pieces about the more "exotic" elements of Chinese life: holidays and celebrations, religious ritual, food, traditional clothing, Confucianism, and family dynamics. In fact, the narrative portions of the novel appear to exist solely to provide an excuse for the author to trot out the kind of formulaic ethnography and exotic travel information familiar to American readers of *National Geographic* and Onoto Watanna's novels such as *The Honorable Miss Moonlight* or *A Japanese Nightingale*.

Another important strand in the development of Asian American literature emerged in isolation. During the weeks, months, and even years of their incarceration on Angel Island in the years before 1940, Chinese detainees awaiting their turn to be interrogated by immigration officials distilled the emotions and stories of their ordeal in poetry inscribed on the wooden walls of their prison. Poems composed early in a period of imprisonment retain shreds of optimism: "I am at the beginning of the road," (Lai et al. 36). Other, later poems are darker and more despairing: "My chest is filled with a sadness and anger I cannot bear to explain" (56), wails one poet, while another reflects that "Sadness kills the person in the wooden building" (52). "Why not just return home," philosophizes one Angel Island poet, "and learn to plow the fields?" (68). In some cases, physical evidence suggests that some of the existing poems are actually revisions of earlier literary attempts, indicating that the creation of those poems may have been a group effort carried on over considerable time.

Before the Angel Island facility was closed in 1940, hundreds of poems had been carved in Chinese characters which now stand as palpable records of the death of hope and the encroachment of confusion and bafflement. These poems are a testament to the loneliness and frustration, and even anger among individuals who, during those dark days, had no idea that they would one day be recognized as some of the pioneers of Asian American literature. Him Mark Lai, Genny Lim, and Judy Yung, who collected and edited the 136 surviving Angel Island poems, suggest that "the poems occupy a unique place in the literary culture of Asian America. These immigrant poets unconsciously introduced a new sensibility, a Chinese American sensibility using China as the source and America as a bridge to spawn a new cultural perspective" (Lai et al. 28).

World War II changed the climate for Chinese immigrants to the United States. The Exclusion Act was repealed in 1943, and China's status as an American ally in the war, coupled with the sufferings of the Chinese people at the hands of the Japanese army, bestowed on Chinese Americans the label of "good" Asians (to distinguish them from Japanese Americans who were held to be "bad"). Literary scholar Sau-ling Wong points out two crucial developments from the war years: First, the relaxed immigration policies made possible the entry of a larger-than-before number of Chinese-born women immigrants (among them the highly educated Helena Kuo, Adet and Anor Lin, Mai-mai Sze, and Han Suyin) who became writers. Second, the coming of age of the second generation of Asian Americans produced Pardee Lowe and Jade Snow Wong, significant writers whose works would reach a wider audience than had any Asian American texts to that point. In the tradition of Lin Yutang and others, Lowe and Wong wrote books that, on at least one level, did serve as armchair travel guides for readers who were seeking to indulge in literary tourism. But Lowe and Wong also left powerful records of the psychological price that was paid by second-generation Asian Americans who were not immigrants, but who were identified by the dominant culture as foreigners because they looked different.

Published in 1943, Pardee Lowe's *Father and Glorious Descendant* benefitted from the prevailing wartime sympathy toward the Chinese, as well as from the fact that its author was a graduate of Stanford and Harvard, had enlisted in the United States Army, and was a member of what was known as America's "loyal minorities," a term created to distinguish, from the enemy Japanese, those Asians from countries allied with the United States. As narrator, Lowe casts himself in the role of travel guide, depicting life in immigrant Chinese communities as quaint and foreign. He assists the reader in experiencing vicariously the exotic life of Chinatown with its singsong houses, Chinese schools, elaborate holiday feasts, sinister tongs (organized crime associations), and hordes of Chinese people dressed in "typical Chinese garments" and clinging to "strange" customs. At the same time, Lowe is at pains to point out his attraction to things American: Buffalo Bill and "Wild Bill Hitchcock" (*sic*), the Revolutionary and Civil Wars, clean restrooms, libraries, and modern homes. Lowe's distaste for the "typical Chinese" is evident in his narrative (he refuses to study Chinese or travel to China, and eventually he marries a white woman), and he does not mask his profound discomfort with his ethnicity or his tremendous desire to disappear into American culture, and to assimilate as thoroughly as possible.

Two years after *Father and Glorious Descendant*, Jade Snow Wong published her memoir, *Fifth Chinese Daughter* (1945), a restrained, elegant account of her early life and education. Only twenty-four when she wrote the book, she had just completed her baccalaureate degree at Mills College. Interspersed throughout Wong's narrative are vignettes of life in a Chinese community, explications of Chinese customs unfamiliar to readers, and descriptions of various elements of Chinese culture. *Fifth Chinese Daughter*, written in the third person (indicating that Wong still conforms to Chinese custom which frowns on the use of "I"), bears witness to the strength of the American Dream; the memoir details Wong's assimilation into and eventual recognition by the mainstream culture. Wong exoticizes her Chinese heritage, repeatedly implying that its very difference is a burden as well as a source of embarrassment to her, and although the book ends with the implication that she has come to terms with her past (she sets up a pottery in Chinatown), it is clear that she prefers the values of the mainstream community. *Fifth Chinese Daughter* became a bestseller, translated into several languages including Chinese, Japanese, and German, and Jade Snow Wong was appointed to the post of cultural emissary to Asia for the U.S. State Department. The book has remained in print, and until the publication of *The Woman Warrior*,

Wong's *Fifth Chinese Daughter* was probably the best-known work by an Asian American writer. For Maxine Hong Kingston, Wong's memoir was a revelation and an inspiration. Kingston told an interviewer that she had no real sense of writing in a tradition "except for Jade Snow Wong: actually her book was the only available one" (Carabi 11). Sadly, for Asian American women of Kingston's generation, literary influence was far more likely to come from writers in the British or European-American tradition—in Kingston's case, Virginia Woolf and Gertrude Stein, and later, William Carlos Williams.

Much of the Asian American writing that emerged from the 1950s and 1960s continued in the apologist/assimilationist tradition. These books tend either to beg the reader's indulgence as the writer elucidates the "exotic" culture in which the book is set, or else to make a point of delineating the similarities between the "exotic" culture and mainstream America. They engage the imaginations of readers by providing windows into life in America's ethnic Asian communities. Although Chin Yang Lee was not a Chinatown resident, his *Flower Drum Song*, published in 1957, provides readers with a comic literary tour of life in a fictional Chinatown and a humorous account of Chinatown's problems. The book portrays generational discord, the dearth of women and the accompanying threat of permanent bachelorhood, and job discrimination as they are experienced by the hapless Wang Ta, son of a wealthy, reclusive, completely unassimilated immigrant from Taiwan. *Flower Drum Song* was a popular novel, and was eventually adapted into a Broadway musical and later a Hollywood film. Asian American readers, however, rejected the novel for its perpetuation of negative stereotypes, as well as for its farcical treatment of the social problems that were all too real to inhabitants of real Chinatowns. Louis Chu's later *Eat a Bowl of Tea* (1961) is a far more sympathetic portrayal of the Chinatown existence. Chu neither ridicules nor idealizes the aging Chinese "bachelors" whose lives he chronicles; these men are not bumbling pidgin-English-speaking aliens, nor are they passive grateful immigrants cheerfully enduring dehumanizing treatment and hard labor, nor even are they model minority individuals. They are simply old men trapped by their ambition and pride in a subculture that is in the throes of massive change from an orientation toward China and their home villages to a focus on America and her immigrant communities.

The Chinese were not the only immigrants writing in the assimilationist tradition, sometimes referred to as "good will autobiographies" (Kim 289). From the ranks of writers of Japanese ancestry came Monica Sone's

Nisei Daughter (1953), a narrative of an American childhood interrupted by internment in a camp for Japanese Americans, and then happily resolved by the prospect of an all-American college experience; and John Okada's *No-No Boy* (1957), which examines the confusion that tears at a second-generation American of Japanese ancestry during World War II, when his country of birth is at war with the country of his heritage. In his autobiography, *I Have Lived with the American People* (1948), Manuel Buaken, an immigrant from the Philippines, seeks to elucidate the reasons why Filipinos emigrate to the United States. For Buaken and others, America represents freedom and justice, and despite his experiences of prejudice and discrimination, he concludes his narrative by pointing out that Americans and Filipinos are not only similar in many respects, but also share common values and goals. Like Lin Yutang, Celso Carunungan attempts to explain Philippine customs to American readers in *Like a Big Brave Man* (1960), as does N.V.M. Gonzales in *The Bamboo Dancers* (1964).

The first anthology of Asian American writing was Hsu and Palubinskas's 1972 *Asian-American Authors* (see p. 47), but that effort was eclipsed in 1974 by the now-famous *Aiiieeeee* anthology, edited by Jeffrey Paul Chan, Frank Chin, Lawson Fusao Inada, and Shawn Wong. Although the editors included only American-born writers of Chinese, Japanese, and Filipino ancestry—a limitation for which the anthology has been criticized—these four architects of *Aiiieeeee* bushwhacked a space for Asian American writers in the thicket of American literature. Frank Chin must be acknowledged as a central and radically militant figure in the recovery and dissemination of literary works by Americans of Asian ancestry. In their introductory essays, the editors ignited what is still the ongoing debate about the nature and boundaries, purposes and responsibilities of Asian American literature by articulating certain principles: that an Asian American sensibility is "one that was neither Asian nor white American" (Chin et al. xxi) and that genuine Asian American literature does not and should not exhibit a "dual personality, of going from one culture to another" (vii, xi). A third important anthology was published also in 1974: David Hsin-fu Wand's *Asian American Heritage: An Anthology of Prose and Poetry*.

Anthologies of literary pieces by Asian American women did not appear until the late 1980s and early 1990s. *The Forbidden Stitch: An Asian American Woman's Anthology* (1989), edited by Shirley Geok-lin Lim and Mayumi Tsutakawa, included the work of Korean and Indian writers, among them first-generation immigrants. A year later, Sylvia Watanabe and Carol Bruchac edited *Home to Stay: Asian American Women's Fiction* (1990), a collection that also included writers of Korean and Indian ancestry. Asian Women United of California produced two significant collections—*Making Waves: An Anthology of Writings by and about Asian American Women* (1989) and, much later, *Making More Waves: Writing by Asian American Women* (1997)—notable for expanding the range of genres to include memoir, essay, ethnography, and privileging "multiple identities and subjectivities" by featuring work from the various Asian groups, as well as from writers of mixed racial heritage.

In 1991, a follow-up anthology to *Aiiieeeee—The Big Aiiieeeee*—edited by Jeffrey Paul Chan, Frank Chin, Lawson Fusao Inada, and Shawn Wong, was published. Like its earlier sibling, the second volume included an introduction that posited a definition of Asian American literature, but the new definition reflected a decade and a half of controversy by attempting to distinguish between "real" and the "fake" Asian American literature. Unlike *Aiiieeeee*, the second collection did include pieces by first-generation immigrant writers, at the same time creating an even narrower focus with its restriction to works only by Chinese Americans and Japanese Americans. Far more inclusive are Jessica Hagedorn's *Charlie Chan is Dead: An Anthology of Contemporary Asian American Fiction* (1993), featuring the work of forty-eight authors, and Shawn Wong's *Asian American Literature* (1996), compiled according to its editor to represent "the range, variety, and depth of Asian American literature today" (Shawn Wong xvii) and featuring the work of immigrants and American-born writers alike.

Since the 1982 appearance of Elaine Kim's ground-breaking *Asian American Literature*, a number of major studies have continued to focus on the literary productions of American writers of Asian ancestry. Among these volumes are significant analyses by King-Kok Cheung, Amy Ling, David Palumbo-Liu, Stephen Sumida, and Sau-ling Cynthia Wong. Also important are collections of essays edited by Shirley Geoklin Lim, alone and with Amy Ling. Moreover, since the mid-1980s, university faculty positions in Asian American literature have not only proliferated, but have also become highly visible in both public and private major institutions. The increase in both scholarly studies and academic positions suggests that Asian American literature—far from being a temporary and peripheral phenomenon on the fringes of American writing—is now acknowledged as a thoroughly canonical strand of American literature.

MAXINE HONG KINGSTON AND ASIAN AMERICAN LITERATURE

The publication of *The Woman Warrior* in 1976 changed Asian American literature, managing to do what no other literary work by any Asian American writer had ever done—simultaneously earn critical acclaim and popular success. Equally notable is the fact that *The Woman Warrior* expanded the scope and purview of American literature by inspiring readers and literary scholars to begin paying attention to literary works by ethnic minority writers.

Many major studies of Asian American literature repeat—as do biographical and bibliographical entries in reference works—the fact that *The Woman Warrior* is not only the most widely recognized work by an Asian American writer, but also the most frequently assigned book on college and university campuses by a living American author (Perry 172). Sau-ling Wong points out that "It is safe to say that many readers who otherwise do not concern themselves with Asian American literature have read Kingston's book" (Sau-ling Wong, *Multicultural* 249). If some of Kingston's reading communities have embraced and privileged *The Woman Warrior* and, to a certain extent, *China Men*, others have contested the significance of Kingston's popularity, especially among general readers. This popularity has prompted mixed reactions from Kingston's colleagues: While many view Kingston's fame as a positive phenomenon that helps to legitimize writing by other Asian American authors, others are hostile, accusing Kingston of writing "with white acceptance in mind" (Tong, "Racist" 6). The resulting *pen wars* (a Chinese term for literary arguments) are of considerable interest to students of Asian American literature in particular, and minority literatures in general.

Incited by the reception of *The Woman Warrior*, the pen wars have since expanded to include not only angry attacks on the works of Amy Tan, David Henry Hwang, and David Mura, but also laments about mainstream readers' and critics' tendency to stumble into cultural misreadings. Because the details of the literary battle have been elucidated by a number of eminent scholars (King-Kok Cheung, Garrett Hongo, Amy Ling, and Sau-ling Cynthia Wong, among others), a very brief summary must suffice to provide a context for this book's analysis of Kingston's major works.

It is clear that the lines of battle have never been clearly drawn, that participants in the ongoing discussion do not agree on either the identity of the authors to be maligned (although the names of Maxine Hong Kingston, Amy Tan, and David Henry Hwang appear the most frequently), the nature, or even the severity of the literary and cultural "crimes" on which the arguments focus. It is equally clear that the origins of the controversy—and, in fact, the nature of the controversy—have not been completely defined. What is obvious is that many of the attacks do emanate from within the Asian American community of writers, a point made by Asian American scholar Amy Ling, who goes on to codify the nature of the accusations. Ling notes that some of the most virulent criticism of a minority writer can emanate from within the minority community. In the "damned-if-you-do, damned-if-you-don't" atmosphere of some of the pen wars, anything and everything is a target for denigration: "this writer is a traitor to the community and to the cause; she's not telling the story right or she's telling the wrong one . . . she's falling into stereotypes and catering to base appetites for the exotic and the barbaric" (Ling, "Dialogic Dilemma" 153). It should be pointed out that literary attacks from within a culturally and ideologically defined group are not peculiar to the Asian American community. Novelist Alice Walker for example, has been condemned for her negative portrayal of black men in *The Color Purple*.

By most accounts, Frank Chin, who early took exception to *The Woman Warrior*, has been the most vocal and unrelenting of Kingston's critics, accusing her—and later, Amy Tan—of pandering to the popular imagination and parodying Kingston's work in his short story, "The Unmanly Warrior." Accusing Kingston of misrepresenting Chinese Americans, Chin writes that her "elaboration of this version of history, in both autobiography and autobiographical fiction, is simply a device for destroying history and literature" (Frank Chin, "Come All Ye" 3). Although the purported literary battle between Chin and his supporters and Kingston's defenders has raged over most of the crucial issues in Asian American literature, the most public skirmishes (in the press as well as at professional meetings) have focused on issues of gender and on discussions of the differences between "authentic" (radical, polemical) and "inauthentic" (critically successful, popular, award-winning) Asian American literature. Kingston has herself refused to comment at length on the hostility, although some—most notably Shawn Wong—have noticed that Wittman Ah Sing in *Tripmaster Monkey* bears more than a passing resemblance to Frank Chin. Nevertheless, Chin is not alone in his contestation of Kingston's work.

Kingston has been criticized for producing "a work of fiction passing for autobiography" (Tong, "Racist" 6), mistranslating Chinese terms that are central to her text, creating fictional characters who construct their own versions of Chinese folktales, and writing a *very personal* description of growing up in Chinese America. It is *one* story from one Chinese American woman of one out of seven generations of Chinese Americans (Fong 117). Kingston has even been put down for experiencing a childhood in the wrong place—Stockton, California, instead of Chinatown—a place that supposedly renders her incapable of "historical and cultural insight" about the experiences of Chinese Americans (Tong, "Chinatown Popular Culture" 233). In addition, Kingston's critics assert that her worst flaw is her portrayal of Chinese American men as sexists trapped in a Confucian time warp. According to this line of reasoning, Kingston is guilty of creating female characters who conform to white feminists' belief in a universal female experience of oppression and of writing fashionably feminist texts for white readers. Given his intractable stance in the *Aiiieeeee* anthologies, Frank Chin not surprisingly weighs in with his opinion that Kingston "villifies Chinese manhood" (quoted in Kim, "Such Opposite Creatures" 76).

Much of the negative criticism faults Kingston for what are really the shortcomings of her mainstream readers—readers who might be tempted to read *The Woman Warrior* and *China Men* as anthropological texts or tourist guidebooks; readers who extrapolate from Kingston's work to all Chinese Americans and even Asian Americans; readers who attempt to force Kingston into the role of spokesperson for all Chinese, all minorities, all women. Still other critics, complaining that Kingston misrepresents folktales or mistranslates important words, are guilty of denying Kingston the right to basic artistic license—a right that has been claimed by writers in many different cultures. *The Woman Warrior* and *China Men* are not historical texts, although both works incorporate large chunks of factual material interspersed with other forms of narrative. When Kingston's fictionalized protagonists rewrite folklore and ancient history in order to make a point or provide an obscure translation that underscores an idea, their creator should not be taken to task for "falsifying" or "faking" Chinese culture. In fact, the revision of ancient narratives and tales, even of other literary and artistic texts, is a tradition of sorts: Shakespeare rewrote history and Richard III's reputation; playwrite Eugene O'Neill appropriated the classical *Oresteia*; and J. M. Coetzee and Jean Rhys have deconstructed, respectively, *Robinson Crusoe* (a text that Kingston also claims and reconfigures) and *Jane Eyre*. In popular

culture, musicals like *West Side Story* and *Miss Saigon* are revisions, respectively, of Shakespeare's *Romeo and Juliet* and Puccini's *Madame Butterfly*. David Henry Hwang, an Asian American playwright, has taken
Puccini's opera as the shaping allusion in his own *M. Butterfly*. Not unlike other minority writers whose work has broad appeal to the general
reading public, Maxine Hong Kingston is being made responsible by
other Asian Americans, her own ethnic community, for educating the
dominant culture while at the same time protecting that same ethnic
group from further negative stereotyping or cultural misunderstanding.
Kingston does not have the luxury of writing from personal experience
and inspiration if such writing has the potential to "mar" her community's public image. Sau-ling Cynthia Wong sums up the dilemma that
confronts the minority writer, noting that "the ethnic woman autobiog-
rapher victimized by sexism must be ready to suppress potentially damaging (to the men, that is) is material; to do less is to jeopardize the
united front and to prostitute one's integrity for the sake of white approval" (Sau-Ling Wong, "Autobiography" 259).

Kingston is not the only Asian American writer to be subjected to what
Garrett Hongo, also an Asian American writer, calls "internalized oppression" which he defines as a tendency, occasionally manifested in
minority communities, when one group within that community op-
presses another group through the deployment of political clout and the
construction of power hierarchies (Hongo 15). Novelist Cynthia Kadohata has been accused of "falsifying" Asian American history because
her novel, *The Floating World* (1989), focuses narrowly on a single Japanese American family and does not mention internment camps or the
federally mandated evacuations of citizens of Japanese ancestry during
the Second World War. Another novelist, Amy Tan (*The Joy Luck Club*),
whose work is often compared to *The Woman Warrior*, is sometimes the
target of Frank Chin's ire because she writes fiction that appeals to mainstream readers and enjoys a long tenure on best-seller lists. In addition,
Tan has been criticized for creating characters who speak imperfect Chinese—although both she and her characters are American-born and educated, and hence quite likely to speak an Americanized and "incorrect"
form of Chinese. David Henry Hwang's Tony-award-winning play, *M.
Butterfly* (1988), has been condemned for its lack of admirable Asian male
characters, and even historian Ronald Takaki has become the target of
scholarly attacks for his prize-winning study, *Strangers from a Different
Shore: A History of Asian Americans*.

The depth and virulence of the debate that started with *The Woman*

Warrior now encompasses Asian American writing as well as the entire field of Asian American Studies—evidence of the power of Kingston's writing and the centrality of her work not only to Asian American literature, but also to American literature. The fact that one work (perhaps two, if we consider *China Men*) can stand unscathed at the center of such a longstanding and often ferocious controversy says much for the longevity of the work, as well as for the significance of its author to the culture that nurtured her. Moreover, that controversy is evidence that American literature is alive, healthy, and growing—only in a vibrant literary culture can such debates gain momentum and flourish for so long.

Ironically, Kingston's admirers from mainstream literary circles provided another source of anxiety for the author. What dismayed Kingston so profoundly about countless reviews of *The Woman Warrior* was a tendency among reviewers to evaluate her work through the cloudy lenses of long-entrenched cultural and ethnic stereotypes. She had been prepared for readers who would employ "the women's lib angle, and the Third World angle, the roots angle," but she did not foresee that both she and her writing would be judged against existing stereotypes of mysteriously exotic and inscrutable, mysterious Orientals, nor had she truly understood the power of stereotypes to blind a viewer into perpetuating those cliched images ("Cultural Mis-readings" 55).

Specifically, Kingston, who has always considered herself an American writer, was disturbed by the reviewers' repeated use of words like "inscrutable," "exotic," "oriental," or "foreign" to describe her work, as well as by headlines that insisted on labelling her "Chinese." She contends that the use of such labels denies basic humanity by suggesting that individuals of Asian descent are so different from others that they are intrinsically unknowable and indelibly foreign. Stereotypes allow people to hide behind and even defend ignorance. But she adds that Asian Americans also dislike being described as *not* inscrutable, exotic, and mysterious because such labels continue to imply the existence of people who do represent those descriptors. Like so many other American writers from a variety of backgrounds, Kingston's ambition is to write the great American novel; furthermore, she asserts that too many reviewers have missed a crucial point: *The Woman Warrior* is an American book, about an American girl growing up in California.

Maxine Hong Kingston was driven to respond in the essay, "Cultural Mis-readings," to what she considered to be disturbing inconsistencies and errors in otherwise favorable reviews of *The Woman Warrior*. Specifically, she points out that critics and reviewers "praise the wrong things" because they are locked into an aesthetic that privileges the idea of the exotic Oriental (see above), a stereotype that immediately positions Kingston as foreign, as Other. Noting that several early readers and reviewers of *The Woman Warrior* cited "The White Tigers" as their favorite chapter because it narrates a "Chinese" folk story, Kingston firmly asserts that "The White Tigers" is no Chinese myth; rather it is a tale transformed by America, "a sort of kung fu movie parody" ("Cultural Mis-readings" 57). The shaping narrative of that chapter may have had its origins in China, but Maxine Hong Kingston's retelling is American—as any number of literary critics and historians have shown. Moreover, Kingston emphatically pronounces her American identity: *"Because* I was born in Stockton, California, I *am* an American woman. I am also a Chinese American woman, but I am not a Chinese woman, never having traveled east of Hawaii" (58). She would, a few years later, finally travel to China, to be received as an honored American visitor—with an American passport, in the company of American writers, and under the sponsorship of an American university.

In light of the strong reactions to her work, it cannot be denied that Maxine Hong Kingston has had an incredibly powerful influence not only on Asian American literature, but certainly on American literature in the last decades of the twentieth century. But we must not ignore the fact that her impact has been felt in fields other than literature, as well. Informal and admittedly unscientific investigations have turned up the information that *The Woman Warrior* and *China Men* are required in courses in gender studies, philosophy, anthropology, history, teaching methods, counseling, and psychology. Excerpts from Kingston's three books as well as separate essays have found their way into popular college readers and anthologies such as *The Bedford Reader*, *The Conscious Readers*, and *The Norton Anthology of Literature by Women*. It is fair to surmise that a relatively substantial number of high school and college students have been exposed to Kingston's work. Proof of her work's incontrovertible assimilation into the canon of American literature is the fact that Maxine Hong Kingston has earned herself a place in the *Columbia Literary History of the United States*. In addition, the Modern Language Association has published *Approaches to Teaching Kingston's* The Woman Warrior, a collection of essays outlining and describing strategies for engaging students with Kingston's first major work, edited by Shirley Geok-lin Lim (1991). This anthology of essays is a clear signal of *The Woman Warrior*'s canonical status in American classrooms. And finally, in 1999, Sau-ling Cynthia Wong's *Maxine Hong Kingston's* The Woman Warrior: *A Casebook* was released by the University of California Press, further demonstrating the centrality of Kingston's first book to twentieth-century American literature.

Through her work and by her example, Kingston has inspired a younger generation of ethnic writers to excavate their family stories and raise their voices in celebration of those stories. Hawai'i-born poet Garrett Hongo says that *China Men* was, for him, a revelation that the lives of his ancestors were worth writing about: "If it weren't for Maxine Hong Kingston, I wouldn't have my imaginative life. It was a great moment reading *China Men*. That book released human feeling for me. It humanized me, it released my own stories for me" (Hongo 17). Another poet, Marilyn Chin, discovered *The Woman Warrior* while she was an undergraduate in Massachusetts, and later told Kingston in an interview that the book "gave us permission to go on" (Marilyn Chin 62). In Chin's case, "going on" meant choosing a literary career—a somewhat unusual choice for an Asian American in the late 1970s, when so many were studying science, engineering, or medicine.

Evidence of Maxine Hong Kingston's tremendous influence on the American literary world has surfaced from an unlikely source. At a reading of her work at the University of California at Los Angeles, Kingston was approached by several students who gave her the astounding news that some publishers were returning manuscripts with a "generic Maxine Hong Kingston" rejection slip, advising young writers to read Kingston's work before attempting another submission (William Satake Blauvelt 84).

Laura Skandera-Trombley, who has compiled a collection of essential critical articles about Maxine Hong Kingston and her three major works, notes that Kingston has become such a significant cultural icon that she is now a notable presence in cyberspace, having found 419 "hits" associated with Kingston. Among the Kingston websites are pages in *Voices from the Gap: Women Writers of Color*, several syllabi for university courses featuring Kingston and other Asian American writers, student-written biographies of Kingston, and pages from on-line reference works. Moreover, judging from the customer reviews for *The Woman Warrior* on Amazon.com as well as on another readers' website, New Vision, readers continue to discover Kingston's first book, published before many of them were even born.

And finally, the most tangible proof that Kingston has profoundly affected American popular culture is the release, in 1998, of the Walt Disney animated feature film *Mulan*. The release of this film in movie theatres and more recently on videotape is a cultural phenomenon that has firmly installed Fa Mu Lan—the courageous woman warrior with her roots in Chinese folktales—as an American cultural icon, and as a role model for millions of young American girls who are searching for women that they can identify as their own heroes.

MAXINE HONG KINGSTON'S WORK: GENRE AND THEMES

One explanation for the enduring popularity of Kingston's first two books, as well as for the continuing fascination that *Tripmaster Monkey* inspires in readers and scholars alike, is the author's focus on subjects of universal appeal: identity, family, coming of age, and cultural transition. Kingston writes about the search for self and the construction of personal identity, exploring the intersections between individuality and group identity within the geography of a powerful and entrenched family and community culture. She examines family stories, asserting their significance in an immigrant group's attempts to create a space for themselves in a new environment. She portrays the conflicts and misunderstandings that necessarily erupt when the second generation in an immigrant group begins to take the first tentative steps toward assimilating into the dominant culture. Kingston's work resonates with American readers, a good number of them not too many generations removed from their own immigrant ancestors. But the work speaks equally powerfully to colonized peoples and others whose lives continue to be shaped by the master narratives of a culture that considers them alien. The appeal of Kingston's work is, in large part, a function of the work's narrative form and structure, the identification and description of which has occupied the attention of readers and critics alike.

The word that most often surfaces in discussions of narrative form and Kingston's work is "autobiography," although both Kingston herself and a number of scholars have either denied the label or sought to modify and contextualize its implications. Complicating the discussion is Kingston's use of the word "memoir" in the subtitle of *The Woman Warrior*. In addition, *The Woman Warrior* has been read as bildungsroman (a novel about the growth of the main character) and *China Men* as fictionalized history (suggesting a chronological order). *Tripmaster Monkey*, identified by the publisher as Kingston's "first novel," at times *sounds* like a prose poem in the tradition of Walt Whitman and Allen Ginsberg. In the babel of interpretations that continues to grow, a few labels have emerged as perhaps among the most appropriate identifications for Kingston's oeuvre—the most inclusive and descriptive of which may be *postmodern mixed genre*.

Postmodernism resists easy definition, and is, perhaps, best approached through what it *does* rather than what it *is*. As a portmanteau term, it refers to experimental tendencies that have characterized a substantial body of art, literature, culture, and ideology since the 1940s and 1950s. Postmodernism encompasses a wide range of cultural styles and technique. The term "postmodern" is often invoked to identify literary works that are different from the familiar linear narrative. Among these works are William Burroughs's cut-up novels—constructed from prewritten text that has been scissored into segments which are shuffled and then rearranged at random for printing—*The Ticket that Exploded* (1962) and *Nova Express* (1964). Truman Capote's nonfiction novel, *In Cold Blood*; and Gabriel Garcia Marquez's magic realism, with its combination of the fabulous and fantastic inserted into realistic narrative, are also labeled "postmodern." Additionally, Vladimir Nabokov's self-reflexive fiction that overtly investigates its own composition and references its own fictionality, and Thomas Pynchon's cybernetic novels that manipulate different versions of reality within the same text can be identified as postmodern. Instead of manifesting causality or a logical progression, postmodern narratives are often structured like dreams or even home movies, cutting from one scene to another, abruptly moving from point to point, creating uncertainty and indeterminacy about the nature of narrative. Maxine Hong Kingston's major works—especially *Tripmaster Monkey*—share with other postmodern pieces a tendency toward self-referentiality, a leaning toward pastiche and collage, quotation and parody, an eclectic embracing of all genres—both fictional and nonfictional, realistic and fantastic.

Describing Kingston's work as *postmodern mixed genre* reinforces the hybrid nature of her prose, for if "postmodern" implies collage, pastiche, and open-endedness, then the phrase "mixed genre" reinforces the suggestion of multiplicity and eclecticism. Kingston's texts defy simple definition because they embrace a variety of narrative forms, thereby occupying a new literary space that exists both within and without genre borders. Such a space lends itself especially well to Kingston's purpose—to write the experience of Americans whose cultural heritage derives from both China and the United States, and to find the narrative strategy that best represents that experience.

Maxine Hong Kingston deserves credit for introducing talk-story, an ancient folk-art form dating from storytellers of the Sung dynasty, to the general American reading public. While certainly not the first Asian American writer to employ talk-story as a narrative strategy, Kingston—through *The Woman Warrior* and *China Men*—nevertheless added the term to the collective American vocabulary. Talk-story (or *gong gu tsai*), at its most essential, is community discourse, an inherited oral narrative tradition that incorporates family tales and genealogy, history, familiar adages, folklore, myth, heroic stories, even didactic and cautionary pronouncements that have been handed down—and embellished—by successive generations within an extended clan. Popular proverbs, fables, parables, fragments of literature, and ancient philosophy also find their way into talk-story which is so infinitely flexible, so malleable as to allow for the incorporation of such elements as the speaker might wish to include.

Kingston asserts that talk-story "reverberates" in that her stories have neither clear beginnings nor definitive endings, that "every time you tell a story it changes, it grows.... these stories ... generate other stories" (Skenazy, "University" 149). She considers talk-story to be a singularly appropriate vehicle for reimagining the past, as well as rejuvenating—and thus preserving for a new generation—a community's or culture's most significant narratives. Through talk-story, Maxine Hong Kingston is able to engage with her Chinese heritage and reimagine it, to retell it as Chinese American narrative, thus claiming both of her cultures as the inspiration for her art. As she points out: "there has been continuous talk-story for over 4,000 years [spanning] China and America. Once in a long while during these millennia, somebody writes things down; writing 'freezes' things for a bit, like a rock, but the talk-story goes on around and from this rock" (Kingston to Sledge, quoted in "Oral Tradition" 147).

Like most immigrant families, the Hongs preserved their own talk-story, making additions and revisions to accommodate the family's experiences in America, testing multiple versions of individual stories. They—as did others—revitalized the form by embracing American idioms, maintaining tradition by preserving the minority peasant dialect that the parents had brought with them from southwest China and still spoke in Stockton. Family talk-story shapes Kingston's prose, lending it the immediacy of bedtime stories, of family tales recounted at reunions and holiday celebrations. And from family talk-story, Kingston draws the themes that shape her work, providing focal points, strands of thought, clusters of ideas that function as structural foundations for her prose. Among the themes that readers have identified repeatedly in the Kingston oeuvre are ethnicity, identity formation and integration of the self, cross-generational conflict, alienation, the appropriation of America by immigrants, woman as Other, and the difficulties of negotiating the demands of two cultures.

For many readers, the most compelling thematic strand in *The Woman Warrior* is the narrator's attempt to construct and perform an identity that allows her to be an American even while she acknowledges and even—at times—privileges her Chinese heritage. Struggling to reconcile the conflicting messages emanating from her dual heritage, she attempts to find a voice that can speak for both her Chinese inheritance and her American upbringing. To remain silent is to risk erasure. Also crucial to and embedded in her search for identity are a number of parallel and intersecting strands that include questions related to gender, biculturalism, and ethnicity—questions that will ultimately help her shape a literary form that will allow her to narrate her experience and that of others like her.

As she experiments with narrative form and a multilayered structure, Maxine Hong Kingston pieces together cultural elements and literary fragments to create the mosaic that is her fictional world. Employing a variety of linguistic devices—allusions, symbols, motifs, single images and related clusters of images, puns and word games, and auditory signals—she teases her readers into participating in the constructions of her stories, into entering the lives and communities of her protagonists. Among the most pervasive and dominant of Kingston's motifs are storytelling (discussed in chapter 1) and gender-crossing. Equally conspicuous are images of silence and its opposite condition, speech or voice. These motifs and tropes serve as bridges between Kingston's texts and the world beyond the page, as connections with the cultural milieux that have produced both the motifs or images, as well as with Kingston herself.

In Kingston's prose, gender-crossing is a condition that highlights the instability of gender definitions, especially in the context of slippery cultural and ethnic geographies. Both *The Woman Warrior* and *China Men* employ cross-dressing figures as important icons—Fa Mu Lan in the former book, Tang Ao in the latter. Disguised in the clothing of a male warrior and taking the place of her father, Fa Mu Lan vanquishes the powerful baron who has persecuted her family for years. To this clearly articulated example of gender-crossing, Kingston adds another by conflating the Fa Mu Lan legend with the story of Yue Fei, the historical warrior whose mother inscribed a patriotic slogan into the skin of his back. In *China Men*, Tang Ao finds himself in the Land of Women where he is subjected to humiliating and painful feminizing rituals—his feet are bound, his beard plucked, his ears pierced, and his face painted. The gender-crossing trope in *Tripmaster Monkey* is more subtle, involving the author—a woman—who speaks through a young, irreverent, macho San Franciscan named Wittman Ah Sing. Wittman's thoughts and speech are larded with references to gender-crossing. He claims that one of his names is Joang Fu, pronounced "like Joan of Arc," the cross-dressing medieval French heroine (and a sort of European Fa Mu Lan). In the mock sword fight with his wife Taña, however, Wittman is defeated by a woman wielding what he subsequently realizes is a phallic symbol—thus, she figuratively emasculates or feminizes him, vanquishing him with a weapon that represents masculinity at its most potent. Wittman's defeat places him in the company of those immigrants who arrived in the Gold Mountain only to find themselves forced to perform what both they and their employers considered to be women's work—cooking, housecleaning, laundry, and sewing.

Another theme that informs all of Maxine Hong Kingston's work is silence in its multiple forms: those who refuse to speak; those who cannot speak because they lack the language to do so; those who are afraid to speak, or who have been told not to speak; and those whose stories have been deliberately obliterated from human memory, or erased from official histories. In all three of Kingston's major works, the protagonists insist on being heard, on telling their own and other's stories. They struggle to find their individual and community voices, for being silenced is tantamount to being denied existence as a human being, and being silent means collusion with those who would deny agency. Thus, the narrator in *The Woman Warrior* is compelled to tell the story of No-Name Woman, and screams at the silent little girl at school in an effort to force her to speak; the grandfathers in *China Men* dig holes in the ground into which they shout their frustration, anger, and exhaustion; and Wittman Ah Sing brashly demands a stage on which to perform the stories that explain his history in the context of the American story.

The landscape of Kingston's works is a cross-cultural space, inhabited by individuals who are daily forced to negotiate the uneven and treacherous terrain that forms the border between two shaping geographies: China and America. Bounded by the ancient culture of China at one pole, and the culture-in-progress that is the United States at the other pole,

Kingston country is constantly evolving, forever threatening its inhabitants with cultural metamorphoses.

Kingston has created a China that is a fictional construct, a collage of impressions and images, predominantly from her mother's talk-story, some from stories told by the immigrants who visited the laundry and from letters written by relatives in China, others acquired from American popular culture—the movies, books, and television. Kingston reveals that Chinese Americans cling to "a myth of China" that they pass on from one generation to the next, a myth about which they construct stories—other myths. The myth of China hovers over immigrant communities, taking on a presence so strong that eventually that mythic China inspires individuals to build their lives around its fantasy geography (Ross 293).

For the child, Maxine, in *The Woman Warrior*, China is rife with contradictions. In China, the land of emperors and beggars, armies and farm laborers, an aunt is driven to suicide because she has borne an illegitimate child—yet also in China, a girl warrior disguised as a man goes to war in her father's place and saves her people. Girls are despised in China, but girls who manage against all odds to grow to adulthood might become college-educated physicians, enjoying widespread respect and a lucrative medical practice. Old China has ghost plagues and bandits, floods and temples with fighting monks; but modern China is dominated by ideologically rigid Communists who force uncles to kneel on broken glass, drive aunts to hawk firewood in the streets, and teach children to dance with red kerchiefs as they parrot patriotic jingles. Consequently, Maxine is confused—China is both attractive and frightening, she does not know which version to believe, and she has no way of knowing whether either one bears any resemblance to the true China.

Significantly, the contradictions that confuse Maxine are integral to the talk-stories with which Brave Orchid seeks to inculcate Chinese culture and heritage in her children. On the surface, in those tales, China is home and America is simply a temporary place. The successful sojourner is one who is able eventually to return to the home country to grow old with the wealth amassed in America. In China, people keep promises, time moves gently, and human beings live to a great and venerable age. China is tranquil and peaceful, a lovely country with pure air, golden birds, and flowers sweeter than any the immigrants have found in the Gold Mountain. Most important, China teems with Han people just like themselves.

But the talk-stories also inadvertently reveal another and far more riveting China, one that inspires nightmares in the listening children. While
the immigrant generation is able to privilege nostalgic images of home,
glossing over the realities of life in the old country, their children—
American-born and raised, educated in the ways of Western cultures,
lacking in any experience of China—notice only what to them appears
to be unimaginable terror and madness. They absorb stories about whip-
pings, stepmothers who spatter hot cooking oil on the bare toes of their
husband's children, and babies left to die in outhouses. Maxine is especially disturbed by what she is told about the fates of girls: smothered
at birth in a box of ashes kept beside the birth bed; allowed to live, but
imprisoned if they refused to marry the men their parents have chosen;
tied naked on anthills by disapproving in-laws.

BaBa (also known as Ed), the sojourner in *China Men*, tells his children
about a distant land where would-be scholars could sit for the Imperial
Examinations and fail them repeatedly, year after year, for the rest of
their lives. He describes villages that are bottomless pits into which all
earnings go to support parents, aunts and uncles, siblings, nearly forgotten children, second and third and fourth cousins, all demanding
money, all claiming severe deprivation.

The longer the immigrants stay in America, the more established they
become in their adopted country, the more mythical and abstract China
becomes. Moon Orchid's husband in *The Woman Warrior* has virtually
erased China from his emotional geography, his wife is someone who
reminds him of the characters in a book read long ago and half forgotten.
For the "bachelors" and sojourners in the cane fields and railroad camps,
China is a fading memory, a home that becomes more and more unfamiliar as years pass. Five generations removed from China, Wittman Ah
Sing, the trickster hero of *Tripmaster Monkey* (see chapter 5) knows only
what he has learned from kung fu movies and *The Lady from Shanghai*,
from books about the I Ching, from *Flower Drum Song*, and from bits
and pieces of legends recounted by his actor parents. Kingston's China
is a constructed geography of the imagination, an unstable and amorphous landscape that owes its continued existence to fading, unreliable
memories.

By contrast, America is no fantasy. Inspired by tales of the wealth to
be had from the Gold Mountain, the immigrants arrive in Hawai'i and
California to discover that the reality means humiliation, displacement,
and discrimination. It is a society in which respected grandfathers are
mere nameless field hands, a Chinese physician is forced to labor in

tomato fields and in a cannery, and a rigorously trained scholar becomes a laundryman. These immigrants are rendered virtually invisible by discrimination, as well as by their willingness to perform those tasks commonly relegated to servants—who are, in some ways, also invisible. They cluster together in nationally specific enclaves, in Chinatowns, Little Japans, and other similar neighborhoods where they continue to speak their native languages and retain some of the cultural practices that define their countries or regions of origin. For Kingston's ancestors, the Gold Mountain turns out to be several Chinese communities, each one a cluster of immigrants from the same village or a number of nearby villages, each community embedded in but invisible from the mainstream culture.

While China is a looming—if distant—presence in *The Woman Warrior* and *China Men*, so powerfully realized that many fail to notice on first reading that both are American books, America is the undisputed setting for *Tripmaster Monkey*. This America is not the Gold Mountain of mining camps and immigrant villages and tiny Chinatowns, nor the country closed off to immigrants by stringent exclusionary laws. Wittman Ah Sing's America is in the throes of cultural and social upheaval, fighting an unpopular war in Asia and waging battle with newly awakened activists of all causes at home. This is an American whose citizens have surnames like Kamiyama and de Weese and Fong, a country in which the name "Lee" could be "Black or white Southern, Korean, Scotsman, anything" (*Tripmaster Monkey* 12). In this America of the sixties, Wittman can aspire to be a Yale Younger Poet; unlike Kingston's scholar father whose classical training went unrecognized in the Gold Mountain, Wittman is a graduate of one of the major English departments in the United States. And yet, in this America, discrimination and prejudice are still alive, albeit not as blatantly directed toward Asian Americans as during the early twentieth century. Fourth-and fifth-generation Asian Americans, Wittman and his friend, Lance Kamiyama, (educated in London as well as in Berkeley) must still explain that they *are* Americans and that their first language is English.

LeAnne Schreiber of the *New York Times Book Review* has asked a pertinent question: "It takes only one generation to lose China. How many does it take to gain America?" (Schreiber 9). The question has resonance for Kingston's works, portraying as they do the experiences of immigrants and their children, and illuminating the lives of people who are no longer Chinese, but who—despite their best efforts—cannot or are not permitted to assimilate completely into American society. For second-, third-, and fourth-generation Chinese Americans, Schreiber's question is crucial—these individuals have at best a secondhand knowledge of China; they have American educations, yet are often viewed as foreigners, as aliens. Many of these American-born children and grandchildren of immigrants seek a geography that allows them to claim and identify with all of the cultures to which they are entitled. This quest for a cross-cultural space lies at the heart of *Tripmaster Monkey*.

If *The Woman Warrior* is Kingston's "China book" and *China Men* her "Gold Mountain book," *Tripmaster Monkey* is located in what some readers have identified as a third space, between China and America. This is the place where cultures, aesthetics, and ethnicities intersect, collaborate, collide, fuse, and morph together into hybrids, mongrel identities that represent all of their origins even as they identify themselves as Americans. In the third space, difference is foregrounded—Wittman Ah Sing is not Chinese; neither is he stereotypically "American" or Anglo. American-born, raised, and educated, he emphasizes his Chinese complexion by deliberately wearing colors guaranteed to make his skin appear more yellow, and he dreams of bringing a Chinese legend to the American stage. Similarly motivated, Boston residents whose great-grandparents emigrated from County Clare in the nineteenth century might identify themselves as Irish, celebrating St. Patrick's Day, listening to Celtic bands, and learning how to step-dance, despite their never having been to Ireland. In the same vein, African Americans, claiming their African ancestry, celebrate Kwanzaa and wear kente cloth on formal occasions; and descendants of long-ago Mexican immigrants have parties on Cinco de Mayo—the fifth of May—which is a much more important holiday in the United States than in Mexico.

The third space is border country, a largely invisible but no less real personal and communal geography that is of, but not in, two or more cultures, the terrain where new meanings come into being. The third space—a location of cultural hybridity—enables the survival of diasporaic communities, minority cultures, immigrants, and liminal identities in this space, the narrator of *The Woman Warrior* can interrogate her heritages, and talk-story her way into a stable American identity that embraces not only her parents' cultures, but also the dominant culture in which she has grown up. Many border country inhabitants—generally the younger members of immigrant families and diasporaic communities, as well as members of Native American groups who are also border inhabitants—straddle two cultures, often speak two languages, two distinct varieties of English, and are frequently called upon to translate one culture into and for another. These individuals have double identities—they are of both cultures and can negotiate each one separately, but their true identities are bound up with their dual heritage. Shaped by the dominant culture in which they have been educated, these individuals nonetheless feel strongly drawn to the traditions and values of their families and to their parents' ancestral cultures.

An important new strand in American literature and art focuses on the issues and concerns of those whose lives are defined by cultural dislocations and oppositions. Writers who examine cultural borders and who legitimize experiences outside those commonly portrayed in popular culture and art are breaking the profound silence that has, until just after the mid-century point, enveloped America's minority communities. Maxine Hong Kingston is one of the best-known among such writers, along with Toni Morrison, Oscar Hijuelos, and Scott Momaday. Others, from a variety of communities and traditions—Frank Chin, Amy Tan, Carolyn Chute, Shawn Wong, Gloria Anzaldua, Leslie Marmon Silko, Fae Myenne Ng, and Cynthia Kadohata, to name only a very few—are giving voice to those who have not spoken earlier. These writers are including new characters in the ongoing and evolving drama that is American history, creating additional narratives to incorporate into the story of the United States.

The Woman Warrior: Memoirs of a Girlhood among Ghosts
(1976)

The publication of Maxine Hong Kingston's *The Woman Warrior* in 1976 marked a critical point in the ongoing development of the American literary tradition. With one book, Asian American writing entered the mainstream, appealing simultaneously to the general reader and the scholarly community, and eliciting reactions in popular publications, Sunday supplements, and specialized literary journals. *The Woman Warrior* has been identified by the Modern Language Association as perhaps the most frequently assigned twentieth-century literary text by a living author on American high school, college, and university campuses. This fact is made doubly significant by the evidence that is required reading not only in literature classes, but also in courses at many levels across a wide spectrum of academic disciplines. The book is discussed in sociology and anthropology classes, in literature seminars, and in history and political science courses. It is critiqued by feminist theorists, poststructuralists, sinologists, and geographers; and it is analyzed as biography, fiction, history, ethnography, memoir, and autobiography. In addition, *The Woman Warrior* is popular not only among academic readers, but also with mainstream readers, both Chinese Americans and Americans whose ancestry is non-Chinese, and now appears on high school reading lists as well as on book club agendas.

As noted in chapter 1, the response to *The Woman Warrior* on its first appearance was largely positive and enthusiastic; scores of readers responded viscerally to a text that is provocative and engaging, a book that speaks to the intellect and the emotions. "An unusual and rewarding book for a specially attuned readership," was the judgment of *Publisher's Weekly* (1976, 72), capturing in one sentence the work's special attraction—its innovative narrative style and its powerful connection to the sensibilities of readers who surrendered to Kingston's seductively inter-textual prose. Citing Kingston's description of the painful muteness experienced by exiles, refugees, and their children, and lamenting the erasure of ethnic heritages due to silence, *Time* critic Paul Gray says that in *The Woman Warrior*, Maxine Hong Kingston "gives that silence a voice" by recording "triumphant journeys of the spirit through a desolation of spirit" (Gray 91). Sara Blackburn, writing about the book for *Ms.*, labels *The Woman Warrior* "a perception-expanding report for the archives of human experience" (Blackburn 39). Other reviewers reflect on Kingston's handling of a theme that pervades the literature of diaspora and immigrant communities, the theme of cross-cultural conflict. For reviewer Miriam Greenspan, Maxine Hong Kingston captures "the pain of an American-born child who inevitably rejects the expectations and authority of her family in favor of the values of the new land" (Greenspan 108). Linda B. Hall describes the book as "remarkable in its insights into the plight of individuals pulled between two cultures" (Hall 191); and Susan Currier writes in the *Dictionary of Literary Biography* that *The Woman Warrior* is a personal narrative that represents Kingston's effort "to reconcile American and Chinese female identities" (Currier 235).

PLOT DEVELOPMENT

The Woman Warrior is a collection of five short prose narratives that collectively perform several functions: They recount the coming-of-age of a young girl who is not named, but who is, in very significant ways, almost certainly the author, Maxine Hong Kingston (the subtitle signals that the work consists of "memoirs"). They illustrate the cultural tensions that shape the lives of immigrants and their families; and they constitute the reclaimed voices of generations of immigrants whose silence has kept their stories from being told, and from being valued as narratives worthy of inclusion in America's history. Interrelated in their shared focus on the construction of both individual and group identity, the five pieces center on issues that are complicated by gender and ethnicity, and are shaped by the cultural narratives of both China and the United States.

Each narrative elucidates the situation of the women in Kingston's extended family, and as a group, the stories epitomize the contradictions in the cultural messages with which a young Chinese American woman must grapple. "No Name Woman" introduces the unidentified aunt who represents the fate of transgressive women in traditional China, providing a context for Kingston's embedded account of discovering her self by contesting the unwritten rules that she is expected to obey. "White Tigers" implies through the story of Fa Mu Lan (Hua Mulan) that Chinese tradition does provide, as an antidote to the submissive maiden archetype, the powerful image of a warrior woman who wields a sword in battle and vanquishes an enemy army. "Shaman" narrates the story of Brave Orchid, a modern warrior woman who exorcises the malevolent Sitting Ghost, earns a degree from a medical college, and carves out a career as a physician before she emigrates to the United States. Moon Orchid's sad tale in "At the Western Palace" reveals the perils and disappointments that confront a woman whose conformity to traditional norms of submissiveness and silence leads to her being abandoned by her husband for a professional American woman. Moon Orchid consequently succumbs to madness, which allows her to erase the memory of her humiliation. In the final chapter, "A Song for a Barbarian Reed Pipe," Kingston celebrates the realization that she possesses a distinctive voice that allows her at last to communicate candidly with her mother. The book concludes with the rewritten and starkly beautiful story of Ts'ai Yen (Cai Yan), who recovers her voice as she listens to the music of barbarian flutes, and is inspired to write poetry that distills into words her sadness and anger at her long separation from her beloved China.

Discussions of *The Woman Warrior* invariably bring up the word "autobiography," which is frequently used to describe the book. To a certain extent, Kingston's text functions as an autobiography in the sense that it is a personal history centered on reflections about her early life as she attempts to interpret and understand the cultural codes that have shaped her life. But *The Woman Warrior* is less an autobiography than it is a mosaic of memoir, history, and fiction—artistic storytelling in the service of one woman's (re-)creation of her own identity. Through the medium of memoir, Kingston is able to narrate the events of her life, thus giving that life a shape by re-creating herself as the heroine of a story that is told and retold, changing with each telling and adding layers of signification with each new version. To accomplish her artistic purpose, Kingston employs talk-story (see chapter 2), a narrative medium that lends itself admirably to creative shaping, absorbing, and appropriating all other narrative forms, transforming them into a new artistic utterance that can speak for her emerging self. As Shirley Geok-Lin Lim notes, *The Woman Warrior* is "part biography, part autobiography, part history, part fantasy, part fictions, part myth, and wholly multilayered, multivocal, and organic" (Lim, "Preface" x), and the book draws its strength from Kingston's ability to embrace this wealth of narrative forms.

NARRATIVE STRUCTURE

Although *Woman Warrior* is indisputably a kind of autobiographical text, Maxine Hong Kingston's personal account is not the overtly central focus of the narrative, but rather is interpolated in the episodic and loosely related assemblage of family stories, traditional Chinese tales, and reminiscences that combine to make up the book. Kingston's book is unlike most Western narratives, comprised as it is of episodes that do not follow each other chronologically or develop logically, but rather appear to be called into textual being by allusions, reminiscences, and motifs, and are in turn displaced by other texts. The major narratives that comprise *Woman Warrior* represent different decades or eras in Kingston's family history, portrayed in thematic rather than chronological order, and describe not only the narrator's coming of age, but also her mother's story, told through flashbacks and retrieved memories and recollections.

Each of *The Woman Warrior*'s distinct sections, with its own title, comprises a story that is both complete in itself and an integral part of the entire work. Each section incorporates a story recounted by Brave Orchid, paired with the narrator's revision or (re-)creation of that story. Multiple tellings of a single story, separated by days, months, or years, and superimposed over—in some cases—a traditional story or myth, create the impression of time as a series of layers or strata, as well as an awareness of intricate webs of relationships between incidents and their narrators. Kingston herself is positioned at the center of two sections— the second and the fifth—in which she compares herself to powerful legendary women from Chinese myth and history. Quite a few readers have pointed out that *The Woman Warrior* is organized along a circular scheme; the book opens and concludes with sections that portray Brave

Orchid commencing a story which is then completed by Maxine. To avoid confusion, this discussion will identify the author of *The Woman Warrior* as Kingston or Maxine Hong Kingston, and the narrator as Maxine. Kingston, however, has said that the book's narrator is not entirely herself.

Employing talk-story as a narrative strategy, Kingston is able simultaneously to present a rich array of stories—her own, Brave Orchid's history, the tales of legendary Chinese women, the saga of Chinese immigrants to the United States, and Moon Orchid's sad tale of abandonment. Moreover, talk-story allows Kingston to include folktales, legends, and historical episodes that parallel, intersect, or function in contrast with the lives of her protagonists, who are the women of her family and her heritage. Instead of producing an autobiography in the Western tradition which demands a chronological rendering of significant episodes in the life of the subject, historically and culturally contextualized, Kingston shapes the narrative of her early life by locating herself in a long line of women, mythical and historical, strong and weak, slave and warrior, old and young. She embeds the important occasions of her own life in her retellings of the exploits of the warrior women—not only Fa Mu Lan, but also Brave Orchid and Ts'ai Yen—whose lives are the spine of the book. By talking story, Kingston claims her cultural inheritance, transforming it into a new American narrative form that serves to unite her present and her past.

Kingston's text appears not to conform to the conventions that govern the genre known as autobiography. Moreover, *The Woman Warrior* is comprised of substantial chunks of fiction, as well as clear indications that Kingston is creatively constructing her versions of events, and refusing to privilege one telling over another. From the outset, with the story of No Name Aunt, Kingston indulges in conjectures, in revisions, attempting through her variations on her aunt's story to understand not only her ancestor's decisions, but also the contexts in which those decisions had to be made and carried out. Consequently, Kingston speculates on her aunt's pregnancy, asking questions about the events that culminated in the midnight raid and the subsequent predawn suicide. Was the pregnancy the result of a love affair? Or was the aunt coerced into sex, or raped? Kingston attempts, as well, to imagine her aunt as an individual—was she a free spirit? A timid victim? Did she commit suicide out of spite? Kingston's propensity to speculate, to present alternate possibilities for events, is a hallmark of *The Woman Warrior* and its companion, *China Men*. In both works, speculation and creative reconstruction emphasize the tremendous fluidity of memoir and storytelling as narrative genres.

The Woman Warrior is both fact and fiction, slipping easily from one genre to another calling into question the instability of memory as the narrator wonders about Brave Orchid's veracity: How much truth is there in her stories? Might they be somewhat altered by time, by wishful thinking, or perhaps by a desire to rewrite the past? How reliable is Brave Orchid's memory of events that happened in what was essentially another life, in another country? Memory may be the recollection of factual events; it may also be the fictional reconstruction of fragments of experience enhanced by invention; or it may be speculation on how events might have happened had circumstances been different. Kingston leaves these options open, allowing the reader to speculate, to come to conclusions, or to refuse closure.

Another narrative strategy that Kingston employs successfully is the juxtaposition of multiple versions of a single story as told by a variety of narrators. She candidly calls attention to this technique and to the artifice through which she constructs her text. After a detailed account of how her aunt, Moon Orchid, arrives in the United States, only to encounter rejection by her Westernized husband, and eventually succumbs to a descent into madness, Kingston sets about questioning what she truly knows about these incidents, wondering how much she knows about her aunt's humiliation. Not having been present at the confrontation between Moon Orchid and the unfaithful husband, Kingston begins the following chapter with "What my brother actually said" (163), instantly alerting the reader to the probability that the events previously narrated might have happened differently. She immediately undermines her initial version of events still further by adding that her brother has not told her the story—rather he has recounted the events to one of their sisters who, in turn, has passed it on, presumably to the rest of the family. Kingston's knowledge is very much third-hand, and the possibility of invention (by brother and sister) is quite real. Thus, Kingston acknowledges the pliability of stories and the concomitant difficulty of determining the truth which might be obscured in a tangle of talk-story or interpretation.

Yet another Kingston strategy involves the use of a variety of narrative forms, some literary, others from the oral tradition. Included in *The Woman Warrior* are legend and myth (the tale of Fa Mu Lan), memoir (the story of the silent Chinese girl), historical reconstruction (Ts'ai Yen), family talk-story (No Name Woman), and speculation (Moon Orchid's experience). Each narrative form exemplifies a different way of arranging the elements of a story or a different way of privileging information. Through reliance on these forms, Kingston invites consideration of the variety of narrative structures through which memory can be exhumed and examined. Because she synthesizes from disparate and various elements the story of the women in her family—and by extension, the history of other immigrant women—Kingston allows us to imagine innovative ways of confronting and embracing the past. She proves that myth and folktale, family talk-story and memory, as well as a panoply of other narrative forms are convincing vehicles for the construction of history and cultural narratives, as well as for the description of an identity and a life in progress.

A third narrative strategy which is frequently mentioned in analyses of *Woman Warrior* is the work's transgression of borders and boundaries. Kingston's text frequently straddles the lines between fact and fantasy, between dream and waking reality, even between autobiography and fiction. The work's precarious positioning between genres is mirrored in Fa Mu Lan's crossing of gender boundaries during her masquerade as a soldier. By dressing as a man in order to join the army, Fa Mu Lan temporarily ceases to be a "worthless female," instead transforming herself into a valiant and valuable fighter, and thereby contesting the cultural scripts that have dictated the behaviors and identities of men and women in feudal China. Fa Mu Lan proves through her military prowess that women have the ability to excel at those military activities traditionally considered too difficult for females, albeit entirely appropriate for males, and she proves, as well, that a woman can have both domestic and public lives.

Gender-crossing is not the only manifestation of unstable borders in *The Woman Warrior*; the line between Chinese and American proves difficult for Maxine not only to identify, but also to maintain. Kingston asks a crucial question of all Chinese Americans: "When you try to understand what things in you are Chinese, how do you separate what is peculiar to childhood, to poverty, insanities, one family . . . from what is Chinese? What is Chinese tradition and what is the movies?" (5–6). What, she asks, comes solely from her Chinese heritage? What part of her identity is the product of family dynamics? How much is the result of community practice? What does she owe to the kung fu films that she watched on Sunday afternoons? How has her self—and those of other Chinese Americans—been defined by the tension between the dominant culture and the ancestral traditions? Her confusion about Chinese and American elements in her heritage reinforces the narrative's inclination to fluctuate between cultural texts, raising the possibility that *The Woman Warrior* exemplifies thinking through and beyond cultures.

Additionally, Kingston's text is *about* border crossings. In Brave Orchid's recollections of her years at the medical school, ghosts are not nocturnal, insubstantial creatures who emerge only out of darkness. Rather, they are manifest in daylight, inhabiting bridges and empty rooms; they are corporeal enough to bleed and to be butchered and fried in oil. Possessing the traits of both humans and spirits, these ghosts are proof of the permeability of the border between the real and the supernatural. The word "ghost" acquires a new meaning when Brave Orchid comes to the United States. Surrounded by a culture that she does not understand, she teaches her children to refer to all strangers—all human beings who do not fit into recognizably Chinese categories—as ghosts. Ghosts include individuals whose occupations are unfamiliar to immigrants—Bus Ghosts, Mail Ghosts, Social Worker Ghosts, Public Health Nurse Ghosts—as well as people whose behavior is somehow inexplicable—Hobo Ghosts and Wino Ghosts. Thus, the word which has a set of meanings in China is redefined in America to name a new category of unfathomable beings whose actions are puzzling to the immigrant community, and whose speech borders on the unintelligible. Unlike the supernatural Chinese ghosts, these American ghosts are obviously flesh-and-blood individuals; yet they are able to move between worlds, as the Garbage Ghost manages, by mimicking sounds and copying "human language" (98), to say several words in Chinese—a language he does not speak—thus briefly participating in the world inhabited by Maxine and her siblings.

Included among the newly designated ghosts of the Gold Mountain are Maxine and her brothers and sisters, born to an existence between two conflicting ways of life, belonging to neither one completely. Brave Orchid withholds important cultural secrets from her children who have been "born among ghosts . . . taught by ghosts . . . [are themselves] half ghosts" (183). Sharing many of the characteristics of the ghosts who inhabit the American environment, the children are—by Brave Orchid's standards—noisy and talkative, possessed of no memory or finesse. In fact, when Maxine, in defiance of all rules of proper Chinese behavior, summons the courage to verbalize loudly the resentments of her childhood, Brave Orchid angrily shouts that her daughter is "Ho Chi Kuei"—a kind of ghost ("Kuei" can be translated "ghost").

In *The Woman Warrior*, the demarcation between dreams and waking reality is insubstantial. Every night, Brave Orchid talks story until her children fall asleep; and Maxine grows up unable to distinguish the stories from her dreams: "I couldn't tell where the stories left off and the dreams began" (19). To young Maxine, Brave Orchid's voice becomes the voices of the heroines in her dreams. Stories about Japanese bombing raids on China fill young Maxine's dreams with airplanes; letters detailing communist tortures inflicted on aunts and uncles inspire dreams that she too has been put through their agony.

Another narrative strategy employed by Kingston with stunning effect is the juxtaposition of opposites—East and West, China and America, silence and speech, the ballad of a warrior woman chanted by a culture that has oppressed women for centuries. These oppositions provide a context for the tensions that shape the narrator's stories and thus her identity, as Maxine compares her own history with the saga of the family's emigration to America, as she dreams of being a woman warrior instead of a "worthless female." Aligned in uneasy coexistence are the Chinese injunctions to women to keep silent and the very audible loudness of Brave Orchid and her friends, or the contrived shyness of American girls and the American teachers' admonitions to students to speak up in class. Brave Orchid (the bold) contrasts with Moon Orchid (the timid), and silent but rebellious Maxine grows up to become a renowned writer whose voice reaches millions through her books. With her stories, Maxine is able to mediate the conflicting elements of her identity; she is able to recognize that the heroic Brave Orchid and the disenfranchised immigrant nonentity are the same woman. Ultimately, Maxine is finally able to understand and reconcile her own dual identity as a fact of life. As a child who is both Chinese and American, she learns about the woman warrior and about the oppressive culture that enjoins women to docility, while she tries to please teachers who command her to be outspoken; she is a girl who knows that girls are despised unless they grow up to become swordswomen. As a grown woman, she understands that she must construct her own identity out of the fragments of her heritage.

POINT OF VIEW

Most of *The Woman Warrior* is narrated by Maxine, whose personal history is encased in and intertwined with the stories that she recounts about her family and that family's history in China and the United States.

Through Maxine and her stories, the other women about whom she speaks acquire voices, and their words enrich the narrative, adding complexity, depth, and alternate ways of confronting the world. Brave Orchid and Fa Mu Lan, specifically, are able to articulate their identities and their existences through Maxine's memoirs. In Kingston's text, the first-person point of view dominates, as the primary narrative voice is joined by the voices of Fa Mu Lan and Brave Orchid, women who also claim the first-person point of view and employ the "I" to articulate their own experiences of rebellion and anger. That assertive voice comes from a storyteller telling her own story; and the presence of an "I" or first-person narrator signals that narrator's American identity. As Jade Snow Wong indicates in the introduction to her own memoir, *Fifth Chinese Daughter* (1945), a first-person narrator displays behavior that is characteristic of a non-Chinese individual. Unwilling to divest herself of her Chinese identity, Wong writes her autobiography in the third person, as though the events she narrates had happened to another person. She explains her decision in the introduction to her book:

> Although a "first person singular" book, this story is written in the third person from Chinese habit. The submergence of the individual is literally practiced. In written Chinese, prose or poetry, the word "I" almost never appears, but is understood. . . . Even written in English, an "I" book by a Chinese person would seem outrageously immodest to anyone raised in the spirit of Chinese propriety. (Wong vii).

We have already noted that Jade Snow Wong was one of the few Asian American writers whose work was available to young readers of Kingston's generation; thus Kingston's choice of the first-person pronoun for the narrator is doubly significant in light of not only her Chinese heritage, but also her literary and cultural influences. The choice represents Kingston's conscious decision to write as an American and to speak in the first-person Western idiom, in order to find the appropriate words to tell the story of her growing up as an American girl. Her choice reflects the influence of Walt Whitman's poetry on her writing. The distinctive American "I" is both Whitman's voice and his subject, and it is clear that Kingston wishes to claim her own version of "I" by speaking through and about herself. Kingston signals her chosen identity on the cover and title page of the book. Although she has a Chinese name, she uses her American name. Moreover, the Chinese name "Hong," her maiden name, is flanked by two names in English, suggesting that while the author does acknowledge her Chinese heritage, she is Maxine Kingston, American writer.

Like all first-person texts, *The Woman Warrior* records only what the narrator knows and is willing or able to tell. The narrator's tone is dictated by several factors: gender, mood, personality, emotional state, and ethnicity. As a second-generation Asian American, Kingston has created a narrative voice that is alternately conflicted and certain, outspoken and reticent, a voice that is rebellious, angry, and disappointed by turns.

In "At the Western Palace," Kingston abruptly shifts the narrative voice from first-person to third-person, creating between the reader and Moon Orchid a division that is exacerbated when Maxine admits to having heard Moon Orchid's story second or perhaps even thirdhand. Still trapped in the passive feminine ideal of traditional Chinese culture, Moon Orchid is nearly voiceless, possessed of no genuine opinion except that of whoever happens to be speaking with her, generally willing to agree with anything another person suggests, fearful and timid about acting independently. Such a woman cannot narrate her own story, and must rely on another who can conjure up the words to inscribe Moon Orchid's life in the history of female immigrants. The distance between Moon Orchid and the reader also underscores her tragic failure to connect with American culture, her inability to adjust to life in California, and her ultimate insanity, signaling a complete separation from her environment. Persuaded to come to the United States, lured away by Brave Orchid from a comfortable life in Hong Kong, Moon Orchid is unable to discover within herself the independent and resilient spirit that would allow her to make the transition from one way of life to another. At the beginning, Brave Orchid speaks for her; and after Moon Orchid slides into dementia, her daughter becomes her voice. The third-person point of view underscores Moon Orchid's inability to articulate her ideas and desires in her own voice.

CHARACTER DEVELOPMENT

The Woman Warrior is, at its most basic level, a woman's memoir—the loosely constructed narrative of Maxine's discovery of an individual voice, and thus, by extension, the shaping of a distinctive identity. The book foregrounds the stories of women—both legendary and real—whose lives provide Maxine with examples of who she might become, depending on the choices she makes as she undertakes the journey from childhood to womanhood.

Identified as positive role models are women who speak and act, who take control of their circumstances and shape their lives: Brave Orchid, whose voice opens the book and dominates much of the pages that follow; Fa Mu Lan, the legendary female warrior whose life is the focus of "White Tigers"; and Ts'ai Yen, whose story concludes the book on a note of cultural translation. Three other women—No Name Aunt, Moon Orchid, and the silent sixth-grader—represent what Maxine must try to avoid becoming. Embodied in this second trio are passivity, silence, lack of agency, and ultimately, the status of victim—a trap into which an Asian American girl might so easily stumble and remain. Kingston develops the six women as characters by employing three strategies: description of physical appearance; analysis of language and its significance; and discussion of the implications of certain characteristic actions performed by the women.

Brave Orchid is described at thirty-seven as alert, intelligent, and pretty, with thick eyebrows, and naturally curly hair. Posing seriously for a photograph of the graduates of Hackett Medical College for Women, she does not smile. There is no softness in her gaze, and she stares straight ahead into the camera, almost as though she can see not only her grandchildren, but also her grandchildren's grandchildren. The photograph exposes the steel in Brave Orchid's spine, the calm steady resilience that will see her through the vicissitudes of the immigrant experience. On the other hand, Moon Orchid lacks her sister's sturdiness. When Moon Orchid arrives at the San Francisco airport, her nieces and nephews see a tiny woman, clad in a wool suit and pearls, wearing her hair in a gray knot. She is very slim, and her pampered little hands, adorned with gold and jade rings, flutter as she speaks in a sophisticated city accent acquired from years of luxurious living in Hong Kong. Moon Orchid is the antithesis of hardworking Brave Orchid, whose Cantonese speech still bears the accents of their shared rural upbringing. A younger version of Moon Orchid, the silent girl in Maxine's sixth-grade class is delicate, with hair cropped in the China-doll style, pink cheeks, and soft skin, the epitome of young Chinese femininity and everything that Maxine fears she herself might become. Like Moon Orchid, the girl wears clothing that is so inappropriate for daily activities that it brands her instantly as an outsider. So dainty and delicate is the quiet girl that young Maxine is roused to unreasonable hatred, vowing to look as unlike the girl as possible.

Language (or its absence) characterizes the women whose stories Kingston tells in *The Woman Warrior*. The book opens with a linguistic admonition, "You must not tell anyone," that immediately introduces both Brave Orchid's penchant for talking story and her habit of making advisory pronouncements to her daughters. Brave Orchid is generally confident, her speech peppered with understandable self-congratulation when she recalls how her fellow students at the medical school fought over who would sit beside her during examinations. She is decisive when she declares to Moon Orchid that the latter's husband will have to speak with his first wife. Brave Orchid can also be admonitory, as she demands that her children eat, even while they stare in dismay at blood pudding quivering in the middle of the dining table. Moon Orchid, unlike her forthright sister, is tentative and frightened. She whimpers that she wants to return to Hong Kong when Brave Orchid discusses a confrontation with Moon Orchid's husband. In response to a suggestion that she go for a walk, Moon Orchid balks, claiming that she cannot go out into Gold Mountain by herself. For Fa Mu Lan, language literally is self. On her back are etched the symbols proclaiming to the world the oppression of her people, making visible the young woman's motivation for becoming a warrior. And finally, the poet Ts'ai Yen communicates through her words, distilling her experiences in the barbarian camp into language that artistically transmits her emotions to others and translates her subjugation into art.

The absence of language defines other characters in *The Woman Warrior*. Maxine's despised silent classmate is unable to speak up even in the Chinese school, and when she whispers, she produces only a sound so soft that she seems to have no muscles. No Name Aunt maintains total silence throughout the months of her ordeal: She does not cry out when the villagers ransack her home; she refuses to identify the father of her child; she gives birth without a sound; and she dies without a word. Her silence is an act of will, while by contrast, the wordless Chinese American girl displays the silence of inaction, of an overprotected and weak woman who depends on others to speak for her.

Another technique that Kingston employs for characterization is to describe significant actions that reveal the nature of an individual, perhaps even more tellingly than language can. The most spectacular of Brave Orchid's adventures—in a life composed of amazing events—is the encounter with the Sitting Ghost. On discovering that her fellow medical students avoid a room that is said to be haunted, Brave Orchid nonchalantly offers to spend a night in the room and to confront the resident ghost. During the night, she is attacked by a presence that attempts to suffocate her, and the next morning, she asks her classmates to go through the ritual of calling her back to life to mitigate the effects of the nighttime encounter. Then, the young women purge the room with fires in buckets, chanting as they fill the room with smoke. This incident highlights Brave Orchid's best qualities: leadership, courage, the ability to improvise; the fortitude that allows her to bear six children after her forty-fifth birthday. Another trait, the astute reading of character, marks the episode in which Brave Orchid negotiates with a slave vendor for the purchase of a girl who can help with Brave Orchid's new medical practice. Slyly concealing from the vendor her interest in a specific girl, Brave Orchid fires off a series of questions that are guaranteed to elicit certain kinds of responses if the girl is as clever as she seems—responses that the vendor is unlikely to decipher.

Different from her sister, Moon Orchid is tentative, childlike, dependent, and easily distracted. While Brave Orchid attempts to show her younger sister to the guest bedroom, Moon Orchid pauses to look at family photographs, pick up bits of colored string, and turn the fish tank light on and off. During her visit, she interrupts a nephew who is studying, creeps up behind a niece and tries to comb her hair, and loudly announces what the other children are doing. Although she offers to help with the laundry, she dresses for work in a suit, stockings, and dress shoes, and is completely baffled by the equipment, giggling when she burns a garment with the iron or folds a shirt incorrectly. Kingston portrays Moon Orchid's cultural displacement through the conflicts that erupt between Brave Orchid's children and their aunt. Absolutely unaware that she is irritating her nieces and nephews, Moon Orchid follows them around the house, marveling aloud as though talking to herself about everything with which she is unfamiliar, and occasionally prodding Brave Orchid's children as if to determine their reality. "Stop poking me," roars a child; whereupon Moon Orchid remarks, "Now the child is saying, 'Stop poking me!' " (135). Newly arrived from a culture in which adults and children interact constantly, Moon Orchid is a stranger to her sister's independent American children and their behavior; and they, in their turn, find her annoying and intrusive as well as hopelessly foreign.

Although Kingston focuses on recounting the stories of both real and legendary warrior women, as the unnamed narrator, she is herself central to *The Woman Warrior*, her character also revealed primarily through her voice, but also through her thoughts and her actions. She is unsure of herself, yet she is creative and curious; she has difficulty asserting herself or voicing her thoughts, yet she has strong opinions. More than anything else, she is confused about her place in the world, her identity, and her self.

Maxine's small, high-pitched voice suggests that she is young, unsure, and confused, and because of her tiny voice, she is unable to make authority figures take her seriously. At one point, while she is employed at an art supply store, her boss demands that she order additional supplies of a pigment that he describes as "nigger yellow" (48). Disturbed by the racial epithet, Maxine informs her supervisor that she dislikes the word he has used, but because she speaks in her "bad small-person's voice" (48), he ignores her complaint. At another job, she is fired when she "squeaks" a reminder that the restaurant her boss has selected for a company banquet is being picketed by CORE (Congress of Racial Equality) and the NAACP (National Association for the Advancement of Colored People). Clearly, her voice lacks the authority necessary for assertion of strong opinion, and the representatives of the dominant culture can find no reason to listen to what she has to say. Even within her own community, Maxine faces ridicule from a powerful matriarch who announces that the girl has a "pressed-duck voice" (192) that will make her impossible for the family to marry off.

Frequently during the course of *The Woman Warrior*, Maxine reveals herself through her thoughts, her speculations and attempts to reconstruct events, her articulation of opinions that she has kept to herself for years. Imagining herself in the place of her forgotten aunt, Maxine speculates that the aunt's suicide could have been an act of revenge for the treatment inflicted by the village on that long-dead ancestor. Because Brave Orchid has said little about the aunt, Maxine reconstructs the old story, projecting onto her aunt her own anger, stubbornness, and desire to have a role in the construction of her own identity. It is Maxine who, under the same circumstances, might consider committing suicide out of spite, or might sully the village's water supply, and might refuse to fade into the oblivion to which her family would consign her.

Maxine's childhood is marked by suppressed rage and profound insecurity. She reveals neither of these feelings to anyone, yet her thoughts dwell constantly on the inescapable condition that inspires both her anger and self-loathing: she is female. Unable to protest when a great uncle takes only her brothers on a jaunt to Chinatown, she nurses her mingled disappointment and anger quietly, all the while aware that silence is the mark of a good Chinese girl. But ultimately, she cannot contain her rage, which erupts at the sight of a meekly quiet classmate—a girl who is Maxine's opposite in every way. Driven to ungovernable irritation by the girl's compliant silence, fragility, neatness, and pastel dresses, Maxine confronts her after school in the girls' lavatory, pinching her, pulling her hair, and shouting, "Talk! Talk! Talk!" (180) demanding the kind of bold speech that Maxine herself cannot produce. In a sense, by attacking the girl, Maxine punishes herself for her own inability to articulate her feelings.

SETTING

Setting, which includes geographical location, locale, and specific site, as well as time of day, season, and even weather, creates an atmosphere and environment conducive to an author's intent in a literary work. Through the careful choice of words, images, and rhythms, and author creates the spatial and chronological boundaries within which significant events occur. In any literary work, setting performs innumerable functions, prompting specific emotions in readers, arousing suspicion or anticipation, creating mood, and affecting tone. Furthermore, setting serves as narrative strategy, revealing character, foreshadowing crucial developments, commenting on the action, exacerbating conflict, and paralleling the mental and emotional states of the characters. More practically, the setting of a work indicates geographic location and suggests temporality. In *The Woman Warrior*, China is three places: a mythical country inhabited by fantastic creatures; a romantic half-remembered homeland rendered out of reach for Chinese immigrants sojourning in the Gold Mountain; and a modern nation altered beyond recognition by Communism and Mao Zedong's Cultural Revolution.

China is a construct of myth and tradition, perpetuated by talk-story: a country whose inhabitants tell stories about the dragons who live in caves, mountains, lakes, even the sky; a culture whose layers of tradition govern the lives of Chinese, even when they are far away in America; a psychological geography shaped by paradox, intuition, inexactness, and indirection. In many of the legends, reminiscences, and tales that Brave Orchid tells, China is mysterious, secretive, full of indirection, defined by metaphor, a country in which "summer rested on the mountain" and mountains are the tops of dragons' heads (94). This is the China that the immigrant generation attempts to transmit to their children, the China that Brave Orchid gives her daughter. And yet, contradiction is the norm in Brave Orchid's China, which subjugates women while chanting about a warrior woman, a culture that instructs girls to be silent, yet writes the history of Ts'ai Yen the poet. Brave Orchid's own name is symbolic of these contradictions, pairing the name of a beautiful and fragile flower with an adjective that connotes strength, sinew, and power.

For Brave Orchid and her husband, China is the "home" that they have never given up, and they idealize it more and more intensely as years separate them from the ancestral ground. Brave Orchid tells her children that time moved more slowly in China, where women whiled away long evenings with card games and leisurely cups of tea. In China, where "human beings didn't work like this"—meaning the unceasing, round-the-clock toil in America—she didn't need well-developed muscles didn't even have to hang up her own clothes (104). Her daughter says that Brave Orchid has not stopped "seeing land on the other side of the oceans" (59). The sad truth that becomes more and more evident as years march on is that Brave Orchid and other immigrants like her will never return to China, even for a visit. During their long absence, the China that they remember so wistfully has changed past imagining into a country that has no place for them.

China in its new incarnation is a terrifying place, known to Maxine only from airmail letters full of bad news over which her parents weep. In that alien China, uncles are forced to kneel on broken glass and confess to being landlords, aunts are raped and disappear, cousins must survive on four ounces of fat and a cup of oil each week. The letters beg for money and for bicycles, and recount long days of body-breaking labor, torture, and starvation. Despite the heartbreaking news, Brave Orchid for years clings to dreams of somehow returning to China, but at length, after her children have grown up, she finally admits that for her family, there no longer is a China to which they can return. The country that she remembers has altered beyond her imagining, and the savings that she has earmarked for airfare to China can be diverted to making life in America more comfortable.

Unlike their parents, Maxine and her sisters and brothers see China as a fiction, an unseen world, a place that exists only in talk-story and in didactic pronouncements from their parents. In *China Men*, Kingston refers to China as a country that she has created in her imagination. China in *The Woman Warrior* is the alien and menacing country that looms behind Brave Orchid's exhortations and stories; it is a place in which parents might sell daughters or a father might marry two or three additional wives who would mistreat his children by the first wife. Yet China is also the source of myth, of legendary women like Fa Mu Lan. Faced with these contradictions, the American-born generation finds it difficult to construct a coherent image of the country about which they hear so much. Kingston admits that the China in her books is a construct, that the China in her stories is not the geographical country halfway around the world from the United States. And as *The Woman Warrior* and *China Men* suggest, the myth of China constantly threatens to deconstruct itself. *The Woman Warrior* makes it clear that in the company of other American-born children of immigrants, Maxine and her siblings must find a way to reconcile the imagined, invisible Chinese world created by the emigrants in their talk-story with the reality of life in "solid America" (5).

America is not described, but rather is implied in Maxine's musings about her place in the world around her. If China is feminine and secretive, America is masculine, straightforward, logical, practical. Unlike the convoluted mysteries and myths that permeate immigrant talk-story about China, life in America is orderly. Maxine describes school as a place in which events and activities are highly organized, children are regimented into lines, and stories are reconfigured into the more structured, less imaginative essay form. As a child, Maxine Hong Kingston, who had been raised in a storytelling family, found the essay form baffling, and by her own admission, she did not comprehend the conventions of the essay until she was in college. Instead, she wrote stories, explicating her thoughts and ideas in narrative form. In *The Woman Warrior*, practicality is the hallmark of America. At school, Teacher Ghosts encourage Maxine to be a scientist or a mathematician, careers which hold no appeal for the artistic girl. Even at home, she is told that she must learn to type if she wants to become a real American girl.

If Maxine is ambivalent, even afraid of China, Brave Orchid feels similarly about the United States. To her, America is somehow not real . . . it is "terrible ghost country," populated by beings that she implies cannot be human because only Chinese are human (104). More distressing to Brave Orchid is her sense that America is nothing but motion and energy, exhausting, enervating, draining. She complains that America never shuts down: "Factories, canneries, restaurants—always somebody somewhere working through the night" (105). Yet, for all the years of labor and unstinting effort, immigrants like Brave Orchid find it difficult to get ahead, trapped by their inability to assimilate sufficiently, held back by their marginal status.

LITERARY DEVICES

In the construction of a literary work, a writer has access to a wide variety of literary devices that add richness and intricacy to the text, thereby creating for the reader not only an intense experience that engages both the intellect and the emotions, but also a densely textured work that allows for new discoveries with each reading. The most common literary devices include archetypes (more or less universally recognized figures or tropes), icons, image clusters, linguistic patterns, motifs, and symbols (generally objects, but also places, persons, occasions, or events—even single words). In *The Woman Warrior*, Kingston employs motifs, symbols, and allusions, employing references to storytelling, Chinese embroidery, and ghosts, as well as to Chinese history and mythology, literature, and popular culture. In addition, she invokes images from American culture, juxtaposing those elements with the references to Chinese culture, creating a palimpsest that invites the reader to experience and confront layers of meaning, variations of story, multiples of signification.

Motifs

In *The Woman Warrior*, the controlling motif—an image, pattern, idea, incident, or situation that is repeated in a work—is storytelling, the substance of the book and its method. Storytelling is introduced with the first sentence and implied in the book's final reference to Ts'ai Yen's poem about the twelve years that the poet spent in captivity with the barbarians. Storytelling is both motif and strategy in *The Woman Warrior*, employed by Brave Orchid as the means by which she can transmit the elements of Chinese culture to her American daughter, and as a mechanism whereby she is able to speak with the voice of authority, admonishing that daughter to learn from the story of No Name Woman. As well, storytelling is the method through which that same daughter comes to terms with Brave Orchid's words, examining them as signifiers of a culture she does not understand, reiterating them in order to claim them as her heritage. Ultimately, storytelling becomes the avenue to the self and a means to an articulation of identity.

In *The Warrior Woman*, storytelling functions as ethnography, a medium for recording cultural values, thus as an assertion of cultural identity. Brave Orchid's tales provide a window into a China that now exists only in books like *The Woman Warrior*. With her appropriation of the tales of Mulan, Yue Fei, Ts'ai Yen, the big eaters, the emperor's knot, as well as the family stories passed on by her parents, Kingston engages in an act of self-creation. She reshapes and modifies the stories, paying attention to the demands of the audience for whom she retells them, artistically rewriting them into an American memoir, a narrative about growing up female and ethnic in the United States. She embraces and internalizes the stories of her Chinese heritage, combining them with her own experiences as an American child, creating a fresh approach to describing the American experience.

Storytelling empowers the storyteller. Fa Mu Lan derives strength from the narrative of oppression that her mother and father have etched into her back. Ts'ai Yen's pain is authorized by the poetry it inspires. Brave Orchid mobilizes her fellow medical student by talking story about the Sitting Ghost that they must collectively vanquish. Fortified with talk-story from her mother and other female relatives, Maxine is finally able to break her own silence, tell her own story, and speak her mind. Even as the act of storytelling moves the action forward in a narrative, Kingston's revisionist storytelling authorizes the transformation of her community from oppression and victimization to self-affirmation and cultural survival. Stories validate major events in the existence and development of a community, ensuring that each generation participates in the oral tradition that shapes both a communal history and the lives of the individuals who form that community.

Storytelling is a way to uncover the buried past; it is, as well, a strategy for participating in the rituals and practices of that past. Through her subversive talk-story—prefaced with an injunction to silence—Brave Orchid provides a way for her daughter to reconstruct the life of No Name Woman. Kingston takes up the challenge, retelling the story of her aunt's transgression, thus articulating a portion of family lore that has been concealed. And yet, along with the act of "devot[ing] pages of paper" (16) to her aunt, Kingston also colludes in the silence that continues to punish the transgressor. Kingston does not know her aunt's name, has never requested further details, and even in recounting the story does not completely re-identify her or reinstate her into the family by naming her. Consequently, the aunt remains silenced, her life obscured by the multiple conjectural retellings of her travails and death, the truth of her story buried in words and re-creations.

Storytelling is an avenue for social commentary. Through the conventions of storytelling, a raconteur can interrogate cultural narratives, teasing apart their components, and commenting on the ways in which those narratives shape the lives of individuals. A story can also function as a metaphor for a larger, more universally encompassing narrative. In *The Woman Warrior*, for example, Kingston retells the legend of Fa Mu Lan as a strategy for examining and challenging the construction of gender roles in a patriarchal society.

Kingston's evident fascination with storytelling as both narrative device and motif is the product of her early immersion in the regional Chinese culture that her parents brought with them to the United States—the culture of agricultural villages in which storytelling was practiced and privileged as a strategy for community and survival. Kingston has often pointed out that traditional Chinese culture was frequently handed down orally from one generation to another, because so many people in old China were illiterate. Out of that need to transmit culture came storytelling (Marilyn Chin 70). The oral tradition is a way for a community to transmit its history, culture, and values to the next generation, which receives the stories, reinterpreting and retelling them to their own descendants.

Another dominant motif in *The Woman Warrior* is ghosts, referred to in the subtitle, "Memoirs of a Girlhood among Ghosts." Kingston employs a variety of definitions—most of them incorporating the idea that something is not precisely identifiable—for the word "ghost," emphasizing the fact that her uses of the word come from both Chinese and American culture. She states in interviews that the word is a very loose translation of "kuei," a Chinese word that can also be rendered "demon," which connotes some level of active malevolence, instead of the Western idea that ghosts are characterized by unreality or lack of substance. "Ghost" refers to invisible spirits, evil that must be cursed or exorcised (the Druggist Ghost, the Urban Renewal Ghosts), children to be scolded. In *The Woman Warrior*, ghosts appear in many guises: the invisible hairy creature that harasses Brave Orchid in the haunted room; the "little ghost" (15) who is No Name Woman's never christened baby; even No Name Woman herself; there are American ghosts such as "Taxi Ghosts . . . Police Ghosts," and the "Mexican ghosts," who frighten Moon Orchid into chronic agoraphobia. Ghosts in *The Woman Warrior* encompass uneasy ancestors, white people, figures from the past, and ideas that cannot be readily explained. While some ghosts are frightening, others are more benign.

America, the "terrible ghost country" (104), is inhabited by people whom Brave Orchid does not understand, or with whom she is unable to cope. At various times, she describes her own American-born children as ghosts, generally when their inexplicable (to her) behavior does not conform to traditional Chinese rules of deportment governing interactions between the young and the old. She labels No Name Aunt as a ghost, more than likely because that young woman's behavior defies explanation in a village in which women's actions are prescribed and monitored. Additionally, Brave Orchid considers Maxine to be a ghost—the American-born daughter whose desires and ambitions are baffling to Brave Orchid can be explained only as the product of "ghost country," as an alien being, as one who is not Chinese and can therefore be nothing but a ghost. Ironically, Brave Orchid has passed on her uneasiness about ghosts to the daughter she has labeled a ghost, and as long as Maxine remains in her childhood home and in the city in which she grew up, her life remains circumscribed by the existence of these ambiguous and malevolent beings. She is freed from that fear when she leaves home. On a visit to her parents, when Brave Orchid begs her to return permanently to Stockton, Maxine explains that she has discovered that there are places without ghosts, and she believes that she belongs in one of those places. In ghost-free territory, Maxine no longer has to be quiet; she can speak up. She can write the stories that crowd her imagination, no longer coerced to remain silent by her dread of ghosts.

Ghosts represent the gulf between Maxine and her mother, the ambiguities in their relationship. They are ghosts to one another, strangers in some fundamental way, each finding the other disturbingly incomprehensible. Maxine complains that her mother never explains anything that is truly important, like the phrase "Ho Chi Kuei" that Brave Orchid flings at her daughter on the day that Maxine's throat "burst[s] open" (201) with every grievance, with her painstakingly compiled list of over two hundred "things [she] had to tell" (197) so that Brave Orchid would understand the truth about Maxine. Attempting to decipher the meaning of the phrase, Maxine consults a dictionary, but to no avail. She knows that "kuei" means "ghosts," but the first two words of the phrase carry so much cultural freight that Brave Orchid's exact meaning is impossible to pinpoint. What is clear is that Brave Orchid has relegated Maxine to the company of ghosts. To her mother and the Chinese community—as to the larger Stockton community—Maxine is the complete outsider, not Chinese, not American.

Ultimately, ghosts are reminders of Brave Orchid's separation from both China and America; they are symbols of her lack of tangible connection to either place. She views the people around her as ghosts—as not Chinese; but she eventually has to acknowledge the fact that to those people, she is not American. Because she must live in their space and in their geography, it is she who is the outsider, she who belongs nowhere. In America, Brave Orchid is herself a ghost.

Allusions

Allusions—seemingly passing references to persons, places, events, works of art or literature—enable an author to bring the entire universe into a written text, or to indicate connections between one text and another. Allusions function much like a kind of literary shorthand. Generally, no explanation is provided; an author assumes that the reader will be familiar enough with an allusion to recognize the history or literary tradition to which it refers, as well as to understand the contexts and meanings that the allusion brings to a work. Occasionally, as in the case of Maxine Hong Kingston, the allusions come from a culture with which readers are unfamiliar; such references require cultural translation or research. *The Woman Warrior* is not impenetrable without translation, but recognition and understanding of the allusions richly contextualize the events that comprise Kingston's memoir, adding layers of significance, raising questions, and foregrounding important issues.

Allusions in *The Woman Warrior* invoke Chinese history, legend, folktale, and geography. Because the narrative presence is Maxine's American voice, these allusions serve as markers of the not-too-distant cultural heritage that she must somehow integrate into the identity that she is attempting to construct. Allusions also establish connections between *The Woman Warrior* and other texts—written, visual, performed—from Chinese culture and art, allowing Kingston to bridge the chasm that appears to separate her ancestral heritage from the American culture that is her birthright.

The central allusion in *The Woman Warrior* is Fa Mu Lan—the most obviously identifiable of the warrior women in the book. Kingston introduces Fa Mu Lan in the "White Tigers" chapter, recounting the story of the young girl who is lured away from home by a bird, and trained by a mysterious old couple in the martial arts. Returning home to find her village crushed by an oppressive baron, she takes her father's place in the army, concealing her gender beneath the warrior's armor. Thus dressed as a man, she leads an army composed of hundreds of peasants to victory over the tyrannical landowning aristocracy, whereupon she returns home to take up the more traditional female roles of wife and mother. In telling the story, Kingston alludes to a much-admired Chinese folk heroine whose triumphs have been the subject of legend, poetry, and drama, becoming most popular in a ballad from the Tang dynasty.

In the classic rendition of the tale, "The Ballad of Mulan," the woman warrior Mulan is a paragon of filial loyalty, joining the army to spare her elderly father from the rigors of a military campaign. Disguised as a man, she goes to war against the invading Tartars, thinking only about her parents during her twelve years of military service, refusing official rank offered to her as a reward, and desiring only a swift camel at war's end so that she can return home immediately. The war, which is led by the emperor's troops, is waged against an external enemy, and nowhere in the ballad is there a hint that Fa Mu Lan is participating in anything other than a classic national battle against an invader. She is a defender of China and its borders, a hero for her people, a warrior battling against foreign intruder. Yet after the war is over, she resumes her interrupted girlhood without a qualm, displaying no apparent regret for the freedom that she must give up when she discards her masculine clothing.

Kingston's retelling of the tale differs in nearly every respect, except for the general plot involving the young girl who joins the army and goes to war in her father's place. To begin with, Kingston's version is talk-story, implying creative improvisation that draws material from at least three sources, whereas the original is a sixty-two-line written ballad from the fifth century. To create her female warrior, Kingston invokes not only the written ballad, but also the story of General Yue Fei from the twelfth century. Moreover, she indicates in an interview that the swordswoman figure in kung fu movies also inspired the genesis of the heroine of "White Tigers." In *The Woman Warrior*, Fa Mu Lan is an ambitious young woman, motivated by her own need to prove herself as well as by her parents' desire for revenge. She is energized by martial activity, taking pleasure in extraordinary feats, in battles well-fought and strategy cunningly conceived. Although Mulan—the original swordswoman—remains a maiden throughout her adventure, Kingston's Fa Mu Lan encounters her husband (who married her by proxy in childhood) during a military campaign, conceives a child, and conceals her pregnancy beneath artfully altered armor through a battle. She then bears their son secretly—and because she wishes to focus her attention on winning another victory, sends her husband and son home to his parents for safety. In Kingston's version, the emperor is an enemy and Fa Mu

Lan's army is fighting against an oppressive aristocracy in a civil war, at the conclusion of which the emperor is beheaded by the victorious peasants. In this way, Kingston creates a heroine who balances family and career, fulfilling both her domestic roles and her duty to her people and country. Fa Mu Lan proves that not only can she do men's work, but that she can also bear sons (which men cannot do), thus fulfilling society's expectations for a proper Chinese wife.

Kingston expands the original ballad, elaborating on Fa Mu Lan's story to include additional material, containing a lengthy account of the young woman's early separation from her parents, and training—with the help of supernatural intervention—to be a warrior. In addition, Kingston provides descriptions of battles as well as character portraits of the enemies on whom Fa Mu Lan has vowed revenge. Essentially, Kingston has transformed a Chinese ballad into a Western epic, and Mulan from a girl heroine into Fa Mu Lan, a classical epic hero not entirely unlike those of the Graeco-European tradition, combining aspects of Chinese folklore and Western literature to create a new role model for American girls— especially Asian American girls.

Not explicitly named, yet alluded to and embedded in Fa Mu Lan's story, is General Yue Fei (1103–41), a historical figure who fought the Mongols in the twelfth century, and whose story is the source of the carved inscriptions that adorn Fa Mu Lan's back. In Kingston's book, Fa Mu Lan's parents inscribe words of revenge on her back with sharp knives. They etch oaths and names of victims, as well as a lengthy list of grievances, a testimony to oppression, words arranged in "red and black files" (35) that she must carry into battle as a reminder of why she is fighting. The "Ballad of Mulan" says nothing about the incisions that mark revenge on the woman warrior's back; the word-engraving episode comes from the story of Yue Fei, whose mother *writes* four words—"jing zhong bao guo" or "serve one's country with steadfast loyalty"—on his back to remind him always of his duty to his country (Gao 23).

Concluding *The Woman Warrior* is an allusion that invokes Ts'ai Yen (Cai Yan, in pinyin) China's first important female poet. In historical accounts, Ts'ai Yen, daughter of the famous poet-statesman, Ts'ai Yung (Cai Yong), was kidnapped by the Huns during the second-century Dong Zhuo Rebellion and carried off into barbarian territory when she was twenty years old. She became the concubine of a powerful chieftain, and she bore him two sons whom she loved despite her disgust for the barbarians and her desperate longing for home. When the powerful ruler Cao Cao needed Ts'ai Yen to edit her father's works, she was ransomed and returned to China after twelve years in captivity. Hans Frankel, who has studied the poetry attributed to Cai Yan, notes that little beyond the bare outline above is known about Ts'ai Yen, and the poetry generally ascribed to her has not been reliably identified as having been written by her; nonetheless, the three long poems are frequently quoted as the source of biographical information. Maxine Hong Kingston appropriates Ts'ai Yen's cycle of poems, *Hu Chia shih pa p'ai (Hujia shibapai)*, or "Eighteen Songs from a Barbarian Reed Flute," which is a record not only of the poet's own personal travail, but also the political chaos that engulfed China during her life. The poems reveal a woman who is homesick, psychologically bereft, and somewhat given to self-pity. An exile from her culture, Ts'ai Yen finds her environment harsh and barren, and she is bitter over her abduction, lonely, and sick with despair. Her tender skin is irritated by the fur garments that she must wear, and she finds the barbarian diet of mutton repulsive; yet, when she is ransomed and must abandon her sons, she feels enormous pain at the prospect of leaving her two children despite her joy at the prospect of home.

Like her revision of the "Ballad of Mulan," Kingston retells Ts'ai Yen's story by making intriguing alterations, not the least of which is the change in the poet's attitude toward her circumstances. Ts'ai Yen, in *The Woman Warrior*, is no passive, weeping woman yearning for home, but a capable and even aggressive woman who participates in military combat, fighting on horseback when such action is warranted. Unlike the historical woman who is so delicate that her skin cannot endure fur, Kingston's poet is a plucky woman who gives birth on the sand. More notably, this incarnation of Ts'ai Yen comes to understand that her captors are human beings like herself; and moved by the sound of their flutes one night, she sings her poetry, allowing their music and her words to bridge the linguistic and cultural gap between them. Kingston makes it a point to say that Ts'ai Yen's nocturnal song, the vocal echo of the flute melody, "translated well" (209). In other words, the poet is finally able to communicate beyond the language barrier.

THEMATIC ISSUES

Theme, in a literary work, is an abstract concept that takes shape through language, through symbols and motifs, allusions, characters, actions, and events—all of the elements that comprise a work. Generally expressed as a word or phrase, theme can be simple, paradoxical, multifaceted, profound, speculative; it can be expressed as a series of competing truths. At its best, theme provides new ways of seeing the world and approaching truth, allowing both logical and emotional engagement with the work.

The narrative and cultural complexity of *The Woman Warrior* affords Maxine Hong Kingston the scope necessary for her treatment of several themes, both universal and culturally specific. Frequently identified as major themes in the work are several groups of subjects and clusters of issues: silence (both gendered and racially constituted) and the necessity for speech; the discovery of voice; the construction of identity and the search for self-realization; the mother-daughter relationship and the conflicts that it engenders; memory; acculturation and biculturalism; and cultural alienation.

Silence and Coming to Voice

A theme that pervades *The Woman Warrior* as well as Kingston's other works is *silence* and its corollary, *coming to voice*. Through the use of talk-story, Kingston explores the meanings of silence and speech, particularly as they collide or intersect with, parallel, contradict, or underscore other crucial issues that she also addresses in the *The Woman Warrior*. Kingston writes about the influence on herself of an ancestral culture that defines silence as the virtue that best displays a woman's femininity. She explores the manifestations of silence, the ramifications of an individual's inability to speak, and the consequences of that same individual's discovery of language and a voice—all in the context of the Chinese American community in which her narrator is seeking identity.

Kingston examines several kinds of silence in *The Woman Warrior*. There is the reticence of the marginal individual who refrains from speech because to speak up would be to claim an authority which one does not have. Such is the silence displayed by the unspeaking girl whom Maxine berates and then attacks in the girls' cloakroom at school. Raised by a protective family, the girl whispers, but is otherwise speechless, unable to speak up even in Chinese school. Another form of silence, produced by the lack of fluency in a language, afflicts Maxine when she enters kindergarten. Chinese is her first language—the only one spoken at home—and Maxine has little to no English. Because she is required at school to speak English, she speaks to no one, not even asking before going to the restroom, and consequently fails kindergarten. Similarly, her sister is mute for the first three years of school, not speaking even on the playground or at lunch in the American school. Maxine's silence at its most intense finds its visual representation in the black paint that covers her school paintings. To her, the black represents a curtain concealing houses, flowers, and the sun, a stage curtain hiding the sunlight, and the stories which she describes as "mighty operas" (165), thus keeping her thoughts and the worlds of her imagination private from everyone who might require her to articulate them in a language she can barely speak. She takes refuge in an external silence that masks the creative possibilities that crowd her mind, waiting for the day when she can draw aside the curtains to reveal the drama of her stories to the world.

A third kind of silence confers taboo status on certain subjects that might create problems or jeopardize life in America. The parents remain tight-lipped, withholding information so that their children can grow up with imaginations unencumbered by either ghosts or deities. Enjoined to silence by parents who say, "Don't tell," the narrator notes that she and her siblings "couldn't tell if we wanted to," not knowing what the taboo information might be. Like many second-generation Asian Americans, they know instinctively that there are certain types of secrets never to be said in front of non-Chinese individuals because the revelation of such information could lead to deportation. These children infer the existence of Chinese holidays from certain rituals in which their parents participate, but which they never explain; Maxine is aware of cultural practices only because she is punished for failing to conform to those unarticulated customs.

Cultural strictures about silence become the source of deep confusion to Maxine once she begins her education. Raised to conform to the vestiges of a culture that requires girls to be shy and reticent, yet produces women who speak in loud immigrant voices "unmodulated to American tones" even though they have spent years away from the home villages where their ringing voices "called their friendships out" from one field to another (11), Maxine learns to turn herself "American feminine" (11) by speaking in a barely audible voice. Ironically, it is American teachers who require her to speak up in class, and when she whispers and squeaks her way through a recitation, her teacher demands that she speak in louder tones, and the child is silenced once more. Her early role models are Chinese women whose voices are "strong and bossy" (172) as they talk-story during a piano recital, drowning out the performance on stage; yet she learns at school that she must whisper if she wishes to appear attractive by American standards. Within that Chinese American community, still shaped by allegiances to the traditions of the old country, silence is gendered, connected with and imposed upon women who are expected to manifest the voicelessness expected of the ideal Chinese woman. Those expectations confuse the child Maxine, who has heard all her life that Chinese women must be silent. For her, reality is the reverse; the Chinese women she knows—Brave Orchid included—are vociferous, verbal, unhesitatingly announcing their opinions to anyone within hearing.

Related to silence is the discovery of voice, another theme that Kingston explores in *The Woman Warrior*, portraying women whose silence is permanent, as well as those who move from silence to eloquence. For No Name Woman and Moon Orchid—a woman who breaks the rules and another who adheres to them—silence is unbreakable, and it remains for the narrator to give voice to their lives. These are the women whom Maxine must not emulate even as she articulates their stories. Yet, Brave Orchid—despite her aggressive speech and opinionated conversation—is not entirely the role model that Maxine needs. Vocal among her fellow immigrants and at home, Brave Orchid communicates imperfectly with the non-Chinese world. In that larger milieu, her voice is inadequate, her sphere of influence small. Not only does she lack facility with English, but she also lacks the ability to translate one culture into another. She has clung to China for too long, and her voice is Chinese—incomprehensible to the Americans among whom she lives. Complicating the issue is Brave Orchid's inadequate understanding of American culture, and she frequently mistranslates essential cultural markers or fails to comprehend subtle signs of difference. For instance, when the druggist responds to her demand for "reparation candy" after a delivery error by giving Brave Orchid's children leftover Christmas or Easter candy out of season, Brave Orchid believes that she has won a cultural victory over the druggist by forcing him to conform to her way of life. She does not understand that leftover candy—earmarked for the rubbish bin—represents a charitable offering. The druggist believes that her children are so poor that they cannot afford sweets!

Maxine must find her way to a unique voice that incorporates her ancestral culture in equal measure with that of her American home and native country. She will not tolerate the limits that circumscribe Brave Orchid's world—Maxine wants to lift the metaphorical black curtains that conceal her thoughts; she wants to tell her stories to the world. In order to do so, she must first develop a powerful voice that can speak with enough authority so that the world will listen. For Maxine, finding a voice is an essential initial step toward articulating a self.

Constructing Identity

A third theme—one that Kingston also explores in her next two books—is *identity*, its nature and construction, as well as the issues that an individual must resolve in the formation of a stable and viable self-image. Two types of identity are the focus of *The Woman Warrior*: the immigrant identity, exemplified by Brave Orchid; and the Asian American identity, embodied in the narrator. While the two types share common elements, they are sufficiently distinctive as to warrant separate consideration. Brave Orchid and her daughter must negotiate issues of gender, cultural conflict, and assimilation; they must deal with their alienation from the dominant culture, and ultimately, each one must become adept at performing a balancing act.

Like most immigrants, Brave Orchid has had to come to terms with profound disillusionment. A medical doctor in China, she is unable to find work in the United States, other than menial labor in tomato fields and canneries. Having emigrated to the Gold Mountain, she has come face to face with the reality concealed beneath the glitter of the legends, and she realizes that she has no defined place in the land of her dreams. Brave Orchid, born, raised, and educated in China, manages to adjust, even to acculturate to life in the United States, although she never assimilates completely. While she does not educate her children in the practice of Chinese holiday customs or Buddhist religious observance, she continues to perform the appropriate rituals on significant cultural or religious days, despite the fact that her adherence to those rituals has become perfunctory. As Brave Orchid slowly relinquishes her mental and emotional connection with China, which recedes farther and farther into her memory, she comes to understand and accept that there is little chance of her even returning to the country of her birth. Unfortunately, she has nothing with which to replace China; the United States continues to be a mystery—an alien culture inhabited by strange people to whom she refers as ghosts because to her, they have no definable identities.

To her children, Brave Orchid is incontrovertibly Chinese, and they are constantly embarrassed by evidence of her inability to assimilate. For their meals, she cooks whatever is on hand—raccoons, hawks, owls, garden snails, turtles, even skunks, and she keeps a pickled bear claw in a jar on the kitchen counter. She burns candles for good luck in the laundry, stores old clothes and shoes against hard times, and arrives at the San Francisco International Airport provisioned with shopping bags full of food to sustain her while she awaits Moon Orchid's arrival. When a box of medicine is accidentally delivered to her front door, Brave Orchid fears that a curse of illness has been laid on her family, and she orders Maxine to demand candy from the druggist in reparation for the mistake, as well as to undo the curse "with sweetness" (170). Thereafter, whenever the druggist gives the children candy, they are ashamed because they are well aware that he thinks they are beggars, but Brave Orchid remains convinced that she has managed to instruct the Druggist Ghost in good manners and proper behavior. She is, however, unsuccessful when she attempts to coerce her children into banging pot lids together to prevent the celestial frog from swallowing the moon during an eclipse.

If Brave Orchid is irredeemably Chinese to her children, to Moon Orchid, she is an American, taking charge of events, alarmingly energetic, even pushy. For example, although Chinese custom dictates that it is the children's duty to display framed portraits of their parents, Brave Orchid has taken the bold step of hanging up her own and her husband's portraits on the walls of her house. This aggressiveness manifests itself only hours after Moon Orchid's plane lands in San Francisco. Brave Orchid immediately begins to plan her younger sister's life: Moon Orchid will reclaim the husband she has not seen for three decades, work as a maid in a hotel or as a waitress in a Chinatown restaurant, and dye her hair black or wear a wig to conceal her age. When the scheme to reunite Moon Orchid with her husband fails, Brave Orchid immediately demands that the recalcitrant husband at least treat them to an expensive lunch at a good restaurant. After Moon Orchid's lapses into paranoia and then into insanity, Brave Orchid briefly becomes totally Chinese, treating her sister with traditional plants and discarding the Thorazine prescribed by a physician. When the traditional remedies fail, however, Brave Orchid's brisk American efficiency reasserts itself, and she helps arrange for Moon Orchid's admission to the state mental asylum.

Not until she is an old woman can Brave Orchid admit to herself (and to Maxine) that she is bewildered about the way that her life has evolved; she is now "a sad bear; a great sheep in a wool shawl" (100), no longer the woman warrior who was a physician, crossed the ocean, bore and raised six American children. She has relinquished her dreams of China which no longer beckons with the promise of fragrant flowers and the family home. She is in limbo—a border-dweller, bereft of her Chinese identity yet never emotionally vested in an American self. She no longer saves money for a trip to China; instead, she and her husband have purchased furniture, rugs, curtains, even an automobile . . . the outward emblems of an American life.

Complicating identity is the condition of biculturalism, a double existence that produces in the descendants of immigrants the feeling of belonging to two distinct cultural traditions, yet not feeling completely comfortable in either one. Biculturalism is a fact of life for America's immigrant populations and their descendants, many of whom must deal with not only cultural conflict, but also with issues of race and ethnicity. For Asian Americans who grow up "hyphenated," the bicultural condition is a crucial issue in the construction of identity in that they must negotiate multiple cultures, sign systems, languages, and even communities as they seek to stabilize a sense of self that embraces all aspects of their heritages.

When Kingston asks, "What is Chinese and what is the movies?" she describes the dilemma in which Maxine finds herself. Her knowledge of China is imperfect, fragmentary, possibly fictitious, thanks to the constantly evolving talk-story from which her information comes. It is clear that her parents expect some form of Chinese behavior—Maxine and her siblings are chastised for disregarding customs of which they have no knowledge—yet the rules of such behavior are never articulated. On the other hand, Maxine's awareness of American mores is likewise incomplete. Until she enters school where she meets children from more mainstream neighborhoods, her playmates are Chinese; and even after she commences her American education, she must continue her regular attendance at Chinese school. From an early age, Maxine must deal with cultural confusion and collision.

Unlike her daughter, Brave Orchid is not a bicultural individual; nevertheless, she is forced to deal with the bicultural world in which she lives and works. To her children, she is the embodiment of Chinese culture, and she remains stolidly Chinese—attempting to discover an American identity is not an issue for her. In fact, Brave Orchid finds American culture impossible to decipher, as evidenced in her dismissal of the United States as a ghost country populated mainly by those incomprehensible beings whose existence only serves to complicate life.

Maxine's childhood and young adult years are marked by tremendous dislocation, the result of growing up between the Old World (China) and the New (the United States), of growing up "hyphenated." Aware that the older immigrants in her neighborhood do not consider her to be completely Chinese (she and her siblings are too American), she is nonetheless conscious that at school and in the dominant culture, she is not identified as an American (she looks Chinese). In fact, she occupies a third space, between and outside conventional designations of national identity and ethnic heritage. Through no action of hers, she is alienated from both her ancestral culture and the one into which she is born and in which she grows up. She is triply challenged: female in a Chinese community that retains vestiges of Confucian patriarchy; a Chinese American woman in the white patriarchy; and a Chinese American in a European American environment.

Maxine is virtually homeless, a stranger to China and yet not completely belonging to America. Clearly, she is not of Brave Orchid's world and because of her ethnicity, she fits imperfectly into the country of her birth. Moreover, she is torn between the two heritages with which she has grown up, between two national narratives, two sets of cultural myths. Her most pressing task is to integrate the identities that she has been given—the first step in the construction of an authentic self with which she can be comfortable. And that self will necessarily be neither Chinese nor mainstream American, but will incorporate elements of both into a Chinese American identity. The struggle to create a new and more inclusive definition of the designation "American" is a theme that permeates all of Maxine Hong Kingston's work. In her three major books, she explores the ways in which her protagonists balance the demands of the two cultural systems that simultaneously claim and reject them, that pull them in several directions, threatening permanently to fracture their personas. In *The Woman Warrior*, Maxine learns to mediate between her parents' ancestral culture (China) and the culture into which she has been born (the United States).

ALTERNATIVE READING: FEMINIST CRITICISM

What Is Feminist Criticism?

Feminist criticism, which exists in many forms, has a vast agenda with an array of goals. Very generally, it is a way of examining literature and art based on a philosophical stance that advocates equal rights and equal opportunities for women. Seeking social, cultural, political, and personal changes that will enable an agenda of equality, feminist criticism is grounded in the assumption that social institutions are predicated on a culturally established, uneven distribution of power between men and women.

Feminist criticism's goals have evolved over the last several decades, but generally speaking, those goals first include the recovery of texts (both literary and artistic) by women whose efforts have been overlooked, ignored, or possibly even suppressed by environments in which cultural production is dominated by men. Also sought is the reevaluation of canonical literature and art to discover how these works—generally by men—embody the cultural attitudes that have contributed to the oppression of women.

Although modern feminist criticism has its origins at least as far back as Simone de Beauvoir's *The Second Sex* (1949), its contemporary roots lie in the 1970s. In its first stage, feminist criticism, energized by Kate Millett's *Sexual Politics*, focused on identifying misogyny and gender bias, not only in literature and art, but also in the culture at large. The work of the earliest feminist critics uncovered and analyzed the definitive gender biases evident in literary works generally acknowledged to be canonical or widely accepted. Second-phase feminist criticism—called gynocriticism—involved efforts to uncover women's texts, to identify forgotten works in which female authors privilege the woman's perspective, to discover answers to questions about how women's writing differs from men's. The third historic phase of feminist criticism is the most inclusive, extending its focus beyond overtly feminist texts to include works by all women, label and intersecting with gender studies to concentrate its efforts on examining gender as a cultural construction, as a system of categories in which *woman* and *man* are not complete opposites, not distinct categories, but rather points along a system of identifications.

Feminist criticism approaches literary and artistic texts by asking questions that focus on certain aspects directly related to issues, practices, and institutions that have some influence on the lives of women. Among the important questions are the following: How are women portrayed in the work? How are women's roles interrogated? Subverted? In what ways does gender intersect with race? With class?

A Feminist Analysis of *The Woman Warrior*

In *About Chinese Women* (1974), French feminist Julia Kristeva describes how Confucius categorized women with slaves or *xiaoren*, a word which also means "inferior men." As second-class people in Confucian society, women were considered fit only for procreation and domestic work and were called *nei ren* or "humans for the inside," a phrase that picturesquely describes the circumscribed lives of women in traditional Chinese society. Because women were confined to the home, society considered it unnecessary for them to learn to read or write; moreover, only courtesans—not wives and daughters—were educated in the arts, which were considered essential accomplishments for women with whom men sought aesthetic conversation and entertainment.

A central issue in *The Woman Warrior* is Kingston's portrayal of the culturally embedded patriarchal assumptions that define Maxine and the women in her family. In the China that her parents recall with nostalgia, women's lives are narrowly defined by the Three Obediences and the Four Virtues of Confucian philosophy. Succinctly stated, the Obediences require a woman to obey her father and brothers while she is unmarried, obey her husband after marriage, and finally to obey her sons when she is widowed. The Virtues demand chastity and obedience, reticence, a pleasing manner, and the perfection of domestic skills. Women were enjoined to silence and acquiescence, and the custom of foot-binding ensured women's immobility. Even in America, immigrant communities tended to retain some of the cultural practices of their countries of origin, and Stockton's Chinatown is no different. Even though no one in Maxine's community of immigrants-turned-new-Americans practices female infanticide, and foot-binding is a thing of the ancient past, girl children are still considered less desirable than boys, and Maxine's uncles make it clear that they prefer her brothers. Although when *The Woman Warrior* was published, Kingston had never been to China, she had inferred from talk-story, as well as from the attitudes of older immigrants, considerable cultural information about a woman's place in the ancestral country. In her first book, she explores the power of her inferences about women in Chinese society in the shaping of her own life.

Always in the background for Maxine, her sisters, and girl cousins, is the knowledge that in China, which is still "home" for their parents, a girl is despised and families are disappointed when a baby girl is born: at best, they ignore the infant; at worst, they sell her to someone who wants to raise a servant. A proverb once popular in China announces that boys are born "facing in," while by contrast, girls are born "facing out." In this proverb are embedded certain cultural assumptions: boys marry and bring wives into the family to produce sons who will perpetuate the family name; girls marry and leave the family to produce children for another clan. Thus, girls are not worth nurturing, because

such effort ultimately benefits another family. All her life, Maxine has
heard that "Feeding girls is feeding cowbirds," and that because there is
no profit in raising girls, it is "Better to raise geese than girls" (54). Hoping that she has misunderstood the misogynistic remarks that have
marred her childhood, Maxine demands reassurance from her parents:
Did they roll an egg on her face for good omens at her birth? Did they
celebrate her one-month birthday with a party? Did they send her photograph to China? The negative answers confirm her suspicions—Chinese girls are not valuable enough to celebrate, even in America. Even
good grades are insufficient to overcome her gender: "You can't eat
straight A's" (46).

Chinese American girls like Maxine grow up hearing stories about
arranged marriages. They listen to tales about the punishments inflicted
on women who do not obey the husbands their parents have selected
for them. Although she is an American, Maxine is frequently reminded
by elderly relatives of her lowly position in the ancestral culture. A great-
grandfather waxes irate at the sight of six girls at the dinner table: "Maggots! . . . Where are my grandsons? I want grandsons!" (191). His words
echo the Chinese proverb that compares girls to maggots in the rice.
Despondently, Maxine wonders when and how her parents plan to sell
her into servitude, or how soon they intend to marry her off to an F.O.B.
("fresh off the boat"), one of the recently arrived immigrants who have
advertised in Chinatown tabloids for wives. When some of these young
men begin coming to dinner and visiting the laundry at Brave Orchid's
invitation, Maxine goes out of her way to make herself as ungainly, in-
ept, and unattractive as possible. She grows her hair long to hide her
neck in case it is what the Chinese call a "flower-stem neck" (176), avoids
pastels, and wears black. In addition to her attempts at sartorial disaster,
she affects a pronounced limp and wears rumpled and un-ironed clothes;
she drops dishes and picks her nose while she is cooking so as to disgust
any potential suitors.

More extremely, Maxine denies her gender. When her mother scolds
her, Maxine wails, "I'm not a bad girl!" a denial that is tantamount to
her saying that she is not a girl—girls are, by definition, undesirable,
hence "bad" (46). Asked what she aspires to be when she grows up, she
announces that she is going to become an Oregon lumberjacks, a dis-
tinctly unfeminine choice of occupation, one that requires the brute
strength that Chinese women are not supposed to possess. Later, she
expands that ambition, saying that she not only wants to be a lumberjack
but she also wants to become a newspaper reporter—a profession that

few women chose in the 1950s. She announces to her parents that she intends to fell trees during the daytime and write about the timber industry at night after work.

The Woman Warrior explores Maxine's dawning knowledge of her body, the female body that automatically makes a young woman vulnerable. Brave Orchid reveals No Name Aunt's story in the context of Maxine's menarche (beginning of menstruation), appending the warning that any careless young girl could easily suffer the fate of the unnamed ancestor. Because of her mother's cautionary story, Maxine is aware of what the onset of menstruation implies—vulnerability to the blandishments or coercion of men, possible pregnancy and childbirth (without marriage, almost certain ostracism and erasure from the family narrative), and pain. She is equally aware that the changes in her body and her status are peculiar to femaleness, setting her apart from men. Small wonder then that when Maxine imagines herself into the role of Fa Mu Lan, that budding swordswoman asks for the impossible—to postpone menarche, to put off the physical signs that she has reached womanhood, the age of vulnerability, and certain pain. Like Maxine, Fa Mu Lan prefers to be a boy—boys are valuable, boys have endless opportunities, boys are free. Moreover, although boys grow up to be men and men lead violent lives, violence for them is frequently a matter of choice—they choose to become fighters, swordsmen, or lumberjacks. For women in traditional Chinese society, violence comes from without—perpetuated on or against a woman in the name of cultural practice.

The Woman Warrior is permeated with images of violence against women; in fact, the book begins and ends with the stories of women who have been raped. In each case, the rape is central to the pattern of violence that shapes the women on whom the violence is perpetuated. No Name Aunt's rape results in a pregnancy which in turn prompts the riot in which the villagers vandalize her family's home; and the story ends with her suicide. Ts'ai Yen is forcibly abducted from her home to become a barbarian's concubine. Both rapes culminate in an interrupted motherhood: No Name Aunt kills herself and her infant daughter; and while Ts'ai Yen is eventually returned to China, she must leave her sons behind with their barbarian father and kin. Kingston employs images of violence to expose the darker side of female existence and to implicate society in the violence that dehumanizes and objectifies women. In the ancestral culture that provides half of the cultural context for Maxine's attempts to create her self, women experience bodily harm almost from birth. Unwanted female infants are left outdoors to die of exposure, or smothered in a box of ashes conveniently placed beside a woman in the throes of labor. An ink drawing owned by Brave Orchid and her husband depicts starving peasants scavenging garbage from a river, while at the same time pushing discarded girl babies on down the river. The messages are clear: women are expendable, women must be punished for their transgressive behavior—real or imagined—and women must be firmly put in their place. Violence keeps women aware of their precarious existence, ensuring that they know they are perpetually vulnerable and in need of protection.

Yet violence also empowers women, revealing their strength and willingness to take action. Brave Orchid is associated with violence—in fact, she frequently acts out her agency in the context of violence. While she is a student in China, she defeats the Sitting Ghost by threatening to burn it. As a village doctor, she assists at the birth of babies—often in pigpens to fool the gods; and during World War II, she takes charge of a make-shift hospital, tending the victims of Japanese bombings, the casualties of the violence that is tearing the world apart. In the United States, far from the vicissitudes of life in China, violence continues to shape Brave Orchid's life, but in this new and strange country, that violence is transmuted into mere symbolic action or the imagery of violence. Brave Orchid talks story to Maxine about having "pushed [Maxine's] tongue up and sliced the frenum" (164), a tale of physical violence that absorbs Maxine's attention throughout her childhood. Because Brave Orchid explains her probably apocryphal action as an attempt to ensure that her daughter does not grow up tongue-tied, Maxine is sometimes inclined to view the frenum-cutting episode as powerful proof of her mother's love. Another example of Brave Orchid's use of violent imagery involves the attempt to coerce Moon Orchid's errant Americanized husband into claiming his wife. Brave Orchid fantasizes about hitting the man; then surmising that such action would be ineffective, decides that Moon Orchid should position herself in the middle of the street as though she is an accident victim. Surely a woman in pain will bring the physician husband running to help. In the end, Moon Orchid refuses, the plan is a failure, and Brave Orchid has to admit that for all her aggressive language, she is actually powerless to control events.

Ironically, two violent acts also empower No Name Woman, allowing her to take control of events at the end of her brief life. Her suicide represents her attempt to take charge of events, of the rest of her short life; by killing herself in the village well, she shapes the future, not only her own, but also those of her relatives and their descendants. Moreover, by fouling the community's water supply with her dead body, she takes revenge on an entire village that has rejected and condemned her. Finally, by drowning her newborn daughter, she enacts maternal responsibility, taking care of a child who would otherwise be scorned, even abused and sold into slavery; she saves that child from a wretched lifetime of suffering.

Two other themes merit attention in a feminist analysis of *The Woman Warrior*: the fate of women who do not conform to cultural scripts that define women's behavior, and a young woman's coming of age in a patriarchal environment. Kingston explores in both Chinese and American cultures the consequences of a woman's inability or refusal to fit in; as well, she examines the psychological journey to womanhood of a young girl whose maternal line includes women who don't know or who refuse to stay in their place.

The Woman Warrior opens with the tragic tale of No Name Woman, forever nameless because she has transgressed, shaming her entire family in the eyes of the ancestral village, and then inconveniencing her kin by her revenge suicide in the well that provides the neighborhood's water supply. Becoming pregnant more than a year after her husband has left for the Gold Mountain, the young woman refuses—out of secrecy? out of fear?—to name the father of her child. After the terrible night during which the villagers kill her family's livestock and destroy the farm and the house, she bears her child alone and then drowns both herself and the baby in the well for drinking water. Her punishment is to be deliberately forgotten by her family so that her ghost will forever wander, hungry, unremembered, unable to rest. No Name Woman is in permanent limbo, unmourned and unappeased, deliberately erased from family lore and memory.

If No Name Woman is punished by feudal Chinese society for breaking the rules governing a woman's behavior, Moon Orchid is destroyed by America because she has conformed to those traditional Chinese rules. Allowing Brave Orchid to persuade her to discard a comfortable life in Hong Kong as the well-financed first wife of a Chinese sojourner-turned-successful-American-physician, Moon Orchid is swept along in her forceful sister's plan to confront the Americanized husband and force him to acknowledge a wife whom he has neither seen nor spoken to in decades. His repudiation of Moon Orchid and his clear preference for the young American nurse he has married loosens Moon Orchid's fragile grasp on reality. She is immured in an unfamiliar country, surrounded by people speaking a language that she does not understand, and completely baffled by the turn of events that has landed her in America, only to be refused by her husband. Moon Orchid turns inward, losing her connection with the world around her, and she ultimately has to be institutionalized. America has no place for a discarded first wife whose only skill is to dress well, be ornamental, and giggle prettily.

Well-versed in the story of No Name Woman (an ancestor on her father's side) and witness to the deterioration of Moon Orchid (from her mother's side), Maxine must negotiate the difficult road from girlhood to womanhood, fully aware that women who do not conform are punished in the two cultures that battle for supremacy in her identity. With its portrayal of a young girl's journey from silence to full voice, from confused ethnicity to a clear identity as a Chinese American, from childhood to young adulthood, *The Woman Warrior* can be read as a female bildungsroman, a novel that foregrounds the theme of coming of age. With conflicting signals coming from her ancestral Chinese culture and her American environment, Maxine's dual heritage complicates her efforts to construct a new, more adult identity. Maxine must discover for herself a way to integrate the narratives that define her into a single template for a stable identity, for a self that is true to her desires and needs. That she succeeds is evident when, close to the end of the book, Maxine introduces a vignette about the theatre by noting that her mother shared the story when "I told her I also am a storyteller" (206).

China Men
(1980)

In 1980, Maxine Hong Kingston published *China Men*, her second collection of memoirs and a book that she has often described as a companion volume to *The Woman Warrior*. While her first book honors the women of Kingston's family, *China Men*, which won the National Book Critics Circle Award as well as the American Book Award, celebrates the lives and accomplishments of Kingston's father, uncles, grandfathers, and great-grandfathers. These undaunted, tenacious, and ambitious immigrants from China have individual stories which provide an introduction to the history of Chinese emigration to the United States. In writing *China Men*, Kingston portrays her ancestors as heroic characters rather than as victims; as well, she rehabilitates the image of Chinese men, transforming them from nameless coolies to American pioneers whose lives are worthy to be enshrined in American history.

Although at one time she had considered using the phrase *Gold Mountain Heroes* as the title of her second book, Kingston eventually changed her mind, concerned that the focus on the Gold Mountain in the original title might reinforce an existing negative stereotype of the Chinese as financially obsessed workaholics. The title that Kingston finally settled on—*China Men*—is not only a literal translation of the Chinese ideograph for the word Chinese; it is also Kingston's strategy for redefining the pejorative term "Chinaman" that was used for decades as a generic descriptor for male and even female immigrants from China. Kingston explains that she uses two separate words because "that's the way Chinese language is . . . monosyllabic single words . . . [and] the capital C and capital M add dignity" (Skenazy "Coming Home" 111). To emphasize the significance of the book's title, as well as to highlight Kingston's bold appropriation of a denigrative phrase, the ideograph meaning "Chinese" becomes an iconic introduction on the title page of the book, reappearing as well at the beginning of each of the six major chapters of *China Men*. The ideograph is reproduced as though it were the author's "chop" or traditional Chinese signature seal, thereby signaling—because the author is female—that it refers to women as well as men, even as the phrase "Chinamen" was once applied to men and women alike. Kingston's act of claiming a racial stereotype is a bold gesture that diminishes the power of the word to hurt; and her reconfiguration of the term relieves it of much of its potency. The ideograph also functions symbolically, as a representation of the immigrants whose stories Kingston recounts in the book. She provides no translation, rendering the symbol opaque to those who do not read Chinese—but the very presence of the unfamiliar character denoting another language and orthography is sufficient to emphasize the tremendous gulf between the average reader of English texts and the subject of *China Men*. Like the ideograph that does not yield its meaning immediately to the uninitiated, Asian Americans appear incomprehensible, indecipherable, and "exotic." By leading the reader into the text, the ideograph also bridges the distance between China and America. Kingston's use of it to name and identify her pioneering American ancestors allows her to lay claim to the two national cultures that intersect in the Asian American identity.

As she wrote *China Men*, Kingston was inspired by the work of William Carlos Williams, specifically by *In the American Grain* (1925), a series of meditations on American history and explorations of the myths that inform and shape that history. Williams takes the daring step of identifying the Icelandic sagas as integral components of the American literary tradition, naming them as early texts in American history. By thus opening up the canon of American literature to works from outside the Anglo-Protestant mainstream, Williams significantly modifies and expands the American narrative. He creates a space for the inclusion of the silent and unrepresented individuals whose stories have been submerged beneath the conventional and widely accepted Anglo-centric histories of the United States.

The time-honored story of America's origins has been contested for years, generally in the interest of Americans of non-Anglo origins claiming their right to participate in the ongoing construction of American history. Various "origins" have been proposed: Eric the Red's forays from Iceland; Christopher Columbus's voyages to the Caribbean islands; the creation of the Jamestown settlement; the arrival of the Mayflower immigrants; and more recently than other claims, the contention that the first genuine Americans have always been the indigenous peoples who inhabited the continent well before the Europeans arrived. To the existing list of potential first Americans, Maxine Hong Kingston adds her conjecture that the North American continent, which is identified as The Land of Women in *China Men*, could have been "discovered" by a traveling Chinese scholar as early as A.D. 441, more than five centuries before the Icelandic voyagers arrived on the shores of eastern North America.

In the American Grain ends in 1860 with the Civil War, and Kingston commences her version of American history around 1850, beginning *China Men* in roughly the same historical period by overlapping the arrival of the first Chinese immigrants with the hostilities between North and South, thereby incorporating the stories of her immigrant ancestors' courage, suffering, and hard work into the narrative of the American nation. Kingston still remembers that when she first encountered *In the American Grain*, she was entranced by the book's final image. William Carlos Williams portrays President Abraham Lincoln as a woman who is shrouded in a shawl, as a figure representing the mother of the country, quietly walking through the battlefields and bending down to nurture the wounded and comfort the dying soldiers. Kingston explains her fascination with Williams's work by pointing out that he has revised American mythology—a practice that she considers to be one of the right approaches to recording American history. She notes that Williams begins with Leif Ericsson (unlike historians who begin with the Pilgrims or Columbus), and retells the American narrative up to the Civil War. She is especially taken with Williams's gender-crossing image: "Lincoln is a woman, a feminine force . . . like an old nurse, tending to his soldiers . . . [or] the mother of our country" (Pfaff 24).

Kingston feels that in *China Men*, she is continuing the narrative that Williams began. She is drawn to his portrayal of Lincoln as a woman because in her own work, she blurs gender boundaries, for instance, by conflating the tale of Mulan, a legendary woman fighter, with the story of Yue Fei, a general in the Chinese army, to produce her rendition of the Fa Mu Lan story in *The Woman Warrior*. She depicts the transformation of the male traveler, Tang Ao, into the caricature of a high-class courtesan in *China Men*. With her discovery that a celebrated American author had created an image embodying both female and male traits, Kingston felt vindicated in her choice of methods for depicting the central characters in her work. She considered herself freed from the constraints of ethnicity and gender by Williams's example: "I can now write as a man . . . as a black person . . . a white person; I don't have to be restricted by time and physicality" (Fishkin 784). With *China Men*, Kingston, like Williams, reconstructs a portion of American history—in her case, by foregrounding the personal stories of her male ancestors who helped to complete the transcontinental railroad and to clear mountainsides for Hawai'ian sugar cane plantations.

As she does in *The Woman Warrior*, Kingston employs traditional folklore, myth, historical fact, and talk-story to explore her family's place in America, as well as to confer historical significance on some of her family stories, specifically the life of her silent, bitter father and the experiences of other male forebears on both sides of her family genealogy. Contrasting her scholar father's angry and intellectually impoverished existence as a laundry proprietor in Stockton with the colorful adventures of the great-grandfather in Hawai'i or the grandfather in the railroad camps of the Sierra Nevada, Kingston records the extremes, the highs and lows of the immigrant experience. She does this through the stories of uncles who planted and harvested cane, set dynamite charges, suffered, malnutrition and illness, endured abuse, and fought homesickness, all the while slyly inventing strategies for coping with and subverting institutionalized oppression. As she concludes the narrative of her family's journey toward an American identity by recounting her brother's military experiences in Asia, Kingston exposes the ironies embedded in the family's story. It is a saga that begins with the grandfathers and uncles who emigrated from China on the Asian continent, and culminates with the brother, who represents the American-born generation, being sent to fight on the Asian continent in a war against the Vietnamese, whose physical features are mirror images of his own.

China Men incorporates two very different worlds—the Old and the New, China and America—realized over a span of several generations. Kingston's portrayal of the men in her family, in China before their individual emigrations, and in the United States after their courageous crossings of the Pacific Ocean, situates her own patrimony firmly in two cultures, both of which have powerfully shaped her life and those of her parents and siblings. Moreover, by connecting China and America through the history of her family, she threads several new and essential narrative strands into the tapestry that is American history, creating for

Asian immigrants an incontrovertible contribution to the pattern of historical and cultural events that shaped the American nation. Kingston makes it possible for her ancestors to identify the United States as their country, giving them the chance to claim ownership in its history, through her book in which she claims America as her nation. She cites the Chinese talk-story of her childhood, recalling tales of Chinese explorers arriving in America before the Vikings did, remembering the pride with which one storyteller recounted the purchase of a house in the United States (Pfaff 24). For many immigrants, the act of purchasing real estate is a significant action, a tangible gesture that symbolizes permanence and connection to a community and a place. Ownership of a house provides an immigrant with an identifiable place in which to begin putting down roots; a house is the visible evidence that a place is home, a clear sign that the new owner is creating a new life away from the country of origin. The deed to a house confers on the owner an American address, a physical locus of identity, signaling that an individual belongs to a geographical location.

As has been noted earlier, critical response to Kingston's second volume was as strongly favorable as the commentary on *The Woman Warrior*, with which *China Men* was understandably compared. Reviews in major publications—the *New York Times*, the *New York Review of Books*, *Newsweek*, the *Christian Science Monitor*—called attention to the fierceness and the anger in Kingston's stories, praising the author's ability to combine that anger with finely honed prose and luminous imagery. In fact, quite a few reviewers (John Leonard and Anne Tyler, among others) noted the oppositions and violent juxtapositions that imbue *China Men* with the narrative tension that draws readers into the tales of Kingston's father and grandfathers. Henrietta Buckmaster wrote in the *Christian Science Monitor* that *China Men* is "a fierce book . . . full of horrors, superstitions, occasional obscenities, but when one recovers one sees them as metaphors designed to burrow under preconceptions and blandness" (Buckmaster B4).

One review, published by scholar Frederic Wakeman, has become famous for its assertion that Kingston's revisions of Chinese myth are inappropriate. Describing *China Men* as a compilation of history, myth, and memory, and suggesting that although the myths are initially the most intriguing element of Kingston's book, they are also "the most perplexing," Wakeman argues that: "Precisely because the myths are usually so consciously contrived, her pieces of distant China lore often seem jejune and even inauthentic—especially to readers who know a little bit about the original high culture which Kingston claims as her birthright" (Wakeman 42–43). Kingston's response to Wakeman's criticism highlights the divide between the two writers' perspectives on and attitudes toward Chinese culture. Wakeman's expertise is that of the academic, the scholar who has devoted years of careful study and thought to classical Chinese culture. His attitude is one of respect, and perhaps even reverence, for the artistic forms of a centuries-old literary tradition. Kingston's knowledge derives from her mother's everyday talk-story, from the reminiscences and tales of the Chinese customers who came into the New Port Laundry in Stockton. For her, the myths are living stories that must be altered and edited according to the demands of the telling. Describing Wakeman as "a scholar on what he calls the 'high tradition,' " Kingston acknowledges that he "sees me as one who doesn't get it right, and who takes liberties with it," and she continues by suggesting how she believes that her work should be approached: "In actuality, I am writing in the peasant talk-story Cantonese tradition ('low' if you will), which is the heritage of Chinese Americans. Chinese Americans have changed the stories, but Mr. Wakeman compares our new stories to the ancient scholarly ones from the old country and finds them inauthentic" ("Kingston, Maxine (Ting Ting) Hong" 291). According to Kingston, writers often create their own myths or re-create existing ones, and as a writer, she produces "a living myth that's changing all the time." Furthermore, Kingston requests that she be identified as a storyteller rather than as "an archivist preserving myths, writing the exact, original version" (Iwata 4).

Kingston adamantly declares that an author has a responsibility to go beyond simply recording traditional stories and myths as those tales have always been told. To her, such a practice robs the stories of their vitality and connection with people. "They [her critics] don't understand that I have no intention of just recording myths. . . . I'm not an archivist," she told Kay Bonetti (Bonetti 40). She protests that the practice of precisely recording folk narratives is "just more ancestor worship," in which she has no desire to participate; instead, she argues that she infuses the old Chinese myths with life by retelling them in a new American way. She asserts that as a storyteller, she must be given the freedom to revise and translate the stories that she tells—as storytellers have always done. Claiming that she is neither anthropologist nor historian, she points out. "I wanted the right to play around with stories" (Hoy 54). For Kingston, myth should not be considered petrified narrative; it is an integral *and completely malleable* element of any growing culture. Kingston suggests that myth retains life and vibrancy as long as it continues to change. Immigrants bring with them the myths of their homelands, and these transplanted myths undergo metamorphoses that render them relevant to the immigrants' new circumstances: "if they don't change those myths, those myths are useless and die" (Schroeder 86). Although Kingston is an American author, living and writing in the United States, she works in the tradition of China's classical storytellers, who as early as the twelfth century realized the power of the oral tradition and transformed its individual tales into novels, narrative poems, and plays. The survival of the ancient stories is indebted to those writers who re-created and retold them, adapting each version to the demands of each audience as well as the circumstances of each era. By interweaving these traditional tales into the fabric of her contemporary narratives, Kingston becomes a participant in both the preservation and revitalization of the ancient stories.

PLOT DEVELOPMENT AND NARRATIVE STRUCTURE

China Men is episodic, composed of six principal narratives about the men in Kingston's family, each narrative separated, set off from the others by one or two brief tales or fragments of history. Together, the major sections embrace considerable geographical territory, from imperial China to Stockton, California, temporally covering approximately one hundred years, from the Taiping Rebellion to the Vietnam War; but the sections are not arranged entirely either spatially or chronologically.

The book opens with two brief vignettes—"On Discovery," about Tang Ao's transformation in the Land of Women; and "On Fathers," in which a group of children mistake a stranger for their father. The first chapter, "The Father from China," is the story of BaBa, from his auspicious birth and through his education, to his emigration to the Gold Mountain and the betrayal by his friends in New York. Following are two chapters that recount the adventures of the grandfather: "The Great Grandfather of the Sandalwood Mountains," about Bak Goong and his experiences on the Hawai'ian sugar cane plantation; and "The Grandfather of the Sierra Nevada Mountains," about Ah Goong's life as a worker on the section of the transcontinental railroad that cuts through the Sierra Nevada Mountains in California. In "The Making of More Americans," Kingston introduces other male relatives who have made the journey to the United States: honorary grandfathers who raise vegetables and keep horses; a cousin whose dead mother haunts him, forcing him to visit China in order to make sure that her grave is properly cared for; Kau Goong, the former river pirate, who cannot decide whether or not to return to China; Uncle Bun who is enamoured of vitamins and wheat germ; and the uncle who works in a bakery and brings home lemon pies. BaBa returns in "The American Father," as the manager of the gambling house, a man sunk into depression, the owner of a laundry, and finally, as a new American with a house, a business, a garden planted with fruit trees and gourds, and a yard with chickens, pigeons, and turkeys. The book ends with "The Brother in Vietnam," a chapter devoted to the American generation—the California-born sons who join the military and serve in Vietnam. In *China Men*, Kingston records the odyssey of generations of men in her family who left home to make a new life in the Gold Mountain, showing that the family owes its American identity as much to the early sojourners and immigrants as to the war veterans five generations later.

China Men belongs to Tom Hong—as *The Woman Warrior* does to Brave Orchid—and the book begins with his early life in China, ending with a final chapter about his American son. Between the stories of father and son are sections that focus on Kingston's great-grandfathers, grandfathers, and uncles—other men who undertook the perilous journey to become Americans. In her explanation of the structure of *China Men*, Kingston invokes a homely and familiar American image: "*China Men* is like a six-layer cake and the myths are like icing" (Bonetti 41). The layers—which are the stories of Kingston's ancestors—are interleaved and embellished with icing of traditional tales, revisions of myth, fantasy, and reconstructions of history, tracing the immigrant journey from China in the nineteenth century to the Asian American community in the late twentieth-century United States. In her reworking of the past, Kingston employs several effective narrative strategies that enable her to imagine a new American history that embraces the contributions of Asian immigrants. These strategies provide Kingston with the means to codify, through the histories of her grandfathers, her uncles, and her father, the experiences of men like them who left China in search of a better life in America. By using traditional Chinese texts in conjunction with the reconstruction of memory, she re-creates life in the immigrant enclaves of the Gold Mountain during the late nineteenth and early twentieth centuries. Through the genres of legend and memoir, Kingston initiates her exploration of the book's central issues—the symbolic emasculation of Chinese male immigrants, and her search both for her father and for a way to claim America—that underlie the narratives in *China Men*.

Throughout *China Men*, Kingston reconstructs personal and political history, fracturing conventional narratives in order to arrive as close as she can to the truth of the Asian immigrant experience. Because her father refuses to tell his story, and because most canonical historical accounts exclude these immigrants, she is faced with a dearth of information, and she imaginatively teases out and reconstructs from talk-story heard in childhood, from incomplete records, and from literary texts like the Angel Island poems, the stories of the China Men. As she attempts to excavate her father's buried history and to understand this man whose life has most indelibly shaped her own, Kingston experiments with discovering the right words, finding the appropriate voice for narrating her father's history. BaBa, who is silent and embittered by his lack of status and respect in America, withholds all but the contours of the narrative of his life from his children. Consequently, his daughter must somehow piece together the story of his odyssey from his chance remarks and occasional brief reminiscences; she must use the few nuggets of information, the sparse facts that she has gleaned and somehow invent the rest. In "The Father from China," Kingston tries to imagine and then re-create the essential events of her father's life in China and his eventual emigration to the Gold Mountain; she works toward giving voice through her prose to the silent man who dominated her childhood. Thus, she constructs and reconstructs BaBa's journey to America as a paradigm of all Chinese journeys to the Gold Mountain, shaping five different versions of that perilous undertaking, wondering which story is truly her father's, wondering whether any of the stories even approximate the truth. The story of BaBa is paired with a minichapter, "The Ghostmate," about a young man who is diverted from his journey home by a beautiful woman who seduces him into staying with her for a short time. Finally recalling his duty to his family, he leaves—only to discover when he reaches home that he has been gone for a considerable time, and that the woman with whom he stayed has been dead for centuries. The short tale underscores the dilemmas faced by the immigrants who—with wives and children in China—must cope with and try to withstand the temptations offered by America.

Another narrative strategy that Kingston employs to great effect is the juxtaposition of reconstructed history with what Shu-mei Shih has called "intertexts," quoting literary critic Robert Scholes's definition of "a text lurking inside another" (Shih 66). Each of the six major chapters in *China Men* is paired with one or more intertexts, or inserted minichapters—short tales, myths, vignettes, reminiscences, news items, factual accounts. These intertexts "lurk" before or after chapters, and perform several functions: They reinforce through doubling and paralleling similar accounts of the cultural predicament of the China Men; they serve as ironic commentary on crucial events; they dismantle the hierarchies of power that disenfranchise the immigrants; and they confront the complexities of meaning inherent in Kingston's recasting of narrative forms.

"The Great Grandfather of the Sandalwood Mountains" recounts the adventures of Bak Goong, who travels to the Sandalwood Mountains, as Hawai'i is known, to work in the sugar cane fields. Although he discovers that he has been tricked by the job recruiters who promised high wages and comfortable lodgings like college dormitory rooms, Bak Goong remains undaunted. He manages not only to disrupt the plantation's policy against workers speaking (he sings, instead), but also to play a joke on local church women (he layers fresh red paint on the outhouse seat and then plies the women with very sweet tea). Bak Goong survives the overseers' efforts to quell his energy and silence him. Foiled in one attempt to speak, he simply discovers another method for naming and venting his rage and frustration, coughing to disguise speech or digging a vast hole so that he and the other workers can shout into the earth the words that describe their pain. To the white overseers, this last scheme is so inexplicable, so extraordinary that they hide in fear of the China Men who are "so riled up, who knows what they were up to?" (118).

In addition to the narrative vignettes that introduce and contextualize "Great Grandfather of the Sandalwood Mountains," Bak Goong's story is paired with two formally separated interchapters, both of which emphasize the trickster qualities that characterize Bak Goong. The first, from Chinese legend, is about Tu Tzu-chun, who is reborn four times (Trickster is immortal), emerging as a woman the fourth time (Trickster undergoes transformations, including gender shifts). Although women are enjoined to silence, during the fourth incarnation, the now-female Tu is unable to keep silent when her child is killed, and her cry of despair destroys forever any hope of immortality for the human race (Trickster's energy can be negative for others, although Trickster always survives to return another time). In the second intertext, a fragment from Polynesian mythology, Maui the Trickster very nearly succeeds in stealing immortality from Hina, entering her body through her vagina and taking possession of her heart. As he emerges, a bird laughs aloud at the sight of Maui's legs emerging from the the great goddess, and awakens Hina who tightens and contracts her pelvic muscles, killing Maui. These tales, in addition to allying Bak Goong with Trickster and thereby hinting at the indestructibility of men like Bak Goong and the impossibility of permanently obscuring their exploits, paradoxically also emblazon the silencing of the China Men as well as their erasure from conventional history. To deny a people their place in a nation's narrative is to deny them the immortality that history confers on those whose lives are recorded. Kingston's task is to retrieve those buried stories and to include them in the new American history that she proposes to write.

A third strategy that Kingston deploys in *China Men* is the revision of cultural texts: at times, rewriting Chinese texts into Asian American forms; at other times, recasting narratives from the Western literary tradition into Chinese talk-story. Kingston appropriates an episode, "The Country of Women," from the early nineteenth-century Chinese novel, *Flowers in the Mirror*, by Li Ruzhen. In the original chapter, two men— Lin Zhiyang, a merchant, and his brother-in-law, Tang Ao, a scholar— come upon a place known as the Country of Women during their travels. Lin Zhiyang is captured by the women who feminize him, forcing him into the role of concubine. In Kingston's revision of the tale, it is Tang Ao, the scholar, who comes upon the Land of Women during his search for the Gold Mountain. When he is taken prisoner by the women, he is gradually transformed into a feminine creature who has the outward appearance of a beautiful woman. He is compelled to endure the pain engendered by the beautification ordeals that Chinese women suffered for centuries, is required to maintain silence, reduced to a nonentity, and placed in servitude to the queen and her court. The tale ends with Kingston's note suggesting that some scholars locate the Land of Women on the North American continent. By relocating the site of Tang Ao's emasculation to America, Kingston comments metaphorically on the feminization of her Chinese fathers, doing so, however, by critiquing the subjugation of women by the ancient patriarchal Chinese culture, and hinting at the irony inherent in the China Men's experiencing what they have traditionally inflicted on women.

Another tale, "The Adventures of Lo Bun Sun," represents a different kind of textual revision—the transformation of a Western literary staple into the Chinese idiom. The story is, of course, Daniel Defoe's *Robinson Crusoe*, an eighteenth-century British novel about a castaway who survives for decades by his wits and industry on an uninhabited island after a shipwreck. In the version that Kingston heard in her childhood, probably from her mother's talk-story, the British sailor becomes a Chinese adventurer whose survival strategies include preserving eggs in vinegar and planting rice in paddies. She identifies the source of the story as an unnamed book from China, but does not elaborate further: Is the book a Chinese translation of Daniel Defoe's work? Or is it a collection of English tales revised for Chinese readers? Does it acknowledge the existence of an earlier version of the story? Whatever the tale's provenance, it is clear that the story has already undergone at least one cultural transformation, and that Kingston's revision is not the first (Defoe's version is also a retelling). Her engagement with this most canonical text is a clear signal that Kingston lays claim to the Western literary heritage as her own, while at the same time invoking the Chinese talk-story convention that bestows on a storyteller the license to revise a narrative so that it becomes relevant to the unique circumstances of a specific telling.

The insertion of purely factual material into the creatively retold stories is yet another narrative strategy that enables Kingston to reconstruct history. The most controversial section of *China Men* is "The Laws," Kingston's essay on the legislation enacted from 1868 to 1978 to designate the number of Asians who could legally enter the United States and for what reasons. This embedded compendium of factual information sketches out the historical context for the life of Ah Goong, the grandfather, an existence punctuated by significant events in American history, including railroad strikes, the Rock Springs and Los Angeles Massacres, and the Denver fire. "Alaska China Men" follows "The Laws," extending Ah Goong's story far to the north, and introducing China Joe, the Asian Everyman who made his home on the American frontier. Ah Goong, whose life occupies the center of "The Grandfather of the Sierra Nevada," represents the immigrants who came as far as the mainland, becoming the targets of institutionalized anti-Asian prejudice and legislation. One of the thousands of men who slaved for years on the transcontinental railroad, saw the last spike driven in, and watched as two locomotives came together from opposite shores, Ah Goong also experiences what Asian Americans refer to as The Driving Out—the concerted effort to rid the United States of Asian workers as soon as their services on the railroad were no longer necessary. The Driving Out sent Asian men to the East and South; many settled in out-of-the-way towns and locales where no other Asians had put down roots, establishing small businesses such as restaurants, laundries, and grocery stores. Ah Goong wanders on the road for months, stopping briefly in tiny communities, eventually finding his way to San Francisco where evidence of his movements disappears.

Kingston employs fantasy as a narrative strategy, as ironic commentary on the often hellish conditions of the immigrant experience. The illegal father, incarcerated in the wooden crate hidden in a ship's hold, conjures up in his imagination the mythical Dragon King who reigns over an underwater city. The legal father sings a fantasy about being young in Paris's Latin Quarter (which he has never seen), making love to French girls, strolling beneath chestnut trees, visiting bookstalls along the Seine—yet while he sings, he irons and folds shirt after shirt after shirt. En route to the Sandalwood Mountains, Bak Goong succumbs to the impulse to experiment with opium and loses himself in a phantasmagorical reverie in which his thoughts branch out and flow, and reform into branches, and he imagines people connected with a gold light or a gold net, people walking in parades, people in palaces, on roads and stadiums, people building bridges and streets, although there already is an "amazing gold electric ring connecting every living being" (95). The reality is that Bak Goong never connects with a community of people other than his fellow sojourners. Hawai'i for him remains merely a sugar cane plantation, where the sojourners have an occasional "day offu," when he can visit the Chinese stores in Honolulu to catch up on news from China, and later wander the wooden sidewalks until time to board the last truck back to the plantation.

Kingston finds, in stories from China's folk traditions, from Western literature, and from standard historical accounts, parables for the cultural position of several generations of men who emigrated from China to the United States. As well, she discovers, by unpacking her own memories, episodes that graphically illustrate the uneasy relationship that she has with her father. Her intention to claim America is related to these issues: she seeks a way to redefine the American man to include her ancestors, and she wants to tease out the details of her father's story in order to write it into the American narrative.

SETTING

China Men is dominated by the presence of a mythic destination, the fabled Gold Mountain that looms in the dreams and ambitions of generations of Chinese sojourners. As they prepare for the journey to America, BaBa and the other men who scheme and study to leave China are encouraged by former sojourners who regale the entire village with incredible tales of the Gold Mountain. They describe a land of unimaginable riches, endless opportunity for the hard worker, and unlimited food (one man even claims that fish rain from the sky in Cuba which was a stop en route to the Gold Mountain). The stories invent California roads covered in gold nuggets, rivers rocky with gold ore, soil that twinkles with gold dust. Despite the contrary evidence of personal experience, these men persist in believing that somewhere, the Gold Mountain is real, the ideal destination, the landscape of dreams; and even those men who well know that streets of gold do not exist continue to perpetuate the myth of a fabulous place in which everyone is fat, wealthy, and successful. The reality, however, is that the Gold Mountain is not a mythical place; it *is* California or New York or Hawai'i. In some respects, they are mythic golden landscapes, but they are also actual geographic locations with all of the problems endemic to all human societies; and each destination, while granting the immigrants imagined glimpses of the fabled Gold Mountain, only partially fulfill the promise of that mythical country.

From New York's Chinatown, the mountains of Hawai'i, the cliffs of the Sierra Nevada, and the working-class neighborhoods of Stockton, *China Men* distills the exhaustion, pain, loneliness, and despair—but also the tenacity, ambition, and refusal to accept defeat—of the men who labored in those settings in the late nineteenth and early twentieth centuries. California and New York figure prominently in the majority of immigrant stories because until late in the twentieth century, those two states had been the most common ports of entry into the United States. As well, Hawai'i and the Sierra Nevada share with the American South a common cultural and historical heritage. In these regions, a strong non-European ethnic population has grown, albeit not deliberately, from diasporaic communities—African slaves on the cotton plantations of the South, Gold Mountain sojourners in the railroad camps of the Sierra Nevada and the farms of central California, and conscripted Asian laborers clearing land for pineapples and sugar cane in Hawai'i.

For the men of Kingston's father's generation, New York and California *are* the Gold Mountain. Available in New York is the semblance of bachelor freedom, as well as surface sophistication, cosmopolitan pleasures, and urban excitement—movies, the Rockettes, Coney Island, weekend airplane rides, Central Park in the snow. A shopping mecca that provides young immigrants with the opportunity to spend their earnings on $200 suits, motorcycles, and automobiles, New York is a city in which newly arrived Chinese can metamorphose into Worldster, Roosevelt, Woodrow, and Ed (BaBa's American name), and dance with blondes who compliment them on speaking English well. Looking out into the harbor, the immigrants can reassure themselves with the sight of the Statue of Liberty, and the four friends tell themselves that they are Americans, "men of the twentieth century" (66). New York offers both social and economic opportunities for diligent and ambitious immigrants who are willing to work hard toward success. By contrast, California, which some immigrants insist is the real Gold Mountain, does not welcome the new arrivals, and appears at first impression, to be inhospitable. For many, Angel Island, the bleak holding facility off the coast of San Francisco, is the closest they will get to America. In one version of the father's arrival, he is detained for several days at Angel Island and put through a series of demeaning interrogations before he is allowed to enter the country. In another version, he arrives in California by train via Chicago from New York, after having been swindled out of a partnership in a Mott Street laundry that he has helped to run for years. Yet, despite the lack of enthusiasm for the influx of immigrants, California ultimately also affords the economic opportunity that the father has dreamed about. Even if his loftiest dreams remain unfulfilled, he nevertheless is able to make a living, raise a large family, purchase a house, and own a business. In the final analysis, for BaBa, California *becomes* the Gold Mountain.

The Gold Mountain, for the grandfathers, is embodied by the looming ranges of Hawai'i and the high rocky cliffs of the Sierra Nevada in California—literal mountains that represent the obstacles that the China Men must overcome in their quest for success. Hawai'i is a destination just short of the Gold Mountain, but close enough to make that nirvana seem ultimately accessible. Lured thence by a man claiming to be an agent of the Royal Hawai'ian Agricultural Society, Bak Goong, one of the great-grandfathers, is instantly seduced by the scented air, the bounty of bananas and mangoes, and the masses of brightly hued flowers in more colors than he has ever seen. Vowing to work hard in this Eden and to amass thousands of dollars before he returns home to China for a well-deserved old age, Bak Goong is speedily disabused of his fantasies. The lush Hawai'ian greenery disguises the decrepit shacks in which the Chinese workers live, verdant vegetation blocks the sun, and the uncleared land is harsh. Similarly, California's Sierra Nevada Mountains offer natural grandeur, spectacular vistas, rivers sparkling with gold flecks, rocks threaded with ore, sunny days, and nights in which the stars appear to be diamonds, crystals, silver, or even snow and ice. Offsetting that beauty, however, are ceaseless work, illness, boredom, and exploitation—and in the end, erasure from official records.

CHARACTER DEVELOPMENT

China Men is about Kingston's father, known as BaBa in the book—about his rise from favorite youngest son to honored scholar and New York bachelor, to his depressing descent to failed schoolmaster and thence to gambling den employee and laundryman. But it is also about two grandfathers, perhaps less gifted intellectually than the father, certainly less educated, yet canny and courageous and adventuresome enough to travel to America and return to China.

The most colorful heroes of *China Men* are Great Grandfather (Bak Goong) and Grandfather (Ah Goong) who are sojourners, the former in Hawai'i and the latter in California. To introduce her grandfathers—each man in his own chapter—Kingston employs heroic language and images of physical strength, elevating to almost mythic status these two men who truly should be counted among America's founding fathers. The resemblance of the Chinese immigrants' stories to many epics in the Western tradition is marked: Bak Goong and Ah Goong leave their homes, undertake long and perilous journeys, encounter and overcome monstrous creatures, and perform seemingly impossible feats. Both men undergo experiences reminiscent of the classical epic descent to the underworld. Similarities between them notwithstanding, however, these men are very different sorts of epic protagonists. Bak Goong is a comic survivor, Ah Goong a tragic hero; and neither one is completely cast in the heroic mold. Unlike Odysseus or Beowulf, neither of the grandfathers is superhuman.

Kingston balances the heroic with the human, showing that these men are her flesh-and-blood ancestors, prone to the foibles and emotions that plague the human condition; the grandfathers are not legendary warriors in folktales. A resilient and resourceful man, Bak Goong endures long working hours, laboring diligently and well on the sugar plantation where daily he cuts sugar cane twice the height of a man. So strong is his will to succeed and prosper that he manages to continue working even when he is so ill that he must embrace the cane stalks in order to stay upright. But there is a less heroic and more human dimension to Bak Goong, as well. His first journey to Hawai'i is precipitated by his desire to evade military service in the Taiping Rebellion; and on his arrival in Hawai'i, he is subjected to repeated humiliation, whipped like a recalcitrant child for talking during an enforced silence, treated like a chattel of no value, mocked and scolded by plantation overseers. He endures loneliness, frustration, and pain; yet in lighter moments, he tells stories, plays a practical joke on the women who come to evangelize the men in the plantation shacks, and invents the new camp ritual of shouting desire, fear, longing, and joy into a hole in the ground.

Ah Goong likewise demonstrates relentless physical stamina and power, seeming at times like a Chinese Paul Bunyan. As a laborer on the railroad, he blows up tree stumps with gunpowder, sets dynamite charges into cliff faces, and tunnels through mountains. He spends weeks laying, bending, and hammering the railroad ties and rails. Like Bak Goong, Ah Goong possesses the inner strength to endure humiliation and loneliness, coupled with the realization that in the Gold Mountain, he—a man with a family and sons in China—is nobody, just a faceless railroad coolie. Unlike his trickster father who delights in community pranks, Ah Goong reveals his unheroic side in different, more solitary ways. No prankster, he is affected by beauty, lying awake at night in the mountains to watch the constellations cross the sky; moreover, he is introspective, a quality absent in the most of the men with whom he works. After three years of wielding a sledgehammer to build a tunnel out of rock, he knows that he has confronted the immovability of the earth. Reflecting that men change, even die, as the weather changes, he muses that a mountain is "the same as permanence and time" (135).

Ah Goong displays another unheroic trait—an obsession with his genitals. Working from a basket suspended high on the Sierra Nevada cliffs, he takes intense delight in urinating from great heights, producing a continuous stream seemingly connecting himself almost to the bottom of the valley. Other times, aroused by the great height and the majesty of the scenery, he masturbates and ejaculates into space. Returning home to China after years in the United States, he fathers four sons, but after a failed attempt to exchange his youngest son for a neighbor's baby girl, he appears to lose his connection with reality. He begins taking his penis out of his trousers at the dinner table, "worrying it, wondering at it" (21), asking himself why it has given him four sons but not the daughter that he wants.

Bak Goong and Ah Goong share some common characteristics with the men of the West whose legendary exploits are celebrated in ballad and film, as well as in the novels of Zane Gray and Louis L'Amour. Venturing into unmapped territory in search of adventure and opportunity, they carve tillable and habitable land out of mountains, labor and survive on the frontier, and create spaces for the arrival of the amenities of civilization. Moreover, Bak Goong and Ah Goong live—as did those

Western men—in predominantly male communities in which the accepted codes of behavior are defined by men (either the immigrants or their overseers) and the only women are prostitutes or missionaries.

BaBa, the father, also exhibits a combination of heroic and human traits. Like his forebears, he too undertakes the epic journey, not once, but twice: First, he travels a great distance on foot to sit for the imperial examinations, and his successful performance earns him the rank of scholar. Later, he crosses the ocean to make his fortune in the Gold Mountain. Because BaBa does not talk-story, Kingston tests several invented versions of that epic voyage: the ship journey from an unknown destination, a place like Canton, Macao, or Hong Kong; or the days and nights concealed in a one-square-yard crate on a freighter from Cuba to New York; or the uneventful crossing to San Francisco culminating in the shock of landing at Angel Island. Like Aeneas, the hero of Virgil's epic, *The Aeneid*, BaBa and countless other men from Asia voyage across the sea to a destination where a great nation is struggling to be born. Theirs is a crucial role in the emergence of that nation; Chinese immigrants help to tame the land and to connect its opposite shores by laying iron rails across the continental vastness. They are American forefathers. And many generations later, their descendant, Maxine Hong Kingston—like the Roman poet Virgil—creates a work of literature that shares with the world the story of their epic journey and its impact on history.

As his predecessors have done, BaBa overcomes adversity and is, in fact, rather more fortunate than many of his fellow immigrants in that he is eventually able to send for his wife and to establish an American family. Yet Kingston is careful to reveal the failures that signal BaBa's vulnerability: His teaching career in his village ends in disaster when unruly boys refuse to learn poetry. He is cheated by fellow immigrants out of his share in a New York laundry; and his arduously obtained classical education is worthless in the Gold Mountain where he spends his days in menial labor, invisible, unheard, and unvalued. In the America of Kingston's parents' generation, there is no room for Chinese poetry or exquisitely formed calligraphy, no veneration for men who have spent years memorizing the most important passages from classical Chinese texts.

Other characters, whose stories briefly occupy center stage, emerge as individuals through Kingston's succinct and precisely targeted descriptions of their appearance, speech, and distinctive actions. Say Goong and Sahm Goong, brothers who grow vegetables and peddle them from a horse-drawn wagon, bestow boxes of horse manure as gifts to relatives and close friends. Kau Goong is a massive man, and so strong that he is able to carry loaded trunks, boulders, whole trees, and railroad ties, and so lucky that he wins a television and a vacuum cleaner at a raffle. Uncle Bun, enamored of wheat germ and communism, develops paranoia, becoming convinced that he is being poisoned through all of the white food that he ingests; and the wealthy Hong Kong uncle inexplicably withdraws the entire contents of his savings account from a bank and, in a hallucinogenic trance, gives all of the cash to a stranger. The assimilated cousin, Mad Sao, serves in the U.S. Army during World War II, lives in a ranch-style house, drives an automobile, wears fashionable clothes, speaks English even at home, and appears "more American" than the rest of the family (171).

LITERARY DEVICES

To create the multi-genre text that is *China Men*, Kingston employs an array of literary devices that enrich her narratives. Like a novelist, she relies on symbols and motifs, allusions, and distinctive characters and settings; like a biographer, she calls on flashbacks, repetitions, and patterns; like a poet, she revels in figures of speech and imagery, on rhythm, ambiguities and connotations. The most dominant of these literary devices—*structural elements* (narrative parallels, language), *motifs* (myth, poetry), and *symbols* (food)—produce an intricate web of narrative as textured and multivocal as the lives that *China Men* celebrates.

Structural Elements: Narrative Parallels and Language

Narrative parallels in *China Men* stress connections, showing how the past and present can mirror each other. When BaBa is born in China in a Rabbit year, his older brothers climb onto boxes in order to look through a window at the new infant. Catching sight of their brand-new sibling, they burst into song spontaneously: "Jump like a squirrel . . . Bob like a blue jay, tails in the air, tails in the air" (15–16). A generation later, BaBa's youngest son is born in America, and as the older children peer through the window for their first glimpse of their baby brother, they sing impulsively: "Jump like a squirrel. Bob like a blue jay. Tails in the air. Tails in the air" (265). The song, a ditty that animals in fables sing when they are happy, is a Chinese folk tune that connects two generations and two cultures, and the American-born baby—son of a Chinese immigrant—anchors the family to the United States. BaBa, the first baby, leaves Asia to come to America; BaBa's son, the second baby, leaves America—albeit temporarily—to travel to Asia. Another parallel is that father and son both become teachers, not of eager young scholars but of lumpish boys and men who are destined for menial trades and uninterested in poetry or words. Yet, where the father fails as a teacher, the son manages to galvanize one or two of his students, one in particular who makes it a point to correspond with his former teacher after leaving school to join the military.

While all literary devices are functions of words, phrases, sentences, and paragraphs, language itself becomes a literary device in Kingston's hands. By emphasizing the way in which language functions, Maxine Hong Kingston prompts the reader to examine the ways in which language produces meaning and shapes culture, especially in a community whose inhabitants are bilingual. Language in such a community is more than a means of communication, more than a simple set of signifiers. For BaBa, unable to express himself fluently in English, blunt sexist Chinese expletives and curses become an emotional outlet after he is accused of shoddy work by a gypsy, but those same words alert his daughters not only to his misogyny, but also to its source—the Chinese culture that nurtured their father and taught him to say those offensive and demeaning phrases.

Language also highlights the instability of categories and hierarchies, proving that classifications and taxonomies can be merely sets of words used to describe the same thing. Moreover, language reveals the difficulty of defining borders and assigning meaning. In Cantonese, a common toad can be called a "field chicken" or even a "Sky chicken. Sky toad. Heavenly toad. Field toad" (165–66), depending on a speaker's intonation—although, clearly, in English (the language of *China Men*), the same phrases appear to identify completely different species and subspecies. Male relatives of certain generations are either uncles or grandfathers; yet elderly male friends of immigrant families are also uncles or grandfathers to the children of those families. Bilingual Asian Americans must negotiate these linguistic puzzles in two languages, well aware that failure to recognize Chinese nuances will earn them scorn from the Chinese community, while less-than-perfect facility in English exposes them to rejection and discrimination from the dominant culture. The narrator of *China Men* is aware of the need constantly to translate words, phrases, even actions from one culture to another. In a stunning narrative inversion, Kingston portrays her brother, a Chinese American naval officer, attempting to teach barely educated Caucasian navy recruits to read and write in English. The brother's name, Bright Bridge, indicates his role in the family as the son who spans the divide between China and America.

Motifs: Myth and Poetry

Myth is a signature motif in Kingston's work, a structural template, a well of images and icons, and a touchstone for debates about cultural narratives and their place in literary texts. Kingston robustly defends her use of myth, especially her transformation of myths into new forms, calling them "American myths" because she first heard them during her American childhood: "It is less important what they have to do with China than what they have to do with America. What interests me is which chants and stories survive in America . . . Which things die away; which come with us" (Bonetti 40). Working within the traditional practice in many cultures of passing myths from one generation to another, and noting that the myths change from one telling to the next, Maxine Hong Kingston views the ancient stories as the standards against which people measure themselves, the icons of an ancestral culture, however vestigial. In *China Men*, she shows how Chinese myths can be integrated into the lives of Chinese Americans who have never visited their parents' country of birth, and more immediately, she uses myth as a metaphor for the immigrant condition.

Kingston employs myth not only to reveal character, but also to create connections between the two worlds to which the immigrants belong. While he labors long days on the railroad, Ah Goong endures by pretending to himself that the tracks will eventually lead him home. When, after six years, he is forced to admit that his dream is impossible and the railroad leads deeper into the American continent and away from China, he is overcome with loneliness. To assuage his homesickness, he recites aloud the Chinese legend of Spinning Girl and Cowboy, two stars whose love for each other was so strong that they neglected their duties. In an effort to force them to work, the Queen of the Sky separated them with a river of stars; but the King of the Sky took pity on the lovers, decreeing that they be allowed to meet once each year on the seventh day of the seventh moon. That Ah Goong treasures the romantic story is proof of his sentimental side—a facet of his personality that surfaces elsewhere in the book; and in that legend is embodied what Ah Goong knows he cannot have—the chance, once a year, to experience the warmth of human connection and love. Still, that legend is his salvation from loneliness. Reciting the tale puts Ah Goong in the company of generations of Chinese storytellers who have chanted the same sad love story; and through his action, he maintains his identity as a member of the community of people for whom the tale has resonance. Moreover, he is able to reassure himself that in America, he is gazing at the very same stars that his family in China can see on clear evenings.

As a motif, poetry represents the unattainable beauty that is generally absent from the lives of the China Men who are aware that their lives lack grace. The difference between the poet and the rest of the world is made clear at BaBa/BiBi's birth when his mother, Ah Po, compares him with her other sons. Exclaiming about the baby's slenderness, Ah Po declares that his hands with their long fingers are designed "for holding pens," and she announces that he will be educated for the Imperial Examinations. By contrast, the older sons are built like livestock, designed for manual labor and heavy farmwork. BaBa grows up learning poetry, practicing calligraphy for hours, memorizing long passages of philosophy and poetry. At fourteen, he sits for the Imperial Examinations. For an all-too-brief period in his life, BaBa has the luxury of reveling in his creative impulses: the examinations give him the opportunity to attempt to write one poem in the grass style, as well as to create one humorous poem that "darted down the page like swifts in a clear sky" (28).

A further difference between BaBa and his community is highlighted when he becomes the village schoolmaster, charged with educating adolescent louts who chew sunflower seeds instead of practicing their penmanship. When he recites poetry, they fall asleep. They fight, purloin vegetables from nearby gardens, and generally create disruptions. Worse yet, he finally has to resort to "[shrinking] poems to fit the brains of peasant children" (39), and after years of this kind of mind-numbing effort, he decides to try his luck in America. On his arrival at Angel Island, BaBa is reminded forcefully of both his need for and distance from poetry. He finds walls covered with poems written by earlier inhabitants of the barracks in which he and hundreds of others are incarcerated. But these are not poems artistically calligraphed at leisure by scholars toying with the poetic modes known as *The Beauty Adorns Her Hair with Blossoms* or *The Maid Apes Her Mistress*—this poetry at Angel Island is loneliness, anger, fear, and disappointment distilled into words scratched into a wall. BaBa is inspired to add his own poem about his fervent desire for freedom. For him, poetry becomes catharsis, a means for purging his soul of his bitter disappointment. Poetry also provides him with a way to escape temporarily the drudgery of his everyday life. In the following months, poetry becomes a form of escape when he recites lines from two expatriate poets to help him take his mind off the mountains of dirty laundry that confront him daily.

Symbols: Food

Food plays a significant role in Kingston's work, appearing frequently in three guises. First, food marks the passage of important milestones in Chinese culture—events that define the lives of Kingston's protagonists. At these events, traditional dishes signal observance of proprieties and adherence to cultural practices. When BaBa (known as "BiBi" while he is a child) turns one month old, his family hosts a feast for relatives and friends, setting a lavish table with chicken-feet-and-sweet-vinegar soup and pigs'-feet-and-sweet-vinegar soup, red eggs and and ginger, and oranges. Meanwhile, at the nearby home of an unwanted baby girl, guests are offered only shredded carrots. The disparity in the amount and quality of the celebration food underscores the devaluation of girls in traditional China. The parents' protestations that the infant is "only" a girl are symptomatic of the low esteem in which women are held. Food also represents cultural heritage. Across the Pacific, in the Gold Mountain, Chinese festivals are carefully observed, even in the railroad camps and mining communities. At one such holiday celebration, honoring the fifth day of the fifth month, the packets of salty barley with pickled egg, or of beans and pork, conceal specific instructions to Chinese workers about their role in a scheduled strike by which they would demand more humane treatment and better working hours. By maintaining their cultural ties through the distribution of holiday food, the China Men discover a strategy for taking political action in their adopted country.

Food also defines the immigrant experience in America by embodying the tension between paucity and plenty, between the new and the familiar. Through references to food, the China Men engage in a little mendacity to conceal their true circumstances from their families. In their letters home, they lie to wives and mothers, claiming that they have just dined on luxurious celebration dishes such as duck with buns and plum sauce, perpetuating the canard that life in the Gold Mountain is sumptuous and perfect. Much later, Mad Sao's mother's ghost blames her son for eating well in America, while she and other relatives died of starvation in China. Food also suggests the sojourners' ineradicable connections with their homeland. BaBa and his friends might appear in public to be dapper young men-about-town in New York, yet in their apartment, they cling to the cuisine of their childhoods: crackly pork and pressed duck, soup, and rice. Years later, when Kao Goong dies in Stockton, BaBa's wife makes it a point to decorate the grave with dishes of chicken, pork, beef, and vegetables—symbolic sustenance for Kao Goong's spirit on its journey. While food serves as a link to ancestral cultures, it also signals the immigrants' first tentative attempts to master American behavior. At a tea dance in Manhattan, BaBa, Woodrow, Worldster, and Roosevelt order cookies, cucumber sandwiches, strawberry parfaits, and tea. They make an effort to consume the delicacies like well-mannered Americans—carefully nibbling at their food, chewing with mouths shut, dabbing their lips with their napkins, enacting behavior completely unlike their usual habit of holding bowls to their mouths and noisily gulping soup as they race to see who can eat the fastest.

Finally, food symbolizes the blending of cultures and the immigrants' progress toward acculturation and assimilation. The Chinese appropriation of Robinson Crusoe renames the adventurer Lo Bun Sun, but the most significant sinicization is the alteration in his diet. Defoe's hero hunts for game and raises wheat; Lo Bun Sun concocts bean sauce and tofu. Conversely, for the immigrant community in Stockton, food measures the degree to which an individual has adjusted to American life. BaBa, who has difficulty assimilating, even after years of residence in the United States, plants a garden with pomegranates, loquats, and other fruits and vegetables more common to the gardens of his home village in China. Poles apart from BaBa is Uncle Bun, who has discovered *why-huh-ming* (vitamins) and essential elements. Also thoroughly Americanized is Kingston's youngest aunt, who offers her visiting niece pieces of chocolate cake and lemon pie from the neighborhood bakery where the aunt's husband works.

MAJOR THEMATIC ISSUES

A number of thematic strands thread through *China Men*, paralleling, intersecting, and overlapping, giving shape and coherence to the separate narratives that comprise the book, and providing continuity from one generation of Chinese immigrants to the next. Among the significant issues that emerge from Kingston's richly textured memoir, three stand out as especially dominant. The first theme is the pervasiveness of prejudice against the Asian immigrants, a prejudice that finds its strength in legal and cultural institutions. The foundation of *China Men* is the long history of exclusionary legislation that defined the lives of Asian immigrants for a century, skewing domestic demographics, creating an exoticized population of Americans, and reinforcing stereotypes that have proven resilient to dismantling. So central to the Asian American experience were these laws that Kingston confronts them boldly in an interchapter, in addition to suggesting their impact throughout her text. Another crucial theme is silence in its multiple guises—the silence *of* the immigrants, the silence *about* the immigrants. And finally, a third theme is the claiming of America by those who have been disenfranchised.

"The Laws"

Embedded in the collages of legend and family narrative that comprise *China Men* is a straightforward and unadorned historical survey of anti-immigration legislation from 1868 until 1978. In this section of her book, Kingston provides a concise record of the exclusionary legislation that severely restricted Chinese immigration to the United States from 1868 through the Second World War and afterwards, providing the historical context for the achievements of the men on whose stories the book focuses. While the most stringent of those laws were repealed in 1943, the immigrant Asian community continued to feel their detrimental effects well into the next generation, most particularly in the gender imbalance and lack of children that characterized many Chinatowns.

Maxine Hong Kingston has been the focus of strong criticism for interrupting her narrative with baldly factual statistical material that seems better suited to federal agency reports or historical texts than to a memoir. Some reviewers were, in fact, nonplused by the historical insertions, which they considered disruptive, "somewhat rude," albeit generally informative. Doubtless, some of the criticism is a response to the way in which the chapter "estranges or rather excludes the reader from the customary Eurocentric view of American history" (Li 491). Moreover, it is true that "The Laws" outlines a painful chapter of American history that is as unfamiliar to most readers as was the existence of the Japanese American internment camps until fairly recently. Yet, the reaction to "The Laws" has not been all negative; at least one reviewer has suggested that Kingston's seven-page summary of the exclusionary laws should be required reading for anyone who is interested in American history (Park 591).

Despite complaints from readers and criticism from reviewers, Kingston is emphatic that "The Laws" is crucial to her intent in *China Men*. To be able to narrate fully the story of her male forebears, she needs to help her readers understand the tremendous barriers that BaBa, Ah Goong, and fifth grandfather had to surmount as conditions of their quest for success in the Gold Mountain. Because most readers have little or no knowledge about Chinese American history, Kingston feels responsible in some way for educating them, in part because the widespread lack of knowledge creates tension in her. Frustrated with the rampant ignorance around her, she inserted "right in the middle of the stories, plunk . . . a section of pure history [starting] with the Gold Rush . . . [going] right through the various exclusion acts" (Pfaff 24).

Silence

Another theme that informs *China Men* is silence, a theme that is central to all of Kingston's work; and in this book, she extends and deepens the treatment begun in *The Woman Warrior*. Introducing the subject with the silencing of Tang Ao in the Land of Women, Kingston explores the ways in which male Chinese immigrants have been denied the right to speak their minds or to utter any form of communication. In the Sandalwood Mountains (Hawai'i), workers in the cane fields are whipped for speaking or singing; in the Sierra Nevada on the mainland, Ah Goong has to wait until he is suspended alone in a basket over a cliff before he feels safe enough to shout his emotions to the universe. And in downtown Stockton, Kingston's father—because he lacks fluency in English—becomes the victim of a gypsy's trumped up charges that the laundry has mangled her garments. Unable to muster the necessary English words in defense of himself, Tom Hong pays the fine and is forced thereafter silently to endure his wife's remonstrations about the lost income.

Ironically, the Gold Mountain has imprisoned the Chinese fathers within the very silence that they have prized in—and demanded of—women, and the men discover how powerless an individual feels without the freedom to speak. Throughout *China Men*, Kingston invokes the restrictions on women's speech and agency as parallels to the men's predicament in the Gold Mountain. When Tang Ao speaks to his captors, an old woman threatens to sew his lips shut. In another intertext, Tu Tzu-chun, in his fourth incarnation, is reborn a deaf-mute woman whose husband is unmoved by her disability. Why would she need to talk to be a good wife? Through her silence, she sets an example for women. Both Tang Ao and Tu Tzu-chun function as parallels to Bak Goong who, when denied the right to speak, must find circuitous methods of articulating his emotions, thoughts, and desires.

Another form of silence is voluntary—self-imposed avoidance of communication. BaBa deliberately withholds his life story from his children, denies them any knowledge of his experiences before their births, and shuts them out of his thoughts and feelings. As a result, they feel invisible—silenced—as they imagine the worst possible reasons for their father's refusal to communicate. BaBa's daughter reminds him of the time that he was silent for weeks and months, not speaking to the family, and inspiring the children to invent "the terrible things you were thinking: That your mother had done you some unspeakable wrong, and so you left China forever. That you hate daughters . . . hate China" (14). His refusal to speak essentially negates his daughters, as he himself has been excluded from a community with which he is incapable of interacting verbally. Lacking the stories that could serve as a lifeline between China and America, between parent and child, the daughters are estranged from their father and a cultural heritage that should be theirs. China, which has traditionally silenced daughters, has itself been silenced.

A third form of silence involves the obliteration of individual lives from talk-story and genealogies, as well as from official records. Tom Hong refuses to share China with his children. Commenting that Tom has never told stories and appears to have no narratives of his past, the narrator wonders whether her father might have always been American, or whether he was attempting to provide his children with chance to be genuine Americans by erasing the evidence of their Chinese history. Yet, even as Tom Hong erases China from the family's collective memory, the experiences of men like him are left out of American history. Much more pathetic is the plight of the bachelor sojourners, many of them men without descendants—and thus men with no chance at genealogical immortality. Lacking sons, sojourners are the last remnants of their families, and when they die, no one will be left to erect a memorial tablet or clean the grave each year. Not only are these men no longer remembered in China, a country that they have not seen in more than half a century, but they have also been forgotten in America—their contribution to the building of the West a mere footnote, overshadowed by the myth of the Western hero who conquers the West again and again on celluloid.

Through *China Men*, Maxine Hong Kingston ruptures the silence in which her ancestors have been enveloped for nearly a century. The book is rich in images of individuals discovering speech, finding their voices, and recovering their ability to vocalize their stories. For example, Bak Goong coughs his disdain for restrictive policies. Ah Goong shouts into the Sierra Nevada sky, and Tom Hong mutters imprecations at his ironing board. Illiterate navy recruits laboriously copy letters and learn to write, "Dear Mom. How are you?" continuing with reassurances to their mothers that they are "fine" (290). As Kingston's protagonists move from silence to eloquence, from wordlessness to voice, they begin to develop an American identity.

Claiming America

By foregrounding the experiences of her Chinese fathers against nineteenth-century historical events and her youngest brother's teaching career and military service against the Vietnam War, Kingston deploys her family's history in the interest of interrogating "official" American history—the version of history that is taught in classrooms, portrayed in television documentaries, and exhibited in national parks and monuments. *China Men* implicitly argues that it is time to include the stories of non-European immigrants in American history. Kingston has frequently stated that through her work, she hopes to claim America as the homeland of Asian Americans, and in *China Men*, she returns to that theme again and again, varying its treatment and design, yet never losing sight of her goal.

"My grandfather is an American. My father is an American. So I am an American" (58). With these words, the legal father requests permission to leave Angel Island and come ashore in San Francisco. Despite his lack of English, and never having been in the United States, he is, according to the legal documents that he carries—documents that his father and grandfather have presented several times in their peregrinations back and forth across the Pacific—an American citizen, having been born the son and grandson of male citizens. Although the validity of those documents is questionable, what is clear is that men like the father and like his father consider themselves to be men whose home is the United States. Yet, more than a generation later, Maxine Hong Kingston, writing about Americans who are still considered "exotic" and alien by their compatriots, is forced to consider how best to lay claim to America, not just for herself, but more particularly for her ancestors whose efforts helped to build the country.

Kingston acknowledges the irregularity of her ancestors' arrival and continuation in the United States—the father perhaps arriving as a stowaway from Cuba, the grandfather paying a bag of gold to a man known in Chinese mining camps as a "citizenship judge" who promises to draw up legal papers. In "The American Father," she makes reference to the practice among sojourners of registering "paper sons"—ensuring the existence of birth documents for male babies allegedly born while the sojourner father was visiting China. Sons born to American citizens were themselves legally American, and Kingston speculates on how her father acquired his citizenship:

> My father was born in San Francisco, where my grandmother had come disguised as a man. Or, Chinese women once magical, she gave birth at a distance, she in China, my grandfather and father in San Francisco. . . . or the men of those days had the power to have babies. . . . My father nevertheless turned up in San Francisco an American citizen. (237)

The above quote also makes reference to the fact that for decades, Chinese women were not allowed to enter the United States, making it impossible for many of the sojourners to father children in America.

Their precarious legal status notwithstanding, the Chinese fathers and grandfathers and their descendants consider the Gold Mountain to be their home; and although the first generations live in fear of deportation, they continue to work, save money, purchase property, and describe themselves as pioneers, first inhabitants, forefathers. In nineteenth-century Hawai'i, as he invites the other workers to join him in shouting into the earth, Bak Goong explains the ritual, announcing that they can create new customs because they are the "founding ancestors" of the new culture that is developing in the islands (118). To the young Hong children nearly a century later, the adults recount the family history, always proudly naming the ancestors whose backbreaking labor built the railroad. Despite these assertions of ownership in America, it is only Mad Sao, a cousin, who settles easily and immediately into life in the United States. Not until the youngest Hong brother is sent to Vietnam does the family finally begin to feel completely comfortable as Americans. Because he is healthy, unmarried, and of draft age, the brother knows that sooner or later, he will be involved in the war; and when he weighs his options as the war escalates, he decides against escape to Canada and life as a fugitive. The United States is his country of birth, the only country in which he has ever lived, and he refuses to be driven into exile. Enlisting in the navy, he finds himself first on an American base in Taiwan, and then on the USS *Midway* in the Gulf of Tonkin during the Tet Offensive. Promotion follows, and with that elevation the astonishing and wonderful discovery that security checks on his background have cleared him, and by extension, his entire immigrant family. The results of the investigations produce government certification that "the family was . . . not precariously American, but super-American, extraordinarily secure—Q Clearance Americans. The navy or the FBI had checked his mother and father and not deported them" (299). It is significant that all of the Hong sons have been christened with Chinese names that include the word "Bridge." This son, as well as an older one who has similarly distinguished himself in the United States Air Force, become the symbolic bridges between their Chinese-born parents and American culture, between the older immigrants and the American-born generation. Bak Goong, who flees from China to avoid being conscripted into the army, becomes the ancestor of a man who deliberately enlists in the American military and goes to fight on the Asian continent very near China.

ALTERNATIVE READING: GENDER STUDIES

In the last thirty years, the expanding field of gender studies has radically altered the ways in which human beings respond to, interrogate, and shape their lives and their geographies. Briefly stated, gender studies examines gender roles and their representations, as well as the major issues shaping the construction and manifestations of gender within specific communities and cultures. Among the basic assumptions of gender studies are the following ideas: gender differences, unlike sex, are not biological but are culturally produced, and can change over time; gender constructions are essentially artificial and thus vulnerable to alteration. Biology aside, *man* and *woman* are not necessarily absolute categories, and the terms "masculinity" and "femininity" can clash, press against each other, and rupture the boundaries that separate them.

Although for many people the term "gender studies" is synonymous with either "women's studies" or "feminist criticism," the discipline of "men's studies" has developed since the early 1970s into a vibrant and exciting interdisciplinary field of study. It currently engages the attentions and energies of both male and female scholars whose work has extended to include not only contemporary literary and cultural concerns, but also historical construction of masculinity. Central to the work being done in men's studies are the attempts to define, codify, and classify the variant definitions of masculinity and to understand the contexts—historical, social, cultural, political, religious, and economic—in which masculinity is defined or constructed and perpetuated as an accepted and established behavior. An important concept underlying men's studies is the idea that traditionally constructed and conventionally described masculinity is not necessarily obvious, natural, or innate, that it is, in fact, a social construction or a product of a specific cultural environment.

Studies in Masculinity

The growing body of research on masculinity encompasses several disciplines, including literature, history, psychology, sociology, anthropology, and philosophy. Early in the history of the field, scholarship focused on efforts to conceptualize masculinity and to map out its historical, cultural, and political terrain. In recent years, this work has asserted that more than one kind of masculinity exists, constructed, represented, and perpetuated within very specific cultural circumstances. Moreover, masculinity studies examine the ways in which particular kinds of masculinities are or might be challenged, and by whom.

Like other forms of cultural inquiry (see chapter 5), masculinity studies operate by asking questions, many of them by now standard in the field. What is a man? What roles are most often assigned to men, and how are these roles assigned? What forces shape men's lives? How is masculinity constructed and defined, and what part do race, ethnicity, and class play in these definitions? How do the media and popular culture represent the male experience? How do literature and art represent men? Masculinity studies seek to discover how and why men succeed or fail, to categorize the behaviors and activities associated with men, and to implicate the avenues through which definitions of masculinity are conveyed, not only through overt suggestion, but also through negation or absence.

Because masculinity study is interdisciplinary, its focuses are diverse. Among the recent work is an interesting array of investigations: male sexuality; the male body; versions of masculinity; the performance of masculinity; masculinity and power; masculinity and violence; stereotypically "male" activities—sports, military training, scouting, hunting, and fishing; the relationship between fathers and sons, and fathers and daughters; homosexuality; transvestism; and masculinity and globalization. In addition, the field has initiated new inquiries into the influence of rapidly changing political and economic circumstances on the emergence of new forms of masculinity, especially local definitions and constructions. Another development is the emergence of cultural studies that have attracted wide readership among both academics and general readers. A good example of these studies is Susan Faludi's *Stiffed* (1999), which examines the cultural messages that have defined masculinity for entire generations of American men.

An analysis of *China Men* through the lens of gender studies, specifically through men's studies, might investigate the portrayal of Chinese men in American culture and literature, and examine Kingston's treatment of the major issues that inform debates on Asian American constructions of masculinity, and the historical and cultural contexts that have shaped those constructions.

Issues of Masculinity in Asian American Literature and Culture

Within the Asian American literary community, Frank Chin's name is synonymous with aggressive attempts to interrogate the construction of masculinity among Asian Americans and to reverse what he views as the emasculation resulting from the stereotypes that have defined Asian American men during the last century. Chin is an important literary figure, having written the first Asian American play (*Chickencoop Chinaman*, 1972) ever produced in mainstream theatre, as well as the first Asian American script (*Year of the Dragon*) for national television. He has made it his crusade to undo the effects of what he considers to be the most damaging stereotype about Asian American men: that they are not masculine—at least not in the red-blooded American male tradition that finds its embodiment in the Western hero or the tough-talking law enforcement officer. The Hollywood representation of Asian men as servile (domestic) or sinister (male Mata Haris) insinuates that these men are not American in that they do not conform to the popular image of the American male. In his campaign to redefine Asian men, Chin privileges Guan Goong (Kuan Yu), the god of war, as the symbol of Asian masculinity in his work, attempting thus to counteract the feminine or sexless images that have represented Asian men in American popular culture. He also embraces that outlaw tale, *The Water Margin*, with its glorification of the derring-do of a band of Chinese outlaws who live by their cunning and brute strength. Chin's stance is militant, not unlike that of the Black Panthers whom he emulates, and his remarks on the subject of Asian American masculinity have the ring of combat:

> The white stereotype of the Asian is unique in that it is the only racial stereotype completely devoid of manhood. Our nobility is that of an efficient housewife. At our worst we are contemptible because we are womanly, effeminate, devoid of all the traditionally masculine qualities of originality, daring, physical courage, creativity. We're neither straight talkin' or straight shootin'. (Chin and Chan 69)

Like many Asian Americans, Kingston emulates neither Frank Chin's fiery radicalism nor his extreme rhetoric. Her approach to the issue of damaging stereotypes is less incendiary; nevertheless, like Chin, she is deeply concerned about the negative popular images that have denied her ancestors their individuality and their manhood. She does, however, contextualize her exploration of their experiences within the larger and older pattern of female oppression in which these same men were complicit while they were at home in China. Through *China Men*, she ironically juxtaposes the grandfathers' patriarchal power in China with their nearly total lack of agency in the Gold Mountain.

Masculinity and *China Men*

China Men opens with the story of Tang Ao, a scholar who crosses the ocean in search of the Gold Mountain and finds instead the Land of Women. Captured by the women, he is taken to a canopied chamber furnished with mirrors, and stocked with cosmetics and women's clothing. His captors remove his men's clothing and replace it with women's robes, shackle his wrists and ankles, assign several women to sit on him to prevent struggle, and thereafter proceed to put him through the tortures that women must endure in the name of beauty. A pair of elderly women pierce his ears with needles heated in a candle flame and, completing that operation, proceed to bend his toes under and back, binding his feet tightly with bandages. He is allowed to eat only women's food: chrysanthemum tea, chicken wings, and vinegar soup. As the weeks and months pass, the women replace the threads in Tang Ao's pierced earlobes with gold hoops, which in turn are later replaced with jade studs. He is forced to wash the soiled and smelly embroidered bandages with which his aching feet are wrapped. At last, when Tang Ao's body has been successfully altered to conform to the ideal of feminine beauty, his features are enhanced with cosmetics. His eyebrows are plucked, his face is covered in white powder, his lips and cheeks are reddened—and he is taken to the queen's court where he is assigned the role of serving maid. Kingston concludes the story of Tang Ao with a brief geographical note stating that despite the claims made by some scholars that the Land of Women was discovered during the reign of the empress Wu (A.D. 694–705), other scholars claim an earlier date, A.D. 441, identifying the location as the North American continent.

Its brevity notwithstanding, the Tang Ao episode parallels symbolically the experience of Chinese men who crossed the Pacific Ocean in search of wealth in the Gold Mountain. By identifying the mythical Land of Women as North America, Kingston appears to be suggesting that Chinese immigrants underwent a process of womanization in their new country. By virtue of his willingness to travel in search of the Gold Mountain, Tang Ao advertises his spirit of adventure, his bravery, his masculinity. The men who emigrated were prepared for hard labor, physical exhaustion, and pain in the service of family and eventual success. In the Chinese provinces from which many of these emigrants came, the lack of economic opportunity made it difficult for husbands to support wives, or for sons to support parents—and the dangerous journey to America was often the only viable option available for a man who needed to support a family. Measured against the cultural standards of their home villages and provinces, these men embodied the ideal of the responsible male, ready to sacrifice personal comfort for duty to the clan, perhaps even the entire village. Arriving in the Gold Mountain, these men experience, for the first time in their lives, the cultural practices that limit women's lives: enforced silence, confinement to domestic spaces and activities, invisibility, and lack of agency and control. Confined to kitchens and washrooms, condemned to take orders from *women* of another race, these men who had colluded in the subjugation and silencing of women in China, must go through the novel and unwelcome experience of themselves being oppressed. That they persevere is admirable, but for them, heroism must be redefined. Heroism can no longer be described as a product of physical or even intellectual prowess, but as a heroism that grows out of these immigrant men's persistence in the face of cultural, economic, and social humiliation. It is not the martial prowess about which their families can talk-story or about which ballads are written, not even the bravery of the peasant who has been conscripted to fight in a war he does not understand. The new heroism is quiet, stoic, simple endurance in an alien country far away from all that is familiar.

At least three dominant patterns of emasculation appear in *China Men*. The first is the reduction of the Chinese immigrants to nonentities; they are expendables, or unimportant creatures like the despised girl babies in China. When the legal father arrives at Angel Island, immigration doctors "poked him in the ass and genitals, looked in his mouth, pulled his eyelids down with a hook," and he reflects that what he has just experienced should not be the way a father is treated (53). Fathers in China are revered, treated with great respect, and approached with awe; they are never to be insulted or denigrated in any way. Yet, despite the demeaning medical examination that the legal father endures at Angel Island, his experience is far more humane than the treatment borne by the railroad coolies. In *China Men*, laborers who die while working on the railroad are buried in unmarked cairns beside the tracks, and either no record is kept of the number of men who have died building the railroad, or else the white work supervisors keeping the records do not consider dead Chinese coolies worth including in the death counts. Unfair treatment is not confined to railroad crews and plantation workers; Chinese men in Alaska are summarily shipped out of the territory by whites and Indians collaborating on the expulsion. In "The Laws," Kingston reminds the reader that immigrants and sojourners from Asia were denied admission to American public schools, that Chinese were not allowed to own land or real estate or to apply for business licenses, nor could they be hired by state and local government or testify in court.

Another pattern of emasculation is embodied in the legally sanctioned sexual deprivation that marked the lives of hundreds, perhaps thousands of men during the decades of the exclusionary laws. In the absence of wives or women who might be appropriate candidates for marriage, the men of the bachelor communities sought sexual release with prostitutes, and many Chinatowns became notorious for their brothels that were frequented not only by Chinese sojourners, but also by white men from surrounding towns. Not all of the men resorted to the dubious pleasure to be enjoyed with prostitutes, however. Ah Goong in *China Men* does not spend his money in the red light districts near his camp; nonetheless, he is intrigued when a rumor spreads about a woman who is making her way from camp to camp. He imagines that the woman is a nurse or a missionary; but she turns out to be a bedraggled prostitute, led on a leash by her pimp who sells lottery tickets for her time. Ah Goong does not purchase a ticket that might give him a chance to have sex; instead, when he is alone, he "took out his penis under his blanket . . . bared it in the woods . . . wondering what it was [for] . . . what a man was for" (144).

Kingston explores a third kind of emasculation—cultural conditions that deny the Chinese fathers the opportunity to provide adequately for their wives and children. When the police shut down the gambling house in Stockton, destroying BaBa's source of income, he descends into a deep depression, staying in the house all day, allowing his wife to ridicule and berate him. He stops shaving, refuses to dress in anything but a T-shirt, drinks whiskey all day while he reads the *Gold Mountain News*, and screams in his sleep. During this trying period, his wife—the graduate of a Western medical school and a practicing physician while she was in China—supports the family by working at menial tasks, picking to-matoes in the fields and working double shifts in the canneries of Stockton. A squabble among BaBa's children suddenly rouses him out of his lethargy, and after he beats one of his noisy daughters (a symbolic assertion of his ascendancy over the women in his family), he is suddenly his old self again. Bathed, decently clothed, he finds the energy to negotiate the purchase of a laundry. The new business provides him with the wherewithal to earn a livelihood; unfortunately for him, the work is considerably beneath his educational accomplishments and intellectual tastes. The narrator is well aware that BaBa is reduced to engaging in whatever physical labor he can find so that he can support his family; he makes money, but the work is not satisfying.

The society of *China Men* is almost exclusively male except for the sections that focus on BaBa and his family in Stockton. As we have noted earlier, masculinity is a cultural construct, a state of being that exists in opposition to femininity—and in the absence of women, masculinity becomes difficult to define and the masculine role becomes superfluous. For Bak Goong, Ah Goong, Kau Goong, Say Goong, and Mad Sao, traditional masculinity requires fathering many sons, keeping a family prosperous, and acting in the role of patriarch for a vast clan that is blessed with countless grandsons. Only Bak Goong, the trickster, fulfills that role when he returns to China after his years of labor and exile in Hawai'i. The other men provide the requisite prosperity by sending their earnings to the wives and children left at home in China. Unfortunately, the vast geographical distance separating the sojourners from their homes turns the men into mere income producers, deprived of the social and cultural power they would undoubtedly wield in their villages, denied the customary and appropriate exercise of their sexual potency in the procreation of more male progeny. Ah Goong is an interesting exception to the trajectory of the sojourners' experience. Like Bak Goong, he returns to China where he fathers four sons, but his experiences in the Gold Mountain have altered him and he is incapable of successfully playing the traditional role of patriarch. Furthermore, he displays a softer, more feminine side. After Ah Goong's wife bears the couple's fourth son, Ah Goong — who genuinely wanted a daughter — assuages his disappointment by regularly visiting the baby girl newly born to a neighbor. These visits reveal a latent nurturing talent in the old man. He brings to the baby branches of pea blossoms (thereby putting that season's crop of peas at risk!) and supplies oranges when her parents fail to celebrate her one-month birthday with any fanfare (girl babies do not get lavish celebrations).

By recounting the stories of some of America's forgotten founding fathers, and by insisting on creating a space for these pioneers in conventional American history, Kingston imagines a new kind of American man, one who transcends the popular stereotypes perpetuated by popular culture. In the mythic world of the Western film, the men who settled California and contiguous states are tall rugged Caucasians, the Marlboro Man, John Wayne on a horse, gunslinging cowboys who have no time for play or whimsy, and no taste for the softer side of civilization. These men are the reincarnations of the classical epic hero, transplanted to the American frontier. They are on a quest, during the course of which they overcome severe adversity, fight battles, and vanquish monster. They are solitary individuals with little taste for domesticity, and the few human bonds that they develop are homosocial—based on the camaraderie between men—rather than familial. These heroes move from place to place, never settling for long in any location, always looking for the next untamed wilderness, the furthest frontier, the unknown. That heroic image, of course, does a disservice to all American men of any ethnic or national origins who do not resemble the archetype, yet the idea of the Western hero as the epitome of American masculinity persists. Asian

American men, because of their ethnicity, are automatically excluded from the pantheon of heroes. Those who labored in Hawai'i or who struggled to build the railroad share many of the experiences of classical epic heroes, but in the popular imagination, these men do not *look* like Odysseus or Beowulf and certainly not like Kirk Douglas or Clint Eastwood. Moreover, because Asian American men have been feminized by being portrayed as servants, houseboys, and cooks in popular fiction, movies, and other cultural productions, they are further excluded from conventional descriptions of American manhood.

In *China Men*, Kingston begins her exploration of the possibility of a new definition of the American man, which incorporates new behaviors and values, acknowledges the possibility of multiple origins and cultures—a template for a man who is less prone either to subjugate or silence women. This new American man is partially foreshadowed in Ah Goong, the grandfather whose desperate wish to have a daughter—an unusual and highly controversial desire in son-obsessed, patriarchal China—brings down on him the condemnations of his wife who dotes on the baby boy that he tries to exchange for a little girl. It is also Ah Goong who, on meeting the blonde toddler playing in the road, pauses in his journey to sit down and cuddle the child; and it is Ah Goong who is immortalized in Hong family legend as having been spotted rescuing a child from a fire in the aftermath of the San Francisco earthquake. Unlike many sojourners and immigrant men who focus their waking energies on the pursuit of economic success, Ah Goong responds to and connects with children. Among the most important traits of Kingston's new man is his ability and desire to nurture his children—unlike the Western hero, who has no offspring (and no family); unlike BaBa, whose six children are virtual strangers to him; and unlike the Chinatown uncles, who must make do with the sons and daughters of more fortunate men. Like the figure of Abraham Lincoln in William Carlos William's book, the new American man—regardless of his ethnic or racial heritage—will have traits typically described as feminine: the ability to nurture, to fell strong emotion, to show compassion and empathy, and most important, to talk-story.

The new man that Kingston begins to envision in *China Men* is also playful, like BaBa, who sometimes helps his children turn dragonflies into toy airplanes, transforms the chore of killing moths into a game, or lets his daughter occasionally play with the gambling paraphernalia—hole punchers, the lottery drum, betting sheets—when the gambling house is closed to customers. This new American man loves daughters, as Ah Goong does; and he is a storyteller like Uncle Bun. Like Mad Sao at Kao Goong's funeral, the new American man is not too masculine to weep in sorrow. The new man, however, is not Kuan Yu, the war god who occupies the center of Frank Chin's work, nor is he an outlaw or a hypermasculine fighter. And, like the brother who teaches underprivileged youth in the ghetto before he goes to Vietnam, the new Asian American man is educated, patriotic, peace-loving, and open-minded. Kingston outlines the task ahead, implying that we must learn to envision "the possibility of a playful, peaceful, nurturing, mothering man, and . . . a powerful nonviolent woman and the possibilities of harmonious communities" (Fishkin 783). *China Men* thus concludes with a vision of a new America.

5

Tripmaster Monkey: His Fake Book
(1989)

Expecting a third mixed-genre memoir reminiscent of *Woman Warrior* or *China Men*, readers and critics were momentarily taken aback when Kingston's much-awaited third work, *Tripmaster Monkey* (1989) turned out to be a playful, rambling postmodern novel with the fractured, disjointed, chaotic tone that the term "postmodern" implies. In fact, this book has more in common with James Joyce's *Ulysses* and the poetry of the Beat Generation than with Kingston's first two books and their dominant ethnographic flavor. Despite a few rumblings of disappointment from the few who wanted Kingston to publish additional tales of ghosts and culture shock, exotic names and unfamiliar customs, critical reception of Kingston's radical redirection was generally positive, with some reviewers even coming to Kingston's defense against the criticism that the new book was unfathomable and opaque.

In a review published in *The Nation*, critic John Leonard, one of Kingston's earliest admirers, suggests that *Tripmaster Monkey* may deserve to be labeled the "Novel of the Sixties"; and he adds that having produced her highly acclaimed two-volume memoir, Maxine Hong Kingston has "earned the right to write about whatever she chooses, and if she chooses to write about looking for Buddha in the wild West, we'd better pay attention" (Leonard 768). Leonard's description of Kingston's third book as the quintessential novel of the sixties is not far off the mark—*Tripmaster Monkey* focuses on a young Asian American as he attempts to construct a stable and coherent identity, a common quest during those years in which people claimed to be "finding themselves," and certainly a familiar theme to readers of Kingston's work. In order to accomplish his goal, he must come to terms with both his Asian ethnicity and his American upbringing, even as he negotiates his distinctive needs and desires in the context of San Francisco during the freewheeling culture of the sixties.

Tripmaster Monkey is reminiscent of the twentieth century's most significant experimental narratives—among them Joyce's *Finnegans Wake*, Vladimir Nabokov's *Ada*, and Gabriel Garcia Marquez's *One Hundred Years of Solitude*. The novel is brilliant in its appropriation of the Chinese legend of the Monkey King, as well as in Kingston's transformation of that legend into an encyclopedic postmodern narrative that references, embraces, and absorbs a dizzying variety of sources from all cultures and eras.

Several reviewers realized immediately not only that *Tripmaster Monkey* was never intended as an extension of *Woman Warrior* and *China Men*, but also that *Tripmaster Monkey*'s literary ancestry was global rather than Asian, and definitely American rather than Chinese. For reviewer Herbert Gold, *Tripmaster Monkey* is a combination of magical realism with black comedy—"a little of Lenny Bruce and a whole lot of Gabriel Garcia Marquez" (Gold 1). In his words, Kingston's technique is a combination of "a keen sense of recent history, a generous experience with fantasy fiction masters, a satirical meditation on the black humor picaresques of the '60s and early '70s, and something special, individual and captivating of her own" (Gold 10).

Readers and reviewers respond variously to the novel's energy and vibrance. Novelist Bharati Mukherjee draws attention to *Tripmaster Monkey* as a "brash, punchy, loudmouthed first novel" calling the book a "remarkable display of wit and rage." She situates Wittman as a protagonist in the tradition of the Angry Young Men who transformed English literature in the 1950s (Mukherjee X1). Also focusing on Kingston's central character, critic Ray Mungo interprets Wittman Ah Sing as "a vocalist/revoluntionary in racist America" (Mungo D6). John Leonard, an early and long-time admirer of Kingston's work, points out that *Tripmaster Monkey*, while "less charming" than either *The Woman Warrior* or *China Men*, is "more exuberant" (Leonard, "Of Thee" 769), possibly because of the brash energy that emanates from Wittman.

Yet, praise of Kingston's third major work has been tempered with a certain amount of unease about the novel's shape and structure, both of which defy facile analysis. Although novelist Anne Tyler concludes that *Tripmaster Monkey* is a complex yet satisfying novel (Tyler, "Manic" 46), she also asserts that it is "a novel of excesses—both the hero's and the author's," and she notes that "the effect is exhausting" (45). Michiko Kakutani criticizes the novel's plot as "vague" and Wittman as "long-winded" (Kakutani 30); and Gerald Vizenor, whose own work problematizes genre and literary form weighs in with criticism, feeling that Kingston relies too much on coincidence (Vizenor, "Triumph" 13). Pamela Longfellow, who, on one hand, is deeply moved by Kingston's "pictures drawn with words [that] remain with the mind for as long as a mind has consciousness," also implies that *Tripmaster Monkey* is "both wonderful and awful" because it ends with "a bad-tempered rush of explanation," with a harangue that somehow fails to engage the reader (Longfellow 66).

Other readers' comments reflect their struggles with relating to a text that ebulliently sidesteps expectations about fiction, even as that text attempts to balance on the unfixed border between two cultures. Patricia Holt admits that *Tripmaster Monkey* has a "wild brilliance" and then adds that the narrative often is "deliberately (and successfully) offensive" (Holt 1); and Gail Boyer complains that as she read the novel, she felt as if she were being "force-fed facts about Chinese culture" (Boyer C5). For Nicci Gerrard, Kingston's creation of the "extraordinary and unforgettable" Wittman Ah Sing is marred by the first section of the book, which Gerrard describes as characterized by "bitter repetitious paranoia" (Gerrard 28).

On its release, *Tripmaster Monkey* was publicized as Maxine Hong Kingston's "first novel" to differentiate between this new Kingston work and the two mixed-genre efforts that had preceded it. Certainly, reviewers treated the work as a novel; however, it does not appear on the surface to possess many characteristics in common with more commonly encountered literary novels such as F. Scott Fitzgerald's *The Great Gatsby* or Charles Dickens's *David Copperfield*, or popular novels like John Grisham's or Michael Crichton's well-plotted thrillers. While *Tripmaster Monkey* is not a template of the most familiar and widely-read types of novels, it is an extended prose narrative, focused on a single protagonist and his activities. It represents Wittman Ah Sing as he goes through the process of developing an identity with which he is comfortable, and as he performs the actions that will enable him to perform the various selves that he is trying on, as one does an array of new clothes.

Tripmaster Monkey exhibits characteristics borrowed from other fic-

tional genres. From the episodic narrative genre known as the picaresque, Kingston borrows the unheroic protagonist (Wittman Ah Sing),
the series of more-or-less unrelated adventures in which that protagonist
becomes embroiled and a journey or quest of some kind. From the
stream-of-consciousness narrative technique practiced by William Faulk-
ner and Virginia Woolf come Wittman's disorganized, unpunctuated,
uneven, unstoppable free-ranging monologues. Kingston forages for fictional devices in still other literary forms: the epic, the medieval romance,
the tall tale, the drama, even from the prose poems of Walt Whitman
and his literary descendant, Allen Ginsberg. The resulting pastiche is an
unusual novel, although we should remember that this kind of experimentation with the shape, focus, and tone of fiction dates back, at least
to Laurence Sterne's rowdy and fragmented novel, *Tristram Shandy*
(1759–67), an early work of self-conscious fiction that shares with *Tripmaster Monkey* an unheroic protagonist, a disjointed rambling narrative
of episodic adventures, and a fractured chronology.

PLOT DEVELOPMENT

Set in the sixties—that free-spirited psychedelic bohemian decade of
American history—*Tripmaster Monkey* recounts the picaresque journey
that Wittman Ah Sing undertakes through his imagination, his psyche,
his ethnic heritage and family tradition, and through the mosaic of cultures that comprise the American West Coast. Shaping Wittman's journey is his quest for a clear and stable identity, as well as for an artistic
project that will allow him to perform his exploration of the question,
"What is an American?"

The vast sprawling plot of *Tripmaster Monkey* documents the highlights
of Wittman's life during a two-month period: In that brief space of eight
weeks, he contemplates and then decides against suicide, falls in love
with a former classmate, gets married on a whim (but not to the woman
with whom he falls in love), and loses his job in a department store
because he has created a pornographic toy display involving a Barbie
doll and a monkey. He drops in to see his father, visits his mother and
aunts—all former Flora Dora Girls, drives to Reno in an attempt to find
his missing grandmother, attends a marathon party at which he plays
the role of tripmaster (see p. 8), goes to the movies, writes poetry, reads
the poetry of Rilke aloud on a bus—and constructs an epic play that
incorporates every narrative he has ever read and in which he casts

every individual of his acquaintance. The novel concludes as Wittman directs and performs in a production of his play, ending the final evening of performance with a manic free-ranging monologue about life, war, peace, racism, heritage, culture, and the American identity.

Kingston's text is replete with wordplay and puns, and embellished with an astonishing variety of allusions from a dizzying collection of sources, including: Shakespeare, Hollywood, Broadway musicals, classical Chinese literature, television, American popular culture and writers, Walt Disney, the Tibetan *Book of the Dead*, European authors, California history and geography, and the protest culture of the 1960s. The language of *Tripmaster Monkey* is both highbrow and lowbrow, it is democratic in its inclusion of American English, Chinese, Chinese American, Japanese, and even Hawai'ian pidgin—reflecting Maxine Hong Kingston's years in the island state. The rhythms of Kingston's prose evoke torrents, eruptions, cascades, suggesting jazz riffs and improvisations, allowing the words to wash over and deluge the reader.

The phrase "fake book" in the novel's subtitle identifies jazz as one of the controlling metaphors in the story of Wittman Ah Sing's odyssey through life. Literally, a fake book is a published compilation of standard basic melodies and their accompanying chords, used by jazz musicians as the foundation for improvisation. With a fake book for reference, a musician can create additional melodies extemporaneously, or produce tropes on the basic melody line, confident that the fake book can immediately indicate the way back to the original tune. Wittman's fake books are the cultural and literary myths of his double heritage—with these traditional and frequently recounted stories as his starting point, he creates his play, improvising scenes and episodes, extemporaneously vocalizing speeches for the traditional characters. Kingston says that with *Tripmaster Monkey*, she was "trying to write a prose book with basic plots, suggestions for social action, for trips," with the intention of inspiring the reader to improvise as she herself has done with her material (Blauvelt 77). Wittman himself dreams of becoming the first "bad-jazz China Man bluesman" (27) in America. Significantly, he does ultimately transform himself into the theatrical embodiment of verbal jazz, taking the literary canon—both popular and classical—of Chinese narrative and American literature, and improvising inventively and wildly. He samples narrative texts from other traditions, verbalizing riffs on bigotry, love, community, history, identity, and the Vietnam War, and incorporating snippets, allusions, references, names, and lines of poetry to create his play about America, his place in it, and his identity as an American.

NARRATIVE STRUCTURE AND POINT OF VIEW

Departing from *The Woman Warrior*, which features first-person narrators, Kingston employs an omniscient narrator—a storyteller who
knows and sees all—in *Tripmaster Monkey*. Identifying the unnamed storyteller as a narrator that readers will immediately recognize as a woman
(Blauvelt 82), Kingston adds that the mysterious narrator also possesses
a memory that reaches back to ancient China, while at the same time
divining events at the end of the Vietnam War (82). The narrator manip-
ulates Wittman, telling him to be quiet, providing him with "various
girlfriends," supplying him with an array of human situations to contend
with and to resolve, and "giving [him] a bad time" (Marilyn Chin 59).
This narrator appears to have an intimate familiarity with Chinese history spanning five dynasties, coupled with the uncanny knowledge (before the fact) that America does not stand much of a chance of winning
the war in Vietnam. She knows that the 1960s idealism is misplaced; and
she is aware that the classic Chinese novel, *Romance of the Three Kingdoms*,
is both a favorite with Ho Chi Minh and a classroom text at West Point.
Because she is omniscient, the narrator knows about Gary Snyder's trip
to Japan to learn meditation, and is privy to the beneficial effect of that
trip on Snyder's relationship with his mother. In short, the narrator of
Tripmaster Monkey possesses both the wisdom of centuries and the
knowledge of current and future events; Wittman's antiwar idealism and
antics amuse her, knowing as she does that the ambitious play over
which he labors will have no measurable effect on the war. She scolds
Wittman, attempting in vain to curb his excesses; she passes judgment
on his activities with fond exasperation or benevolent tolerance.

Kingston identifies this all-knowing, all-seeing narrator as Kuan Yin,
the beloved Chinese Goddess of Mercy who, in the traditional Monkey
tales, hurls a boulder on top of Monkey, ensuring his immobility for five
hundred years. Coincidentally, before being introduced into the Chinese
pantheon of deities in the first century, Kuan Yin was better known in
Buddhism as the male deity, Avalokiteshvara, the earthly manifestation
of the Buddha, known as a bodhisattva or "Buddha-to-be." In fact, before
the Sung dynasty, the bodhisattva was represented as a masculine presence, although later images incorporate features of both genders. Thus,
as a gender-crossing deity as well as a mediator between the human and
the divine, Kuan Yin in *Tripmaster Monkey* reinforces the shape-shifting
identity-crossing attributes that characterize both Wittman and Monkey,

underscoring the fact that Wittman Ah Sing inhabits and negotiates cultural, ethnic, national, and artistic borders through his ability to perform in all of the spaces that exist on either side of each border.

In the classic Chinese narrative, *Journey to the West*, Kuan Yin watches as Monkey goes on his pilgrimage, supervising his activities from a distance, although she frequently plays deus ex machina, sometimes mildly interfering with the action, and actually stepping in occasionally to extricate him from tight situations that he has inadvertently precipitated. Her benign interference and maneuvering keep Monkey fairly well-focused on his quest for enlightenment. Maxine Hong Kingston believes that Kuan Yin masterminds Monkey's entire journey, ensuring that the travelers do not stray far, but remain on the right path, thus guaranteeing a successful undertaking for the motley group of pilgrims.

As the narrator of *Tripmaster Monkey*, Kuan Yin controls not only Wittman, but also the reader of the novel. Kingston suggests that the struggle between Wittman and the narrator lends tension to the novel. Because the narrator represents the female principle, Wittman struggles with her, refusing to accept the reality that she controls him, resisting the opportunity to become reconciled with the feminine in himself. He believes that his alienation is merely social, and he initially puts his energy into easy fixes, such as "integrating the buses and the bathrooms"; but his real task is the business of integrating his selves (Marilyn Chin 60).

The narrator's relationship with the reader is a much friendlier one, hinting occasionally at the relationship between Maxine Hong Kingston and her readers. *Tripmaster Monkey*'s narrator interacts with the reader in three ways: through direct or indirect suggestions for action; through amused commentary on Wittman; and finally, through remarks that are calculated to lure the reader into collusion with the narrator, as well as into the same fond tolerance for Wittman's antics. "Go on to the next chapter" (35, 65), instructs the novel's narrator; and another time, "You might as well travel on with our monkey for the next while" (268). To the reader, the narrator offers commentary on Wittman's motivations, ambitions, activities, finances, problems—as well as revelations of what Wittman's fate could have been without the narrator's assistance. At times, she addresses the reader as a colleague who is collaborating in the seemingly daunting task of educating Wittman and helping him move toward complete maturity, repeatedly referring to "our monkey," confiding that "We'll let him tell you about himself by himself" (303), and suggesting, "We're going to reward and bless Wittman with our listening while he talks to his heart's content" (306). The narrator has the final word in the novel, blessing Wittman and drawing the reader into the benediction: "Dear American monkey, don't be afraid . . . let us tweak your ear, and kiss your other ear" (340).

CHARACTER DEVELOPMENT

At the center of *Tripmaster Monkey* is Wittman Ah Sing, a California native in his early twenties who has just earned his baccalaureate degree in English from the University of California at Berkeley (Kingston's academic major and alma mater). Like the disaffected group of writers and artists known in England as the Angry Young Men during the 1950s, Wittman is an alienated and intelligent antihero, at odds with the society in which he has been raised and educated, yet unsure of the exact nature or source of his malaise. Tall, skinny, mustached, and occasionally bespectacled (when he performs at poetry readings), he wears his long hair in a parody of a traditional Chinese queue, loosely braided. Wittman is a theatrical child, the only son of Ruby Long Legs, who is a former Flora Dora Girl, and Zeppelin Ah Sing, who wooed Ruby by buying out the front row of seats at theatres whenever she performed, and became a theatre electrician after they were married.

Wittman Ah Sing's name is a linguistic game—three words that carry within themselves singly and together a multitude of meanings that resonate in contrast throughout the novel, adding depth and complication, and thereby meaning. The entire name is an obvious reference to that quintessentially American poet, Walt Whitman, both in "Wittman" which is a version of the poet's surname, and in "Ah Sing," a phrase which alludes to lines from Whitman's great "Song of Myself."

Kingston's Wittman is the Whitmanesque protagonist who dreams of creating community through his art and affirming himself through poetry. Like the poet, Wittman wants to "sing the body electric . . . [and] sing the body from top to toe" ("Song of Myself"). Even as Walt Whitman celebrates the American identity, Wittman must sing the Chinese American self; he must celebrate the Chinese American body. In her choice of names for the protagonist of her novel, Kingston surely was aware that readers would be tempted to manipulate the puns in Wittman Ah Sing's name: "Ah Sing the body electric . . . Ah Sing the body from top to toe." The puns inextricably link Walt Whitman's "Song of Myself" with Maxine Hong Kingston's *Tripmaster Monkey*; Wittman Ah Sing vocalizes the "I" that he is attempting to create—the American "I" that

Kingston so powerfully claims in *The Woman Warrior*, discarding centuries of Chinese tradition that frowns on the use of the personal pronoun, especially by a woman. Like Walt Whitman after whom he is named, Wittman Ah Sing envisions the emergence of a new kind of human being whose existence will empower America, a new kind of American who represents all of the people who have made the United States their home, a new American man only hinted at obliquely in *China Men*.

Wittman's name can also be read as "Wit Man," two words that resonate in two cultures. In English, the name is a testament to his ambition to be a poet, to his linguistic acrobatics, and love affair with words. He is a poet who has the verbal agility to sound like the Beats or like an African American writer. Yet, although Wittman has been educated at the University of California in one of the top English departments in the country, he is also fluent in Chinatown patois. He frequently lapses deliberately into Chinese pronunciations—for example, rehearsing the sound of "Fu-li-sah-kah Soo" instead of "Fleishhacker Zoo" to remind himself that in order to retain his dual identity, he must remain bilingual. Another possibility is that "Wit Man" is an apt identification for the playwright and actor who unleashes the torrential monologue that concludes his play and Kingston's novel. And finally, the name also alludes to "Wit Man," Monkey's nickname from Chinese popular culture which reveres Monkey for his verbal dexterity and his talent for talking his way out of difficult situations.

Kingston uses Monkey as a device for creating Wittman Ah Sing, as a metaphor for Wittman's concealed—and authentic—self. Like Monkey, Wittman has very little respect for authority, and his attempts to subvert the power structure frequently get him into trouble from which he must extricate himself through his ability to perform a variety of selves. As though in affirmation of Wittman's multiple monkey identities, readers have compared him to Stephen Daedalus, Huck Finn, and Holden Caulfield—all of them young male protagonists in search of answers, of self, of the unexpected. To that list of identities, Kingston herself adds Abbie Hoffman and Allen Ginsberg, icons of the sixties and patron saints of protest, rebellion, and free speech.

Monkey is China's beloved traditional troublemaker, the incarnation of mischief, and a central personage in the classic Chinese epic, *Journey to the West*. In Chinese mythologies, the Monkey King is the personification of mischief and rebellion, the simian imp who flouts authority by gobbling up the rare peaches that belong only to the immortals; Monkey's greedy hunger places him in defiance of taboos restricting the fruit solely for the consumption of the gods. Resorting to his seventy-two comic transformations to alter his appearance when he wishes to evade potentially problematic dilemmas, Monkey constantly overturns power structures, leaving chaos and mayhem in his wake, as he continues on his quest for enlightenment.

Like Monkey, Wittman Ah Sing embodies a collision of personas. He is a draft-dodger, a would-be Beat poet, a closet reformer, an actor, and the child of performers. He is both a loner and a man who has multiple friendships and other human connections, a man in search of the perfect love and a bridegroom-on-a-whim, a drifter who is, nonetheless, fired with an obsessive grand ambition—to write, produce, and perform in an epic drama. Wittman is alternately manic and depressed, ecstatic and tortured, oblivious and insightful, expansive and selfish. He is a Chinese American, but five generations removed from the original immigrant ancestor, and he is as indelibly American as anyone whose ancestors made the journey from Europe in the nineteenth century. Yet, his physical appearance, his black hair and eyes, and his sallow skin—characteristics which he ironically goes out of his way to emphasize—identify him to many of his compatriots as a foreigner. Even his name conflates the literary and linguistic traditions of two countries: Wittman/Whitman from the United States, Ah Sing from China. The contradictions multiply. Wittman, the English major who quotes Rilke, is perfectly capable of deliberately lapsing into Chinatown jargon; to Nanci Lee, a classmate with whom he is infatuated, he describes the plight of sojourners: "Wokking on da Waywoad. Centing da dollahs buck hom to why-foo and biby" (33). Faced with the prospect of a long bus ride seated next to a garrulous Chinese girl, he pretends to be Japanese. And although he has earned a university degree, he seems unable to find employment commensurate with his education. A dominant strand throughout the novel is Wittman's deep-rooted desire to be identified as an American, a desire that he nonetheless thwarts by dressing in colors that exacerbate the sallowness of his Chinese complexion. All of these ongoing contradictions—which are clear manifestations of conflicting selves—are parallels to Monkey's six dozen transformations in the legends. Each time Wittman enacts a new self or identity, he does so in the service of evading or avoiding confrontation or debate, even as Monkey frequently transforms himself in his attempts to stay out of trouble or forestall censure.

Although not as completely realized as Wittman, the supporting cast of characters in *Tripmaster Monkey* comes distinctively alive through

Kingston's ability to create character snapshots with a single phrase, name, capsule description or linguistic trait. Judy Louis, the talkative girl on the crosstown bus, becomes a blue boar/bore as Wittman notices her blue-black silhouette in the darkened bus, and takes in the sight of the pointed teeth that glint in her mouth as she drones monotonously about her classes, the dances that she attends at her church, and her negative opinion of Chinese men. Judy is Kingston's parallel for Pigsy, dim-witted and clumsy, slow on the uptake, and one of the trio of animal familiars who accompany the monk Tripitaka on the pilgrimage from China to India. Wittman's Chinese aunts appear in a verbal group photograph, clearly delineated through their bright red manicured fingernails, dyed jet-black hair, and the English names that they acquired during their careers as vaudeville dancers and showgirls: Marleese, Maydene, Sophie, Dolly, Mabel, Jadine, Bessie, Lilah, Peggy, Sadie, Sondra, Lily Rose, Jean, and Carmen. Now retired from show business and respectably married, they introduce each other as "Madame S. Y. Chin" and "Madame Gordon Fong," attempting to relive through the formal titles the glory days of imperial China and the international fame of the much-admired Soong sisters, Madame Sun Yatsen and Madame Chiang Kai-Shek. In contrast to these professional beauties, the elderly woman whom Wittman encounters in the unemployment office has spent her long working life packing "molly-see-no" (maraschino) cherries into fruit cocktail cans— three cherries per can! The work has deformed her hands so severely that she wears prom gloves to disguise her gnarled fingers. So frequently has she been laid off that she has memorized the correct responses to the questions that the job counselors read perfunctorily from a printed list, and she offers to assist Wittman with his application for unemployment benefits.

Kingston's talent for creating memorable characters, including the very minor participants in Wittman's escapades, enables the reader to visualize the incredible variety of humanity represented by the members of the cast that Wittman assembles for his theatrical extravaganza. All of the characters who populate his life—the Yale Younger Poet and Taña, Nanci Lee and Zeppelin Ah Sing, Popo and Ruby Long Legs, the crowd of showgirl aunties and Lance Kamiyama, former Berkeley schoolmates—becomes a member of the troupe that performs for the play; and Kingston's American characters in *Tripmaster Monkey* metamorphose into the central figures in the classical Chinese narratives as reconceived by Wittman Ah Sing.

SETTING

Tripmaster Monkey's San Francisco has a double reality, existing on two levels: it is a geographical location, recognizable to those who know the city through firsthand experience or from travel features in glossy magazines, or even from films set in its streets and neighborhoods; and at the same time, it is a geography of the imagination, a phantom landscape, an abstraction that is no less real than the neighborhoods, streets, and hills of the physical city.

The physical San Francisco is the famous "city by the Bay," home of the Golden Gate Bridge and Golden Gate Park, the Coit Tower and other landmarks. This metropolis is a living organism criss-crossed by buses and the automobiles, locked up with traffic jams. It is a commercial entity composed of restaurants and fast-food joints, fire sales, going-out-of-business sales, pawn shops, bookstores, cafes, department stores—an urban entity "full of schemes" (67). In this incarnation, San Francisco is the familiar city portrayed in tourist brochures, the city immortalized by Tony Bennett in a popular ballad. It is also a city indelibly associated with the Beat poets, and later with the hippies of Haight Ashbury.

The other intangible San Francisco is a space inhabited by a multitude of cultures, an indeterminate and imaginary geography that mirrors Wittman's shifting personas. This city is multilayered—the province of Californian and immigrant (from another country, from the other coast) alike, a babel of languages, a place in which cultures, subcultures, and countercultures exist in parallel, overlap, subdivide, even collide. And out of this urban ethnic/regional chaos emerge Wittman and his cast of thousands, ready to perform the reconstituted, expanded, adapted Chinese legend on an American stage, thus creating a a cultural space in which Chinese tradition and American art can coalesce into a new form that incorporates the best energies of both cultures. Amorphous and fluid, this San Francisco is the third space that Wittman needs as an incubator for his emerging self. In this place, with its multitudes and variety, with its endlessly shifting mix of humanity, Wittman can perform his identity, and sing his Self as well as that of all Chinese Americans. San Francisco's myriad faces are Wittman's faces, its moods are his, its energies encourage and feed his manic activity. As the site of a fusion culture and as the port of entry into which thousands of the first Asian immigrants came, San Francisco offers Wittman the most appropriate setting in which to dramatize the history of the Asian American experience by performing heritage and community on the stage.

Kingston's city is what anthropologist Mary Louise Pratt describes as a *contact zone*, which Pratt defines as a social space in which cultures "meet, clash, and grapple with each other, often in contexts of highly asymmetrical relations of power" (Pratt 6–7). Her use of the word "asymmetrical" highlights the imbalance of power operating in the contact zone—generally one culture dominates over the others, and that dominant culture's values, institutions, language, social rules, and perspectives become the norm, effectively silencing all other perspectives in the interest of smooth interaction between cultures. Pratt notes also that subordinate cultures within a contact zone tend to feel marginalized and invisible—and that individuals from these cultures often feel that they have no choice but to try to fit in.

San Francisco has always been the site of cultural struggles—from its earliest days as the entry point for would-be miners from the eastern states and immigrants from Asia (also known as "the East"), through the poetic revolution of the Beat Generation to the clashes between hippies and the Establishment, war protesters and the military, Asian American students and a university curriculum that privileged European culture. Yet, despite the fact that many individuals in San Francisco's marginalized groups chose to assimilate, still others resisted, subverted, even undermined the dominant culture in their attempts to define a recognizable and distinctive place for themselves. Wittman belongs to the latter group. Initially, he attempts simply to negotiate his role in the dominant culture; however, later, growing bolder and more self-assured in his monkey role, he publicly performs his resistance and his new identity through his play. At the beginning of the novel, Wittman is the classic English major—surely one of the most assimilationist choices possible in the American curriculum—despite his desultory attempts to maintain his connection with his Chinese heritage. He writes poetry in the style of the Beat poets, dresses in conventional suits, frequents Bay Area bookstores and coffeehouses. Wittman himself is a contact zone, a man in whom the various cultures of his environment collide and grapple for purchase. By the end of the book, however, he is no longer a nearly completely assimilated individual—rather, he is aggressively and vocally Chinese American—an American who embraces and publicizes the bicultural heritage that makes him different.

LITERARY DEVICES

Language

For most readers, the most immediately noticeable characteristic of
Tripmaster Monkey is the novel's fantastically playful language. The extended pun on Wittman's name has already been discussed above; in
addition, Kingston's text features other equally delightful linguistic feats
reminiscent of other verbally acrobatic texts, especially James Joyce's
Ulysses and *Finnegans Wake*. Kingston draws her linguistic inspiration
from a variety of sources, most notably from the sixties' culture, Walt
Whitman's poetry, and Chinatown speech—both the genuine and the
stereotypical. As a writer and teacher, Kingston has always been fascinated by the developments in American English that were inspired by
cultural changes and political upheavals in the 1960s. During that decade, American society was evolving to accommodate new ideologies,
emerging lifestyles, careers, and occupations—and these major cultural
developments required a radical overhaul of the language. Kingston
maintains her fascination with the linguistic inventions of that era, a
decade that saw the coining of new words and phrases to describe psychedelic states, innovative strategies for social protest, new ways of being
and living and confronting the world (Blauvelt 78). For *The Woman Warrior* and *China Men*, Kingston created an American idiom that would
replicate the language of people in the immigrant communities, people
whose daily communication moves back and forth between Chinese and
English. These two books of memoirs privilege the voices of Kingston's
ancestors, talking story in Chinese and through Kingston's translation
blending their stories into American history and culture.

In *Tripmaster Monkey*, Kingston no longer mediates between two languages—she revels in the richness and power of modern American English. She talks story with American rhythms in the American idiom,
employing nouns and verbs that she remembers as inventions of the
1960s to describe psychedelic states, drug-induced visions, Zen rituals,
the peace movement, popular culture, and activism—language that she
describes as consisting of words that people made up. In this new idiom,
Wittman can describe Chinese American culture as "knickknackatory"
(27). The new language describes a San Francisco that is populated with
trippers, beatniks, people who freak out or get high or get stoned—a
city in which Wittman and his friends are the new hip generation. Like

his creator, Wittman is exhilarated and even transported with the freedom and fluidity of the new American language, as words and phrases
evolve to describe states of being and actions relatively unknown to
earlier generations. As a poet, playwright, and wordsmith, Wittman ma-
nipulates the language, savors words, dazzles his audience with his linguistic pyrotechnics and radical ideas that are reminiscent of the
wordplay of Walt Whitman a century earlier.

The connections between Kingston's novel and Walt Whitman extend
well beyond the obvious puns on Wittman's name. From the nineteenth-
century poet's masterpiece, *Leaves of Grass*, come several of the chapter
titles that Kingston uses in *Tripmaster Monkey*: "Trippers and Askers" and
"Linguists and Contenders" are lines from "Song of Myself"; "A Song
for Occupations" is an allusion to Walt Whitman's poem of the same
name; the title "Ruby Long Legs' and Zeppelin's Song of the Open Road"
echoes Whitman's own "Song of the Open Road." Moreover, even when
Leaves of Grass does not directly supply Kingston's novel with an apt
phrase or succinct description, the spirit of Walt Whitman, speaking
through Wittman Ah Sing, vocalizes a litany of maxims by which an
individual must conduct life, as well as a series of pronouncements by
which Wittman hopes to explain his actions, his dreams—himself, in fact.

Wittman frequently reminds himself that he must conduct his life according to the rules that he has devised, rules that echo Walt Whitman's
"dialect of common sense." These maxims include "Never tell the same
story twice," a maxim that Wittman later amends to "Don't say the same
thing in the same way to the same person twice" (19); and "Better be
dead than boring" (19); and "Feed the storyteller" (40). The pithy pre-
cepts for daily living enable Wittman to negotiate his way through his
suicidal impulses at the beginning of the novel, and as he begins to
emerge from his brief flirtation with depression, the commonplaces
evolve, becoming more definitive, more Wittman/Whitmanesque. "I am
not a boulevardier," says Wittman, describing himself instead more specifically as a "bum-how" and a "fleaman" (68). Rebelling against Beat
poet Jack Kerouac's phrase, "the twinkling little Chinese" (69), Wittman
admonishes himself that a man "does not twinkle" (69), yet shortly before the impromptu ceremony in which he and Taña are married, he
invokes his intention always to indulge in the "more flamboyant thing"
(163). As he and Taña enjoy an expensive restaurant meal during their
trip to Nevada, Wittman suddenly becomes uncomfortably aware that
his life is devoid of any structure and that his existence lacks grace,
whereupon he silently constructs a new set of rules for living, reminding

himself to wash coffee cups after each use, to stop eating out of the refrigerator or from pots on the stove, and especially not to work and eat simultaneously. He tells himself that he must learn to live more consciously: "End the day gracefully. See each day out, toast it, feast it, sing its farewell" (213). He concludes by reminding himself that at the very least, he must sit down occasionally and dine with another human being.

Allusions

Through her judicious use of allusions, Kingston clarifies the connections, parallels, and resonances between *Tripmaster Monkey* and the global culture, but more specifically between the novel and China and America. Kingston, who is herself the product of a Chinese heritage and an American upbringing and education, a political activist, graduate of Berkeley, and connoisseur of 1960s culture, forages in the collective psyches of her multiple cultural heritages, creating a novel that can best be described as a cultural mosaic. The novel's allusions encompass and embrace all of the world and time—Shakespeare, Buddhism, Hollywood movies and Eastern European art films, California history and geography, Chang and Eng, the Ku Klux Klan, Chinatown slang, German fiction—a dizzying panoply of soundbites that create the impression of a text that belongs everywhere and yet nowhere specific, a novel that is the 1960s incarnate, but at the same moment is also timeless. Even as she harvests her allusions from the cultures of her universe, however, Kingston draws most heavily on three sources: Chinese folklore and literature, American popular culture and literature, and film.

From Chinese folklore comes the mischievous figure of the Monkey King (described earlier), the most recognizable and decipherable allusion in the novel, introduced immediately in the title and appearing frequently thereafter in Wittman's references to himself, as well as in the narrator's remarks about Wittman. Through Monkey, Kingston's text is linked with and alludes to not only any number of folktales and folk heroes from around the world, but also to trickster narratives and other significant cultural fictions. Monkey embodies the multilayered texture of the novel, as well as the polycultural milieu that has produced and shaped Wittman. As the legendary Chinese simian hero, Monkey transfers his comic universe into Kingston's novel, emphasizing the striking similarities between himself and Wittman, and making possible Wittman's multiple transformations, antic maneuverings, and manic schemes. As a monkey (lower case), Wittman takes his place in the global folklore that revolves around a mischievous and clever primate, the inspiration for works such as Henry Louis Gates's *The Signifying Monkey*, which, thanks to the Monkey King, can be added to the expanding library of references that open up readings of Kingston's novel. Finally, at the most basic level, the Monkey King calls up references to popular sayings, proverbs, and doggerel. "Monkey see, Monkey do" is a phrase that perfectly describes Wittman for whom the entire universe is a limitless source of the raw material for his art; moreover, popular jokes about monkeys and typewriters conjure up images of Wittman feverishly laboring to complete his play. Commonly used expressions such as "monkeying around" or "monkey on his back" are also particularly appropriate to Wittman, whose every thought and action are imbued with the spirit of play and mischief.

The Monkey King is the central character in a key work that shapes Kingston's text—Wu Ch'eng-en's *Journey to the West (Hsi-yu-Chi)*, a sixteenth-century comic picaresque tale that recounts the historic seventh-century pilgrimage of the monk Hsuan-tsang to India in search of the sacred Buddhist scriptures. Hsuan-tsang's story was transformed into a novel when Wu Ch'eng-en compiled the several existing oral versions and transformed them into a single unified text. In the literary version, Hsuan-tsang becomes the monk Tripitaka (note the auditory parallels between "Tripitaka" and "Tripmaster") and a variety of folk heroes and popular figures become entangled in the story of the fateful journey.

In *Journey to the West*, Monkey emerges fully formed from a stone egg. Responding to a dare from the monkey inhabitants of the surrounding forest, he leaps through a waterfall and discovers a paradise for the monkeys; and for his courageous act, he is crowned King of the Monkeys. Because he wishes to learn the secrets of immortality, he enters a monastery where he perfects the art of seventy-two transformations which allow him to change shape and size, to travel great distances in seconds, and to perform magic. A short section of *Journey to the West* details the story of Tripitaka and his mission to recover the sutras. The bulk of the novel, however, chronicles the eighty-one adventures that Tripitaka and his companions—Monkey, Sandy, and Pigsy—encounter as they make their way to India, battling villains and monsters, enduring unheard-of trials, contending with the policies of petty bureaucracies, and ultimately attaining the prize for which they have undertaken the journey—the sacred Buddhist texts. In similar fashion, Wittman must vanquish his own imaginary monsters, overcome the sensation of being tugged between two heritages, and deal with the bureaucracies of California social services offices and the Benevolent Association in Chinatown—so that he will be able at last to stage his play, a creative work that he hopes will reveal to him the path toward enlightenment and Self.

A second important allusion in *Tripmaster Monkey* invokes *Romance of the Three Kingdoms*. A portion of the play that Wittman wants to stage is his revision of that classic Chinese text, another rambling sixteenth-century narrative glorifying the third-century power struggle for the throne of China. *Romance* is a fast-paced tale of battle, martial prowess, cunning strategy, and death, and Wittman's appropriation of sections of the tale for his play about community and peace is both ironic and interesting. Specifically, he chooses the famous "oath scene," the first meeting of the novel's three heroes: Liu Pei (Liu Bei, in pinyin), a major claimant to the throne who has been reduced by ill luck to the lowly position of sandal-maker; Chang Fei (Zhang Fei, in pinyin), a farmer and butcher who comes to the aid of Liu Pei; and Gwan Goong (Kuan Yu in pinyin, although Kingston spells the name Guan Goong in *China Men*), the god of war. Standing in a peach orchard, the three men swear to each other the oath of eternal loyalty—clear proof that strong bonds can be forged even among men who have no blood relationship—and they agree to fight together as though bound by ties of kinship.

The third important Chinese narrative to which Kingston alludes is *The Water Margin* (also translated as *The Water Verge, Tale of the Marshes, The Marshes of Mount Liang, All Men Are Brothers*, and *Outlaws from the Marsh*), a novel that is said to have been written by Shi Naian and Luo Guanzhong, who lived during the Ming Dynasty (1368–1644). Yet another of China's four great fictional narratives, the novel is loosely based on the adventures and exploits of a legendary gang of 108 twelfth-century outlaws who thrived by their wits in the swampy marshes at the juncture of the Yellow River and the Grand Canal in Shandong Province. Renowned for their loyalty to each other, the outlaws in *The Water Margin* achieve both fame and notoriety for contesting and subverting government policy and taking the law into their own hands; and the novel teems with episodes of betrayal, murder, revenge, duels, and ambushes. *The Water Margin* is often compared with the Robin Hood tales because the Chinese outlaws display a penchant for assisting the oppressed as well as for taking the side of the poor against the government and the ruling class.

Each of the three Chinese texts originated as a historical event that captured the popular imagination so completely that the event found its way—through talk-story—into legend, folktale, and popular drama, and thence to written narrative, in which form it gained a new kind of popularity. In each case, both historical fact and early narrative have been altered repeatedly through the centuries, revised, reconfigured, modified, edited, and enlarged—all in the interest of creating a riveting story or a performance piece. Moreover, all three texts continue to be reconstructed and expanded to appeal to new audiences; *The Water Margin* has recently become a controversial revisionist film in China, as well as an on-line role-playing game. In *Tripmaster Monkey*, Wittman borrows from each of the three texts only those specific episodes that fit into the grand scheme for his play; and he takes artistic liberties with each episode, combining events as he desires, and interpolating elements from other texts as he deems necessary. Likewise, Maxine Hong Kingston appropriates familiar traditional texts and re-creates them to respond to the demands of the new narratives that she is creating.

Another major source of allusions in *Tripmaster Monkey* is American culture (especially that of the sixties), both high and low. From literature come references to and quotations from that decade's iconic poets—among them Diane Wakoski, Jack Spicer, Peter Orlovsky, Lew Welch, Charles Olson, and LeRoi Jones (now Amiri Baraka). From stage and screen come references to Marlon Brando, *Flower Drum Song*, and *The World of Suzie Wong*. From music come the Monterey Jazz Festival, Louis Armstrong, and John Cage; and from the culture of childhood, war toys, a plush Snoopy, Barbie and her playmates—Malibu Skipper, Malibu Ken, Malibu Christie. In the spirit of the decade for which the word "trip" signified physical, psychological, emotional, spiritual, and hallucinatory journeys, Wittman embarks on the classic American road trip, driving from San Francisco to Berkeley, to Sutro, to Sacramento, and on to Reno, and from thence back to San Francisco, all in the space of two weeks. During that fortnight of peripatetic activity, he also attends an all-night party, gets married on a whim, goes on his honeymoon, takes his new wife to meet his mother and aunts, and embarks on a search for his allegedly missing Popo, or grandmother. He returns to San Francisco in just enough time to finalize the plans for staging his epic drama. Wittman's trip resonates with Jack Kerouac's *On the Road*, as well as with Walt Whitman's "I take to the open road / Healthily, free, the world before me" ("Song of the Open Road"). Newly married, bursting with ideas, and fired with enthusiasm for the theatrical scheme that he plans, Wittman has his world before him—Chinatown, San Francisco, California, the United States, China, the global culture that inspires him and provides the cast for his play.

One of the most intriguing allusions in *Tripmaster Monkey* points to *The Saragossa Manuscript*, a film that catches Wittman's attention because its design so closely parallels what he is attempting to bring to the stage through his play. Wittman never actually sees the film. At Lance Kamiyama's party in Oakland, another guest named Charley regales his fellow party-goers with a lengthy and somewhat disconnected plot summary of *The Saragossa Manuscript*, a film that he claims is so provocative and life-altering that he is anxious for all of his friends to be aware of its existence.

Filmed in Poland in 1965 and barely distributed in the United States, *The Saragossa Manuscript* is a three-hour, black-and-white gothic epic based on a novel by Count Jan Potocki. The plot of both novel and film consists of a series of interlocking stories within stories that are themselves embedded in still other stories. The film's framing device focuses initially on the tale of a soldier who, in the midst of a battle during the siege of Saragossa, Spain, discovers an old book in a ruined house. He begins reading, and becomes so engrossed by the book that he is captured by a Spaniard. That book turns out to be the story of the soldier's ancestor, a seventeenth-century captain whose tale then becomes the focus of the rest of the film.

In the book, the captain travels through Spain, and encounters a series of individuals who feel compelled to narrate stories which focus on characters who likewise have a passion for storytelling; and their tales, in turn, feature stories told by still other storytellers. The film, which has been described as possibly the most extreme treatment of the story-within-a-story device, thus takes on the form of an extraordinarily complicated puzzle in which individual stories eventually parallel others, recast them, or even extend them. Complicating the structure of the film is the atmospheric gothicism of the cinematography, a tour de force of chiaroscuro (contrasts between dark and light) that underscore the film's surreal juxtapositions. At one point in the film, several characters engage in a fruitless attempt to unravel the web of stories in which they are impossibly enmeshed, trapped in a convoluted tangle of their own manufacture. A recurring motif—and a metaphor for the conundrum of the film—shows the captain awakening under a gallows tree, realizing that the events he has witnessed are a dream, awakening once again to realize that the gallows is a dream image—and finding himself under a gallows tree once more in yet another awakening.

The Saragossa Manuscript becomes Wittman's template for the piece of epic theatre that he is attempting to create. Not only is the film an experiment in narrative structure, but it also is a compendium of the fantastic, incorporating ruins, ghosts and other supernatural phenomena, Moorish slaves and barely clothed princesses, a gallows tree with dangling corpses, magic, and a cabalist who vies with a mathematician for control of the captain's soul. Like *The Saragossa Manuscript*, Wittman's play tests the limits of narrative and dramatic form, seeking to be all-inclusive in both imagery and allusions. And even as *The Saragossa Manuscript* features a huge cast of characters with several dozen speaking parts, Wittman's play includes a role for every individual in his orbit of acquaintances, every person with whom he has had a meaningful interaction, however briefly. And finally, instead of a philosophical duel between cabalist and mathematician for his soul, Wittman is pulled in several directions by his multiple heritages: by the ancient compelling legends of China, by the freewheeling exuberance of 1960s America, and by the literary and artistic legacies of China, Europe, and the United States.

Wittman is never able to view *The Saragossa Manuscript*, although for years he attempts unsuccessfully to find a copy of the film. Eventually, he quite naturally begins to wonder whether he has hallucinated or dreamt the film, although his friends who heard Charley narrate the film's plot at Lance Kamiyama's party in Oakland have begun to believe that they have, indeed, seen *The Saragossa Manuscript*. Like the captain who awakens repeatedly beneath the gallows tree, Wittman is forced to examine his experiences, his perceptions of them, and the effect they have on him—and to attempt to determine which of his stories must be told and how that telling must be accomplished for maximum effect.

Symbol

Although as a multivocal text, *Tripmaster Monkey* is replete with symbols, as well as with symbol clusters, two of those dominate the novel, shaping it—and Wittman—far more significantly than do the others. These two major symbols are Monkey and the theatre.

The novel's title makes clear the importance of its simian hero by identifying that hero as the reader's guide on a rollicking literary journey through 1960s America. During that era, when a group of friends experimented with hallucinogenic substances, one individual was designated the tripmaster. This person refrained from ingesting any drugs, remaining sober and assuming the responsibility of verbalizing imagery that guaranteed a pleasant "trip," enabling hallucinators to envision calm, peaceful scenes or safely exciting imaginary landscapes. A tripmaster is responsible for shaping the experience of a psychedelic "traveler" who has embarked on an imaginary trip through a landscape created by the tripmaster. Similarly, Wittman Ah Sing, as the contemporary incarnation of the King of the Monkeys, becomes the tripmaster who shapes our reading experience as we "travel" through Kingston's re-creation of the American landscape. Thus, it is Monkey who occupies the center of the novel, strutting and cavorting and dancing his way through the text, pitching ideas, creating scenarios, overturning long-held assumptions, and otherwise performing.

Kingston points out that writing about the 1960s opened her eyes to the arrival of Monkey in North America. She describes the Chicago Seven as "seven monkeys bringing chaos to the establishment," adding the Monkey also manifested himself in happenings, and events—love-ins, demonstrations, Woodstock. Describing Monkey as a party-loving creature, Kingston remarks that a truly stupendous party can actually effect change (Blauvelt 78–79). Monkey, with his love of frenetic activity and improvisation, symbolizes chaos and change, and ultimately, enlightenment. As Monkey, Wittman Ah Sing represents a new definition of "American" and an entire repertoire of strategies for performing the revised American identity. Like Monkey, Wittman is inherently liminal and possesses little power; consequently, he is forced to resort to trickery, to create new selves that allow him to "sing the body electric," as well as to perform the Chinese American self.

The second important symbol cluster in *Tripmaster Monkey* involves the theatre and all aspects of performance. For Wittman, life has always been one grand performance, and he revels in his freedom to take on and discard roles at will. Born backstage while his parents were touring with a vaudeville show, he spent his infancy not in the standard bassinet or crib, but in a theatrical trunk—the very same trunk in which his great-grandfather stored the seventy-two costumes that represent Monkey's transformations for a performance of *Journey to the West*. As a toddler, Wittman was outfitted in a monkey costume and sent into the theatre to run through an audience dispensing Dr. Woo's pills and elixirs during a Chinese medicine show. Not surprisingly, Wittman's points of reference for life are performance and audiences. As he attempts to explain himself—his life, interests, desires, and ambitions—to Nanci Lee, with whom he is infatuated, he spins a yarn about the history of popular Chinese theatre on the West Coast, especially in Chinatowns before and during the Second World War, and he embeds in that history the tale of his birth which he recounts as though he is describing a play. To Nanci, he recalls his first sensation, the feeling of watching curtains that "rose and rose" to reveal "lights, footlights and overheads" (16).

Wittman, in fact, expends a great deal of his energy in staging performances—his own and those of others. He assumes a succession of roles, each one with its distinctive gestures and language, and even costume—the equivalent of Monkey's many transformations. At one moment, he speaks as a citizen of Chinatown—"Welcome to my ah-pok-mun," he tells Nanci Lee (30)—yet scant minutes later, he is reciting, in perfect English, his Gig Poems, railroad poems, and bane poems, attempting to be a Beat poet, but prompting Nanci's observation that he sounds "like a Black poet" (32). In theatre jargon, Wittman is "always on"; that is, he is constantly performing, always aware of an audience's reaction to him, always playing a role, never himself. In order to acquire the necessary permission to stage his play in the Chinatown headquarters of the local Benevolent Association, he spontaneously breaks into a performance of the character of Monkey for the caretaker, whose initial refusal changes to approval as he guffaws at Wittman's mimicry of Monkey's tricks. Wittman's greatest triumph—the epic play—allows him not only to direct the performances of everyone in his life, but also to perform his one-man song of himself, his community, and his nation.

Theatre is the dominant motif of Wittman's life. His all-consuming ambition is to be a playwright and to revive the long-defunct tradition of Chinese American theatre. He dreams of starting a theatre company that he will name The Pear Garden Players of America, in homage to the legendary pear garden where, according to Chinese tradition, both civilization and theatre had their genesis. His theatre will be the late twentieth-century link in a 1,630-year-old tradition of Chinese performance, a tradition that crossed the Pacific Ocean with his ancestors and flourished in the Western states until World War II. He woos Nanci Lee by announcing that he is writing a play for her, and showing her his great-great-grandfather's trunk, Wittman says that he cannot die until he fills that trunk with poetry and theatrical pieces. The morning after Lance's party, Wittman entertains the last lingering guests by reading aloud, from the manuscript for his play, the episodes that portray Monkey's life. Inspired by the reading, he casts his play on the spot, assigning roles to the other guests as well as to the host. When he marries Taña, his wedding gift to her is the story of Lady Sun from *Romance of the Three Kingdoms* and the opportunity to play the desirable role of Lady Sun in the coming play. Even when Wittman is finally driven to file a claim for unemployment benefits and to submit to an interview with an Employment Counselor, he finds it impossible to eradicate theatre from his mind, and he insists on listing "playwright" as the job for which he is searching.

In a discussion of the symbolic importance of theatre (and related elements and references) in *Tripmaster Monkey*, Maxine Hong Kingston explains that she is recounting the history of theatre, including traditional forms from the many shores of the Pacific Ocean: monkey theatre, talk-story theatre, story boats, song boats, Ramayana, minstrel shows, and one-man shows (Blauvelt 78). In another interview, she suggests that *Tripmaster Monkey* reveals Wittman's extraordinarily complete vision of the theatre which she describes as integrated theatre. Like the Monkey King, Wittman possesses the spirit of play, an essential characteristic for an actor or performer (Marilyn Chin 60). Wittman's play, when it is finally staged, reveals its roots in folk theatre and performance art, as well as its borrowings from the great theatrical traditions of the world. The production of Wittman's play is completely integrated theatre, performed playfully and collaboratively as a community effort, speaking from within and to the varied cultures that make up the United States.

MAJOR THEMES

So dense a text is *Tripmaster Monkey*, so studded with symbol and motif, with reference and allusion, that its richness of thematic exploration is hardly surprising. Among the themes that are frequently identified as the major shaping forces in Kingston's novel are the following: alienation and assimilation (or completely fitting into a culture), appropriating America, and inventing a self and an identity.

Alienation and Assimilation

Kingston explores the interconnected themes of alienation and assimilation through her portrayal of Wittman, a thoroughly assimilated young American who, nevertheless, feels alienated from his own culture for reasons mainly related to race and ethnicity. What Wittman perceives is not merely the disaffection of the youthful intellectual who feels misunderstood by society, but more importantly the profound separation felt by Americans of non-European extraction whose physical features mark them as Other, as noticeably different from the majority of the population. Asian Americans are, in fact, often mistaken for foreigners or international students. Wittman's alienation—like that of many young Asian Americans—is the product of confusion about his place in his own country. He is American-born, his native tongue is English, and he has been educated in American schools. Because of his upbringing and education, he shares the dominant cultural values of the United States; and indeed, he is familiar with no other country or culture except through what he has read in books and magazines. Like the brother who goes to Vietnam in *China Men*, Wittman has never lived anywhere but the United States; and as one might expect of a fifth-generation American, he is completely assimilated. Yet, when he arrives for a job interview, the interviewer, reacting only to Wittman's Asian facial features, immediately asks if Wittman has a green card—that much-coveted document that allows a legal immigrant who is not yet an American citizen to find permanent employment in the United States. In the one-man show that concludes his marathon drama, Wittman launches into a magnificent and spectacularly angry diatribe about the questions that unthinking individuals regularly ask him to answer: "Where do you come from?" they ask, or "How long have you been in the country?" or sometimes, "How do you like our country?" and finally, "Do you speak English?" (317). As a Berkeley graduate with a degree in English, he finds the last question especially disturbing. "On the phone I sound like anybody, I get the interview, but I get downtown, they see my face, they ask, 'Do you speak English?' " (317).

What Is an American?

Another theme that informs *Tripmaster Monkey* is the question: What is an American? Kingston asks this question in *The Woman Warrior* and *China Men*, and she revisits the issue in her third book by focusing on the individuals in a generation far removed from their immigrant ancestors. Unlike his great-great-grandparents who retain vivid memories of their native China and more than likely never lose their Chinese accents, Wittman has no country other than the United States, no firsthand knowledge of an ancestral culture to which he might owe emotional allegiance. He thinks, dreams, speaks, falls in love, gets angry, writes in English—in the hip sixties jargon, in literary phrases, in imitation of the authors whose works he has studied in college. LeAnne Schreiber articulates the provocative conundrum at the center of *Tripmaster Monkey*, stating unequivocally that Wittman is an American man, comparing him with Jack Kerouac, James Baldwin, Allen Ginsburg, even Walt Whitman, and noting that Wittman Ah Sing is "as American as five generations in California and a Berkeley education in the 1960s can make him." And Schreiber raises the question: "[If] he's so American, how come everybody thinks he's Chinese? How can someone raised on Mickey Mouse and *Life* magazine still seem so exotic, so 'inscrutable' to his countrymen?" (Schreiber 9). Wittman is, as Schreiber recognizes, an American, yet he must—like the grandfathers in *China Men*—find a way to appropriate America and claim it for himself. For him, as for Maxine Hong Kingston, the most powerful strategy for claiming his own country is to ensure the incorporation of the stories of his ancestors into the fabric of American history. Consequently, he interpolates the theatrical traditions of frontier towns—Chinese traveling theatre as well as Wild West melodrama—into his play, clearly signaling that a Chinese American play can also be a drama of the American West. Thus, Wittman incorporates himself into the narrative of America—by embedding in that narrative the stories of his grandparents, the contributions of his parents not only to the cultural life of California, but also to the war effort in the 1940s, the characters and symbols of Chinese legends that came to America with the immigrants. Similarly, by creating a Chinese American protagonist for a novel of the sixties, Kingston inscribes a new character among the protesters, politicians, activists, hippies, beatniks, and soldiers that populate cultural and historical accounts of that decade. In doing so, she adds a vibrant new element to America's cultural landscape.

Identity and the Self

A third major theme in *Tripmaster Monkey* involves the intertwined issues of identity and the creation of the self. The driving force in Wittman Ah Sing's life is his need to define himself, both to his own satisfaction and that of the dominant American culture in which he lives. While the search for self is a common theme in fiction, Wittman's quest is complicated by race and ethnicity. Ultimately, his definition of self must take into account the Chinese ancestry that so visibly defines him although he is many generations removed from China and has never visited that country.

A crucial component in Wittman's quest to define himself is his bi-cultural background—the inescapable fact that, like Maxine in *The Woman Warrior*, he must constantly mediate between the two cultures that contribute to his heritage. We have noted that one of the central puzzles in *Tripmaster Monkey* is that Wittman is an American who is ethnically Chinese, an ethnic Chinese who is an American. Thus, he must translate each culture into the other, must go beyond, must think and speak through them, and ultimately transcend their limitations. He is Monkey who dwells on the borders between worlds, and he must create himself—Wittman—in a new setting that is neither mainstream America nor China, but a third cultural space. Early in the novel, Wittman displays his awareness of the bifurcation of his psyche. Noticing an immigrant couple walking toward him on a sidewalk, barring his way, he immediately commences an internal monologue ridiculing the two as "F.O.B.s" (fresh off the boat), especially the wife who is wearing an unfashionable shapeless nylon pantsuit, chewing sunflower seeds, and spitting out the hulls onto the path. Wittman, of course—despite his physical resemblance to the scorned couple—is different from F.O.B.s, having himself descended from immigrants who arrived in the nineteenth century on the *Nootka*, a ship that many describe as the Chinese Mayflower; yet he is acutely conscious that others passing both him and the immigrant couple on the same sidewalk would see only the similarity in facial features and assume that he, too, is not quite an American. Hence his preoccupation with defining his place in America.

Defining the self is a process of invention that requires careful attention to the multifarious facets that an individual presents to the world. As a performer, Wittman is conscious that he must marshall the correct verbal and visual codes in the service of his role-playing; he must deliberately select from his cultural environment only those elements that will enhance the identity he is scripting for himself, and he must also devise the appropriate costume for his new role.

Wittman is a recognizably postmodern hero (see chapter 2 for a full discussion of the term "postmodern"). He is both product and producer of a world in which change is the only constant, impermanence a way of life, and multiplicity and multivocality are cultural givens. In such a world, identity becomes complicated and even contradictory. Wittman's desire to integrate his many selves into a single one, and to create a whole identity is not surprising, given his current liminal position—one that requires him to go through life with a double consciousness. For him, life is a balancing act—between his dream of becoming a writer and his need to earn a living, his obviously Chinese features and his complete American-ness, his university education in the Western canon and his fascination with the Chinese legends of his childhood.

More importantly, Wittman is acutely aware that the "I" who is himself, the "I" that he inhabits, is always also the object of another individual's interpretation. He feels, moves, speaks, dreams, *is* an American; yet others interpret his appearance as different and alien. To them, he belongs to the category of Other. Do what he will to define and redefine himself, his identity will also inevitably be shaped by external conditions that are considerably beyond his control.

Hence Wittman's ambition to establish his own theatre, a venture that will allow him to exert some measure of control over his life. As a theatrical impresario, he plays God. He calls into being a third space in which, under his direction, scenes of his own choosing from important cultural texts can be acted out. On the stage, he can invent and reinvent the kind of world in which he wants to live—a democratic community composed of diverse voices and multiple cultural texts, a society in which every inhabitant is "scrutable" (310). In this brave new world, he and Taña, who are bound to each other in a marriage that some might identify as unusual because he is Asian and she is Caucasian (forgetting that they are both Americans), can prove to society that any two individuals can "get together" and can "learn to care for each other" (337). In such a community, Wittman's "I" has the chance to flourish, as can other identities that have come into being on cultural and racial borders.

ALTERNATIVE READING

Cultural Studies

Cultural studies is the interrogation of how we live. It takes as its province contemporary modes of human production and consumption, examining and critiquing social groups, the media, cultural events, work and leisure, institutions, popular arts—and the literary and popular narratives that inscribe them in the human imagination. The phrase "American culture" implies a common set of social practices to which all Americans adhere. In reality, however, America is composed of several cultures as well as subcultures, distinguished by region, race, ethnic heritage, education, gender, and by numerous other alignments. Individuals do frequently belong to or identify with several groups—Wittman Ah Sing, for example, identifies with more than one group: he is a Californian, also an Asian American, and a Berkeley alumnus; he is also a poet who favors the Beats and the counterculture, and he is a man. Cultural critics are interested in everyday life; they are fascinated by social contexts, or economic and political terrains; they analyze the ways in which a culture creates the narratives by which it defines itself. One especially fascinating strand in cultural studies is the examination of the strategies that allow members of subcultures to contest the dominant culture that silences and disenfranchises them. Such a study often focuses attention on subversive literary forms, including narratives that empower the oppressed—for example, rap lyrics that recount the vicissitudes of life in the 'hood, or folktales that feature trickster figures.

A cultural critic might approach *Tripmaster Monkey* by noting that the novel's title invites comparison with trickster narratives from several cultures. The word "Tripmaster" sounds like "trickster" and the role of the sixties tripmaster—that individual responsible for guiding the imaginary journeys of individuals temporarily existing on the borders between complete wakeful attention and hallucinatory visions—carried with it the potential for the tripmaster to be Trickster. More significantly, the fact that Kingston's tripmaster is Monkey—and therefore a universally recognized Trickster—suggests that Kingston's entire narrative is a trickster text.

Tripmaster Monkey as Trickster Text

Appearing in narratives extant in so many different cultures, Trickster might be described as a universal archetype, recognizable in many cultures, an indestructible cross-cultural incarnation of the spirit of chaos and play and (mis)interpretation. Trickster is a shadowy figure who is said to inhabit crossroads or borders, and who is often described as dwelling between worlds. Trickster has several faces and dons many guises; he is impossible to confine to any single form, being, in fact, a shape-shifter, notable for facility at metamorphosis, transformation, disguise, and masquerade. Trickster is allied with change, constantly instigating disruption of the status quo or interrogating long-cherished rituals and beliefs, generating outrage mixed with laughter in the process.

Trickster is the rebel who respects no taboos and tolerates no restrictions. He is both lovable and irritating, hero and imp, sage and dimwit, destroyer and creator.

Trickster is not confined to any single cultural or historical period, but rather he inhabits the margins of history, always managing to reappear in some form in each era. Trickster materializes whenever those who control power have grown complacent; he disrupts authority, instigates disorder, creates chaos, and then moves on—disappearing so that he can reappear when circumstances demand his presence.

> Trotting, skulking, whining, lurking, ranting, leering, laughing, always hungry, never satisfied, he is an animate principle of disruption, about to precipitate chaos and humor through sacrilege, self-indulgence, and scatology. . . . he exercises his trickery, displays his foolishness, sparks some sure flash of imagination and insight. Then he departs the circled light into the surrounding darkness. (Wiget 86)

In Native American culture, Trickster's most common incarnation is Coyote, although he also appears as Raven, Hare, Wolverine, and Spider. In at least one African American oral tradition, Trickster is Br'er Rabbit. The European manifestation of Trickster is Reynard the Fox, Reinhard Fuchs in German tales. Cultural critic Henry Louis Gates, Jr., has examined trickster texts in *The Signifying Monkey*, pointing out that the Yoruba words for "monkey" and "riddle" are very similar; he adds that Elegba, the divine avatar of the monkey, is a dweller of the crossroads, with one foot on earth and the other in heaven. While these tricksters exhibit significant cultural differences, they do share a number of traits—liminality, energy, disruptiveness, self-indulgence, and humor—that are also evident in literary tricksters such as Prometheus and Milton's Satan, as well as in Monkey, the Chinese trickster who is one of Maxine Hong Kingston's gifts to American literature. Monkey, a border denizen, is semi-divine and is suspended between heaven and earth. Possessed of unlimited energy, he is capable of transforming himself into countless forms, appearing variously as a human being, a plant, a bird, a mosquito, a fish, a demigod, a monster, even a temple. He is indestructible, and irrepressible, and he calls attention to cultural inconsistences by challenging authority.

Trickster texts are characterized by paradox and contradiction, functioning as strategies for challenging oppression and authority, deconstructing stereotypes, and giving voice to a group or culture that has been silenced. Trickster texts are also subversive. Through surprise, subterfuge, excess, invention, and play, they create community among the oppressed, providing continuity for a culture that is on the verge of extinction through silence. Into the company of American tricksters, Maxine Hong Kingston has introduced a third American trickster, the immigrant Monkey who infuses contemporary American narrative with new vitality, by bringing with him the cultural baggage of an ancient civilization whose daughters and sons are now Americans.

Monkey inhabits the body of Wittman Ah Sing, who identifies himself as the incarnation of that legendary hero. As the American manifestation of Monkey, Wittman Ah Sing becomes the contemporary American trickster. Inhabitant of several border spaces, negotiator of several milieu, he is equally comfortable in a stark Chinatown walk-up flat and in Taña's artistically decorated Oakland apartment. He drives her Porsche as easily as he takes the bus, exchanges banter with a group of Berkeley alumni and with his mother's Mah-Jongg circle, subsists on stolen white chocolate candy or dines with panache on escargot and rum steak followed by mousse au chocolat with strawberries. He fits into both mainstream culture and the Asian American subculture; he falls in love with a Chinese classmate and marries a blonde almost-stranger. For Wittman, dress is symbolic of his multiple identities to the world, a device that permits him to enact different roles in the service of his quest to discover a self with which both he and his circle of family and friends are comfortable. Highlighting his Asian ancestry by emphasizing the Chinese pallor of his skin with a green shirt, he nonetheless affects hippie-ish long hair and a wispy beard that guarantee scorn from the Chinatown community, which sees him as "saang-hsu lo, a whisker-growing man," the derisive words that the immigrants use to describe beatniks (11). Thus, he manages to straddle the border between the ethnic enclaves and the white counterculture, complicating his geography by going to his job—until he is fired—in a three-piece Brooks Brothers suit that signals authority and mainstream values. Wittman's costumes allow him to move between the cultures to which he belongs, literally to shape-shift by altering his appearance. His facility with language allows him to assume other identities: Wittman's ability to converse in Chinatown speech, to write poetry that "sounds Black," to read and appreciate Rilke, are all forms of linguistic shape-changing. Trapped in the cultural divide between his worlds, forced to perform a balancing act between cultures nearly every hour of his life, he has developed a functional survival strategy—a fluid identity, a slippery persona that allows him to merge with, blend into, or virtually disappear within any culture that he is trying to negotiate. Taking his cue from Monkey, who transforms and reshapes himself when events become too difficult to handle, Wittman changes himself by performing new identities that enable him to escape from uncomfortable situations.

Wittman possesses other traits that identify him as Trickster. He creates chaos wherever he goes, disrupting the status quo, interrogating dearly-held beliefs and practices, and inserting humor into nearly every situation. Also Trickster-like is the energy that emanates from Wittman—he seems unstoppable, his enthusiasm cannot be contained, and despite everything, he is indestructible. Nothing will get in the way of his performing his play—not the Benevolent Association, not the police, and not the neighbors who are alarmed by his staged theatre fire.

Wittman's play is the trickster text that is embedded in Kingston's trickster text; the play shares a number of common characteristics with that larger work. Both works position Monkey at the center of a vast collection of cultural narratives; both are comprehensive appropriations of cultural elements culled from the lives of their creators; both incorporate a "cast of thousands"; and both subvert the genres to which they appear to belong. Both works are so all-inclusive that they cannot be defined or classified easily, so all-encompassing as to involve an entire community. Like *Tripmaster Monkey*, Wittman's play is the trickster narrative incarnate: the play is fragmented, disruptive, subversive, polyvocal, and playful. It is "an enormous loud play," a "script that [has] lots of holes for ad lib and actors' gifts" (277).

The play happens outside of "real life," allowing participants to exist for its duration beyond the rules that govern everyday conduct—and although the play operates by its own rules, those rules frequently subvert social and cultural norms. The play encourages fantasy, creativity, and experimentation, facilitating the genesis of new ways of being and of new narratives to chronicle those new identities.

The singular decade of the sixties—with its chaos of political turmoil, social activism, spiritual experimentation, drugs, violence, demonstrations and riots, and the war in Vietnam—was also the decade of Flower Power, bright pop music, teach-ins, Peace, and Love. With its contradictions, its juxtaposition of play and seriousness, improvisation and tradition, love and violence, it was the ideal decade for Monkey to emigrate from China and for Trickster to reappear on the American scene, reincarnated as a new kind of American.

Bibliography

WORKS BY MAXINE HONG KINGSTON

Prose

China Men. New York: Alfred A. Knopf, 1980.
Hawai'i One Summer, 1978. San Francisco: Meadow Press, 1987.
Through the Black Curtain. Berkeley, CA: The Friends of the Bancroft Library, University of California, Berkeley, 1987.
Tripmaster Monkey: His Fake Book. New York: Alfred A. Knopf, 1989.
The Woman Warrior: Memoirs of a Girlhood among Ghosts. New York: Alfred A. Knopf, 1976.

Poems

"Absorption of Rock." *Iowa Review* 12 (1981): 207–208.
"Restaurant." *Iowa Review* 12 (1981): 206.

Essays and Short Fiction

"A Chinese Garland." *North American Review* 273.3 (1988): 38–42.
"The Coming Book." *The Writer on Her Work*. Ed. Janet Sternburg. New York: W. W. Norton, 1980.
"Cultural Mis-readings by American Reviewers." *Asian and Western Writers in*

Dialogue: New Cultural Identities. Ed. Guy Amirthanayagam. London: Macmillan, 1982.

"Duck Boy." *New York Times Magazine* (12 June 1977): 54–55.

"Literature for a Scientific Age: Lorenz' King Solomon's Ring." *English Journal* 62 (January 1973): 30–32.

"The Making of More Americans." *New Yorker* 55 (11 February 1980): 34–42.

"The Novel's Next Step." *Mother Jones* (December 1989): 37–41.

"On Understanding Men." *Hawaii Review* 7 (1977). 43–44.

"Reservations about China." *Ms.* 7 (October 1978): 67–68.

"Rupert Garcia: Dancing Between Realms." *Mother Jones* (October 1988): 32–35.

"San Francisco's Chinatown." *American Heritage* 30 (December 1978): 36–47.

"A Writer's Notebook from the Far East." *Ms.* 11 (January 1983): 85–86.

WORKS ABOUT MAXINE HONG KINGSTON

Biographical Information

Alderson, Jill, Lindsy Martin, and Angela Manassero. "Maxine Hong Kingston: A Brief Biography." www.geocities.com/Athens/Delphi/2979/kingston.html.

Chan, Jeffery Paul. "Jeff Chan, Chairman of San Francisco State Asian American Studies, Attacks Review." *San Francisco Journal* 4 (May 1977): 6.

Chan, Mimi, and Roy Harris. *Asian Voices in English.* Hong Kong: Hong Kong UP, 1991.

Cliff, Michele. "The Making of Americans: Maxine Hong Kingston's Crossover Dreams." *Village Voice Literary Supplement* 74 (May 1989): 11–13.

Currier, Susan. "Maxine Hong Kingston." *Dictionary of Literary Biography Yearbook,* 1980. Detroit, MI: Gale Research, 1981. 235–41.

Duke, Michael S., ed. *Modern Chinese Women Writers: Critical Appraisals.* Armonk, NY: Sharpe, 1989.

Iwata, Edward. "Word Warriors." *Los Angeles Times* 24 June 1990, 4.

"Kingston, Maxine (Ting Ting) Hong." *Contemporary Authors: New Revision Series,* Vol. 13. 289–94.

Kubota, Gary. "Maxine Hong Kingston: Something Comes Outside onto the Paper." *Hawaii Observer* 28 July 1977, 27–28.

Mandelbaum, Paul. "Rising from the Ashes: A Profile of Maxine Hong Kingston." *Poets and Writers* 26.3 (1998): 46–53.

Morey, Janet Nomura, and Wendy Dunn. *Famous Asian Americans.* New York: Dutton, 1992.

Simmons, Diane. *Maxine Hong Kingston.* New York: Twayne Publishers, 1999.

Smith, Joan. "Creating Peace Out of Pathos." *San Francisco Examiner* (29 October 1991): B1, B4.

Talbot, Stephen. "Talking Story: Maxine Hong Kingston Rewrites the American Dream." *Image: The San Francisco Examiner* (24 June 1990): 6–17.

Who's Who in America, 1997. New Providence, NJ: Marquis Who's Who, 1996. 2312.

Interviews

Blauvelt, William Satake. "Talking with the Woman Warrior." *Conversations with Maxine Hong Kingston*. Ed. Paul Skenazy and Tera Martin. Jackson: UP of Mississippi, 1998. 77–85.

Bonetti, Kay. "An Interview with Maxine Hong Kingston." Audiocassette. Columbia, MO: The American Audio Prose Library, 1986.

Brownmiller, Susan. "Susan Brownmiller Talks with Maxine Hong Kingston." *Mademoiselle* (March 1977): 148–49, 210–11, 214–26.

Carabi, Angeles. "Special Eyes: The Chinese-American World of Maxine Hong Kingston." *Belles Lettres Interview* (Winter 1989): 10–11.

Chin, Marilyn. "A *Melus* Interview: Maxine Hong Kingston." *MELUS* 16.4 (Winter 1989–90): 57–74.

Fishkin, Shelley Fisher. "Interview with Maxine Hong Kingston." *American Literary History* 3.4 (Winter 1991): 782–91.

Hoy, Jody. "To Be Able to See the Tao." *Conversations with Maxine Hong Kingston*. Ed. Paul Skenazy and Tera Martin. Jackson: UP of Mississippi, 1998. 46–66.

Islas, Arturo. "Maxine Hong Kingston." *Women Writers of the West Coast: Speaking of Their Lives and Careers*. Ed. Marilyn Yalom. Santa Barbara, CA: Capra, 1983. Extended version printed in *Conversations with Maxine Hong Kingston*. Ed. Paul Skenazy and Tera Martin. Jackson: UP of Mississippi, 1998. 21–32.

Janette, Michele. "The Angle We're Joined At: A Conversation with Maxine Hong Kingston." *Transition* (Spring 1997).

Perry, Donna, ed. "Maxine Hong Kingston." *Backtalk: Women Writers Speak Out*. New Brunswick, NJ: Rutgers UP, 1993.

Pfaff, Timothy. "Talk with Mrs. Kingston." *New York Times Book Review* (15 June 1980): 1, 24–26.

Rabinowitz, Paula. "Eccentric Memories: A Conversation with Maxine Hong Kingston." *Michigan Quarterly Review* 26.1 (Winter 1987): 177–87.

Robertson, Nan. " 'Ghosts' of Girlhood Lift Obscure Book to Peak of Acclaim." *New York Times* 12 February 1977.

Ross, Jean W. "Interview." *Contemporary Authors: New Revision Series*, Vol. 13, 1983. 289–94.

Schroeder, Eric. "As Truthful as Possible: An Interview with Maxine Hong Kingston." *Writing on the Edge* 7.2 (Spring 1996): 83–96.

Seshachari, Neila C. "An Interview with Maxine Hong Kingston." *Weber Studies: An Interdisciplinary Humanities Journal* 12.1 (Winter 1995): 7–26.

Skenazy, Paul. "Coming Home." *Conversations with Maxine Hong Kingston.* Ed. Paul Skenazy and Tera Martin. Jackson: UP of Mississippi, 1998. 104–17.

——. "Kingston at the University." *Conversations with Maxine Hong Kingston.* Ed. Paul Skenazy and Tera Martin. Jackson: UP of Mississippi, 1998. 118–58.

Thompson, Phyllis Hoge. "This Is the Story I Heard: A Conversation with Maxine Hong Kingston and Earll Kingston." *Biography: An Interdisciplinary Quarterly* 6.1 (Winter 1983): 1–12.

Vitale, Tom. "Maxine Hong Kingston Reads from *Tripmaster Monkey: His Fake Book* and Talks about Psychedelic Experience of Theatre and Life in the 1960's." Audiocassette. *A Moveable Feast* No. 207. Columbia, MO: The American Audio Prose Library, 1989.

REVIEWS AND CRITICISM

The Woman Warrior

Begum, Khani. "Confirming the Place of 'The Other': Gender and Ethnic Identity in Maxine Hong Kingston's *The Woman Warrior*." *New Perspectives on Women and Comedy.* Ed. Regina Barreca. Philadelphia: Gordon and Breach, 1992.

Blackburn, Sara. "Notes of a Chinese Daughter." *Ms.* (January 1977): 39.

Cheung, King-Kok. " 'Don't Tell': Imposed Silences in *The Color Purple* and *The Woman Warrior*." *PMLA* 103.2 (March 1988): 162–74.

Chu, Patricia P. " 'The Invisible World the Immigrants Built': Cultural Self-Inscription and the Anti-Romantic Plots of *The Woman Warrior*." *Diaspora: A Journal of Transnational Studies* 2.1 (Spring 1992): 95–115.

Chun, Gloria. "The High Note of the Barbarian Reed Pipe: Maxine Hong Kingston." *Journal of Ethnic Studies* 19.3 (Fall 1991): 85–94.

Fifer, Elizabeth. "Review of *The Woman Warrior*." *International Fiction Review* (January 1978): 69.

Fong, Bobby. "Maxine Hong Kingston's Autobiographical Strategy in *The Woman Warrior*." *Biography: An Interdisciplinary Quarterly* 12.2 (Spring 1989): 116–26.

Frye, Joanne S. "*The Woman Warrior*: Claiming Narrative Power, Re-creating Female Selfhood." *Faith of a (Woman) Writer.* Ed. Alice Kessler Harris and William McBrien. Westport, CT: Greenwood, 1988.

Garner, Shirley Nelson. "Breaking Silence: *The Woman Warrior*." *The Intimate Critique: Autobiographical Literary Criticism.* Ed. Diane P. Freedman, Olivia Frey, and Frances Murphy Zauhar. Durham, NC: Duke UP, 1993.

Goldman, Marlene. "Naming the Unspeakable: The Mapping of Female Identity in Maxine Hong Kingston's *The Woman Warrior*." *International Women's*

Writing: New Landscapes of Identity. Ed. Anne E. Brown and Marjanne Gooze. Westport, CT: Greenwood, 1995.

Gray, Paul. "Book of Changes." *Time* (6 December 1976): 91.

Greenspan, Miriam. "slj/Adult Books for Young Adults." *School Library Journal* (January 1977): 108.

Homsher, Deborah. "*The Woman Warrior*, by Maxine Hong Kingston: A Bridging of Autobiography and Fiction." *The Iowa Review* 10.4 (1979): 93–98.

Hunt, Linda. " 'I could not figure out what was my village': Gender vs. Ethnicity in Maxine Hong Kingston's *The Woman Warrior.*" *MELUS* 12.3 (Fall 1985): 5–12.

Johnson, Diane. "Ghosts." *New York Review of Books* (3 February 1977): 19–21.

Kramer, Jane. "*The Woman Warrior: Memoirs of a Girlhood Among Ghosts.*" *New York Times Book Review* (7 November 1976): Section 7, 1.

Lappas, Catherine. " 'The Way I Heard It Was . . . ': Myth, Memory, and Autobiography in 'Storyteller' and *The Woman Warrior.*" *CEA Critic* 57.1 (Fall 1994): 57–67.

Leonard, John. "In Defiance of Two Worlds." *New York Times Book Review* (17 September 1976): C21.

Lidoff, Joan. "Autobiography in a Different Voice: Maxine Hong Kingston's *The Woman Warrior.*" *A/B: Auto/Biography Studies* 3.3 (Fall 1987): 29–35.

Lim, Shirley Geok-Lin. "The Tradition of Chinese American Women's Life Stories: Thematics of Race and Gender in Jade Snow Wong's *Fifth Chinese Daughter* and Maxine Hong Kingston's *The Woman Warrior.*" *American Women's Autobiography: Fea(s)ts of Memory*. Ed. Margo Culley. Madison: U of Wisconsin P, 1992. 252–67.

Lim, Shirley Geok-Lin, ed. *Approaches to Teaching Kingston's The Woman Warrior*. New York: MLA, 1991.

———. "Preface." *Approaches to Teaching Kingston's* The Woman Warrior. New York: MLA, 1991.

Ling, Amy. "Thematic Threads in Maxine Hong Kingston's *The Woman Warrior.*" *Tamkang Review* 14, 1–4 (Autumn–Summer 1983–1984): 155–64.

McPherson, William. "Ghosts from the Middle Kingdom." *Book World—The Washington Post* (10 October 1976).

Miller, Margaret. "Threads of Identity in Maxine Hong Kingston's *The Woman Warrior.*" *Biography: An Interdisciplinary Quarterly* 6.1 (Winter 1983): 13–33.

Mitchell, Carol. " 'Talking Story' in *The Woman Warrior*: An Analysis of the Use of Folklore" *Kentucky Folklore Record: A Regional Journal of Folklore and Folklife* 27, 1–2 (January–June 1981): 5–12.

"*Publisher's Weekly* Forecasts." *Publisher's Weekly* (9 August 1976): 72.

Robertson, Nan. " 'Ghosts' of Girlhood Lift Obscure Book to Peak of Acclaim." *New York Times* 12 February 1977, 26.

TuSmith, Bonnie. "Literary Tricksterism: Maxine Hong Kingston's *The Woman Warrior: Memoirs of a Girlhood among Ghosts.*" *Anxious Power: Reading, Writ-*

ing and Ambivalence in Narrative by Women. Ed. Carol J. Singley and Susan Elizabeth Sweeney. Albany: State U of New York P, 1993.

Wang, Veronica. "Reality and Fantasy: The Chinese-American Woman's Quest for Identity." *MELUS* 12.3 (Fall 1985): 23–31.

Wong, Sau-Ling Cynthia. "Autobiography as Guided Chinatown Tour? Maxine Hong Kingston's *The Woman Warrior* and the Chinese-American Autobiographical Controversy." *Multicultural Autobiography: American Lives.* Ed. James Robert Payne. Knoxville: U of Tennessee P, 1992. 248–79.

———. "Necessity and Extravagance in Maxine Hong Kingston's *The Woman Warrior: Art and the Ethnic Experience.*" *MELUS* 15.1 (Spring 1988): 4–26.

China Men

Broner, E. M. "Stunning Sequel to *Woman Warrior.*" *Ms.* (August 1980): 28, 30.

Buckmaster, Henrietta. "China Men Portrayed with Magic." *The Christian Science Monitor* (11 August 1980): B4.

Cheung, King-Kok. "Talk Story: Counter Memory in Maxine Hong Kingston's *China Men.*" *Tamkang Review* 24.1 (Fall 1993): 21–37.

Collins, Anne. "Intoxicating Myths, Fermented Dreams." *MacLean's* (28 July 1980): 48.

Gordon, Mary. "Mythic History." *New York Times Book Review* (15 June 1980): 24–25.

Gray, Paul. "On the Gold Mountain." *Time* (30 June 1980): 26.

Jacoby, Tamar. "*China Men.*" *San Francisco Review of Books* (September 1980): 10–11.

Kaufman, Linda. "*China Men.*" *The Georgia Review* 35 (Spring 1981): 205.

Leonard, John. " 'Books of the Times': *China Men.*" *New York Times* 3 June 1980, C9.

Li, David Leiwei. "*China Men*: Maxine Hong Kingston and the American Canon." *American Literary History* 2.3 (Fall 1990): 482–502.

Neubauer, Carol E. "Developing Ties to the Past: Photography and Other Sources of Information in Maxine Hong Kingston's *China Men.*" *MELUS* 10.4 (Winter 1983): 17–36.

Park, Clara Claiborne. "Ghosts on a Gold Mountain." *The Hudson Review* (Winter 1980): 589–95.

Shih, Shu-mei. "Exile and Intertextuality in Maxine Hong Kingston's *China Men.*" *The Literature of Emigration and Exile.* Ed. James Whitlark and Wendell Aycock. Lubbock, TN: Texas Tech UP, 1992.

Sledge, Linda Ching. "Maxine Kingston's *China Men*: The Family Historian as Epic Poet." *MELUS* 7.4 (1980): 3–22.

———. "Oral Tradition in Kingston's *China Men.*" *Redefining American Literary History.* Ed. A. LaVonne Brown Ruoff and Jerry W. Ward Jr. New York: MLA, 1990. 142–54.

Strouse, Jean. "Dis-oriented Men." *Newsweek* (16 June 1980): 88.

Taliaferro, Frances. "Spirited Relatives." *Harper's* (August 1980): 76–77.

Tyler, Anne. "*China Men.*" *The New Republic* (21 June 1980): 32–34.

Wakeman, Frederic Jr. "Chinese Ghost Story." *New York Review of Books* (14 August 1980): 42–43.

Wu, Qing-yun. "A Chinese Reader's Response to Maxine Hong Kingston's *China Men.*" *MELUS* 17.3 (Fall 1991–1992): 85–94.

Tripmaster Monkey: His Fake Book

Boyer, Gail. "One American's Heavy Load of Chinese Ancestry." *St. Louis Post-Dispatch* (30 April 1989): C5.

Caldwell, Gail. "Playing Fast and Loose with a Playwright." *Boston Globe* (16 April 1989): B51.

Chang, Hsiao-hung. "Gender Crossing in Maxine Hong Kingston's *Tripmaster Monkey.*" *MELUS* 22.1 (Spring 1997): 15–34.

Chu, Patricia P. "*Tripmaster Monkey*, Frank Chin, and the Chinese Heroic Tradition." *Arizona Quarterly* 53.3 (Autumn 1997): 117–39.

Crow, Charles L. "*Tripmaster Monkey: His Fake Book.*" *Western American Literature* 25.1 (1991): 85–86.

Furth, Isabella. "Beee-e-een! Nation and Transformation and the Hyphen of Ethnicity in Kingston's *Tripmaster Monkey.*" *Modern Fiction Studies* 40.1 (Spring 1994): 33–49.

Gerrard, Nicci. "Wittman Ah Sing." *The New Statesman and Society* 2.64 (25 August 1989): 28.

Gold, Herbert. "Far-Out West." *Chicago Tribune—Books* (16 April 1989): 1, 10.

Holt, Patricia. "Monkey Business." *San Francisco Chronicle* 30 April 1989, 1.

Ishihara, Toshi. "Meanings of Translation in Maxine Hong Kingston's *Tripmaster Monkey: His Fake Book.*" *Asian American Librarians Association Journal* 2 (1995): 25–38.

Kakutani, Michiko. "Being of Two Cultures, and Liking and Loathing It." *New York Times* 14 April 1989, C30.

Koss, Nicholas. " 'Will the Real Wittman Ah Sing Please Stand Up': Cultural Identity in *Tripmaster Monkey: His Fake Book.*" *Fu Jen Studies: Literature and Linguistics* 26 (1993): 24–50.

Leonard, John. "Of Thee Ah Sing." *The Nation* (5 June 1989): 768–72.

Li, David Leiwei. "*Tripmaster Monkey: His Fake Book.*" *Amerasia Journal* 15.2 (1989): 220–22.

Loke, Margarett. "The Tao is Up." *New York Times Magazine* (30 April 1989): 28, 50, 52, 55.

Longfellow, Pamela. "Monkey Wrenched." *Ms.* (17 June 1989): 66.

Monsma, Bradley John. " 'Active Readers . . . Observe Tricksters': Trickster-Texts and Cross-Cultural Reading." *Modern Language Studies* 26.4 (Fall 1996): 83–98.

Montgomery, Priscilla. "On Swinging between the Branches of Two Cultures." *Washington Times* (24 April 1989): E7, 9.

Mukherjee, Bharati. "Wittman at the Golden Gate." *Washington Post* 16 April 1989, X1.

Mungo, Ray. "The Adventures of a Hip Tripmaster." *USA Today* (28 April 1989): D6.

Ong, Caroline. "Demons and Warriors." *Times Literary Supplement* (15 September 1989): 998.

Painter, Charlotte. "In Search of a Voice." *San Francisco Review of Books* 14 (Summer 1989): 15–16.

Pollard, D. E. "Much Ado about Identity." *Far Eastern Review* (27 July 1989): 41, 44.

Schreiber, LeAnne. "The Big, Big Show of Wittman Ah Sing." *New York Times Book Review* (23 April 1989): 9.

Smith, Jeanne R. "Rethinking American Culture: Maxine Hong Kingston's Cross-Cultural *Tripmaster Monkey*." *Modern Language Studies* 26.4 (Fall 1996): 71–81.

Tyler, Anne. "Manic Monologue." *The New Republic* 200 (17 April 1989): 44–46.

Vizenor, Gerald. "Postmodern Monkey." *American Book Review* 11 (January 1990): 17, 22.

———. "The Triumph of Monkey Business." *Los Angeles Times Book Review* (23 April 1989): 1, 13.

Whitehouse, Anne. "*Tripmaster Monkey: His Fake Book*: A Transformation in Life and Fiction." *Atlanta Journal Constitution* (7 May 1989): 4.

Wilhelmus, Tom. "Various Pairs." *Hudson Review* 43 (Spring 1990): 147–54.

SECONDARY SOURCES

Asian American Women's Scholarship and Perspectives. Minneapolis, MN: The Center for Advanced Feminist Studies, 1990.

Chan, Jeffery Paul, Frank Chin, Lawson Fusao Inada, and Shawn Wong. *The Big Aiiieeeee!: An Anthology of Chinese American and Japanese American Literature*. New York: Meridian, 1991.

Chen, Victoria. "Chinese American Women, Language and Moving Subjectivity." *Women and Language* 18.1 (Spring 1995): 3–7.

Cheung, King-Kok. *Articulate Silences: Hisaye Yamamoto, Maxine Hong Kingston, Joy Kogawa*. Ithaca, NY: Cornell UP, 1993.

———. "The Woman Warrior Versus The Chinaman Pacific: Must a Chinese American Critic Choose between Feminism and Heroism?" *Conflicts in Feminism*. Ed. Marianne Hirsch and Evelyn Fox Keller. New York: Routledge, 1990.

————. *An Interethnic Companion to Asian American Literature.* Cambridge: Cambridge UP, 1996.

Cheung, King-Kok, and Stan Yogi. *Asian American Literature: An Annotated Bibliography.* New York: MLA, 1988.

Chin, Frank. *Aiiieeeee!: An Anthology of Asian American Writers.* Washington, DC: Howard UP, 1974.

————. "Come All Ye Asian Writers of the Real and the Fake." *The Big Aiiieeeee!: An Anthology of Chinese American and Japanese American Literature.* Ed. Jeffery Paul Chan, Frank Chin, Lawson Fusao Inada, and Shawn Wong. New York: Meridian, 1991. 1–92.

Chin, Frank, and Jeffery Paul Chan. "Racist Love." *Seeing through Shuck.* Ed. Richard Kostelanetz. New York: Ballantine, 1972. 65–79.

Chin, Yang Lee. *The Flower Drum Song.* New York: Gollancz, 1957.

Chua, Cheng Lok. "Golden Mountain: Chinese Versions of the American Dream in Lin Yutang, Louis Chu, and Maxine Hong Kingston." *Ethnic Groups* 4, 1–2 (1982): 33–59.

Condit, Ira M. *The Chinaman as We See Him.* Chicago: Revell, 1900.

Donovan, Josephine, ed. *Feminist Literary Criticism: Explorations in Theory.* Lexington: UP of Kentucky, 1989.

Eakin, Paul John. *Fictions in Autobiography: Studies in the Art of Self-Invention.* Princeton: Princeton UP, 1985.

Fessler, Loren W. *Chinese in America, Stereotyped Past, Changing Present.* New York: Vantage Press, 1983.

Frankel, Hans. "Cai Yan and the Poems Attributed to Her." *Chinese Literary Essays and Reviews* 5.2 (1985): 133–56.

Gao, Yan. *The Art of Parody: Maxine Hong Kingston's Use of Chinese Sources.* New York: Peter Lang, 1996.

Gentry, Curt. *Madames of San Francisco.* New York: Doubleday, 1964.

Hall, Linda B. "Internal Wars of a Chinese-American Woman." *Southwest Review* (Spring 1978): 190–91.

Henke, Suzette A. "Women's Life-Writing and the Minority Voice: Maya Angelou, Maxine Hong Kingston, and Alice Walker." *Traditions, Voices and Dreams: The American Novel Since the 1960s.* Ed. Melvin J. Friedman and Ben Siegel. Newark: U of Delaware P, 1995. 210–33.

Hongo, Garrett. "Introduction: Culture Wars in America." *Under Western Eyes: Personal Essays from Asian America.* Ed. Garrett Hongo. New York: Anchor Books/Doubleday, 1995. 1–33.

Hsu, Kai-yu and Helen Palubinskas. *Asian-American Authors.* Boston: Houghton-Mifflin Co., 1972.

Hune, Shirley, Hyung-chan Kim, Stephen S. Fujita, and Amy Ling. *Asian Americans: Comparative and Global Perspectives.* Pullman: Washington State UP, 1991.

Juhasz, Suzanne. "Maxine Hong Kingston: Narrative Technique and Female

Identity." *Contemporary American Women Writers: Narrative Strategies*. Ed. Catherine Rainwater and William Scheick. Lexington: UP of Kentucky, 1985.

Kim, Elaine. *Asian American Literature: An Introduction to the Writings and their Social Context*. Philadelphia: Temple UP. 1982.

Kim, Elaine H. "Such Opposite Creatures: Men and Women in Asian American Literature." *Michigan Quarterly Review* 29.1 (Winter 1990): 68–93.

Lai, Him Mark, Genny Lim, and Judy Yung. *Island: Poetry and History of Chinese Immigrants on Angel Island, 1910–1940*. San Francisco: HOC DOI Project, Chinese Culture Foundation of San Francisco, 1980. Seattle: U of Washington P, 1991.

Leitch, Vincent. *Cultural Criticism, Literary Theory, Poststructuralism*. New York: Columbia UP, 1992.

Li, Marjorie H., and Peter Li. *Understanding Asian Americans*. New York: Neal-Schuman Publishers, 1990.

Lim, Shirley Geok-Lin, Amy Ling, and Elaine Kim. *Reading the Literatures of Asian America*. Philadelphia: Temple UP, 1992.

Ling, Amy. "Maxine Hong Kingston and the Dialogic Dilemma of Asian American Writers." *Bucknell Review* 39.1 (1995): 151–66.

Ling, Huping. *Surviving on the Gold Mountain: A History of Chinese Women and Their Lives*. Albany: State University of New York P, 1998.

Madden, Janet, and Sara M. Blake. *Emerging Voices: A Cross-Cultural Reading*. Fort Worth, TX: Holt, Rinehart, and Winston, 1990.

Maitino, John R., and David R. Peck, eds. *Teaching American Ethnic Literatures*. Albuquerque: U of New Mexico P, 1996.

McDonald, Dorothy Ritsuko. "Introduction to Frank Chin's *The Chicken Coop Chinaman and the Year of the Dragon*." *Three American Literatures*. Ed. Houston A. Baker, Jr. New York: MLA, 1982.

Morante, Linda. "From Silence to Song: The Triumph of Maxine Hong Kingston." *Frontiers: A Journal of Women's Studies* 9.2 (1987): 78–82.

Nachmanovitch, Stephen. *Free Play: The Power of Improvisation in Life and the Arts*. New York: G. P. Putnam's Sons, 1990.

Nelson, Cary, Paula A. Treichler, and Lawrence Grossberg. "Cultural Studies: An Introduction." *Cultural Studies*. Ed. Lawrence Grossberg, Cary Nelson, and Paula A. Treichler. London: Routledge, 1992.

Nishime, LeiLani. "Engendering Genre: Gender and Nationalism in *China Men* and *The Woman Warrior*." *MELUS* 20.1 (Spring 1995): 67–82.

Pratt, Mary Louise. *Imperial Eyes: Travel Writing and Transculturation*. London and New York: Routledge, 1992.

San Juan, E., Jr. "Beyond Identity Politics: The Predicament of the Asian Writer in Late Capitalism." *American Literary History* 3.3 (Fall 1991): 542–65.

Schmidt, Jan Klotnik. "The Other: A Study of the Persona in Several Contemporary Women's Autobiographies." *CEA Critic* 43.1 (1980): 24–31.

Skandera-Trombley, Laura. *Critical Essays on Maxine Hong Kingston*. New York: G. K. Hall, 1998.

Sui Sin Far. "Leaves from the Mental Portfolio of an Eurasian." *Independent* 66 (1909): 125–232.

———. *Mrs. Spring Fragrance and Other Writings*. Ed. Amy Ling and Annette White Parks. Urbana, IL: U of Illinois P, 1995.

Tong, Benjamin. "Chinatown Popular Culture: Notes toward a Critical Psychological Anthropology." *The Chinese American Experience: Papers from the Second National Conference on Chinese American Studies 1980)*. Ed. Genny Lim. San Francisco: Chinese Historical Society of American and Chinese Culture Foundation, 1984.

———. "Critic of Admirer Sees Dumb Racist." *San Francisco Journal* 11 (May 1977): 6.

Wand, David Hsin-fu. *Asian American Heritage: An Anthology of Prose and Poetry*. New York: Washington Square Press, Pocket Books, 1974.

Wang, Alfred S. "Maxine Hong Kingston's Reclaiming of America: The Birthright of the Chinese-American Male." *South Dakota Review* 26.1 (Spring 1988): 18–29.

Wang, Qun. " 'Double Consciousness,' Sociological Imagination, and the Asian American Experience." *Race, Gender, and Class* 4.3 (1997): 88–94.

Whitman, Walt. "Song of Myself." *Leaves of Grass*. Ed. Harold W. Blodgett and Scully Bradley. New York: New York UP, 1965 (originally published 1855). 28–89.

Wiget, Andrew. "His Life in His Tail: The Native American Trickster and the Literature of Possibility." *Redefining American Literary History*. Ed. LaVonne Ruoff and Jerry W. Ward, Jr. New York: MLA, 1990. 83–96.

Williams, Raymond. *Keywords*. London: Fontana, 1976.

Wong, Jade Snow. *Fifth Chinese Daughter*. Seattle and London: U of Washington P, 1989. New York: Harper and Row, 1945.

Wong, Sau-Ling Cynthia. *Maxine Hong Kingston's* The Woman Warrior: A Casebook. New York: Oxford UP, 1999.

Wong, Shawn. *Asian American Literature: A Brief Introduction and Anthology*. New York: Longman, 1996.

Yung, Judy. *Chinese Women in America: A Pictorial History*. Seattle: Published for the Chinese Culture Foundation of San Francisco by the U of Washington P, 1986.

Index

About the Author

E. D. HUNTLEY is Associate Dean for Graduate Studies at Appalachian State University in Boone, North Carolina. She is author of two previous volumes in the series, *V. C. Andrews: A Critical Companion* (Greenwood 1996) and *Amy Tan: A Critical Companion* (Greenwood 1998). Huntley has begun working on a study of gastronomy and detective fiction.

Critical Companions to Popular Contemporary Writers
First Series—*also available on CD-ROM*

V. C. Andrews
  by E. D. Huntley
Tom Clancy
  by Helen S. Garson
Mary Higgins Clark
  by Linda C. Pelzer
Arthur C. Clarke
  by Robin Anne Reid
James Clavell
  by Gina Macdonald
Pat Conroy
  by Landon C. Burns
Robin Cook
  by Lorena Laura Stookey
Michael Crichton
  by Elizabeth A. Trembley
Howard Fast
  by Andrew Macdonald
Ken Follett
  by Richard C. Turner
John Grisham
  by Mary Beth Pringle
James Herriot
  by Michael J. Rossi
Tony Hillerman
  by John M. Reilly

John Jakes
  by Mary Ellen Jones
Stephen King
  by Sharon A. Russell
Dean Koontz
  by Joan G. Kotker
Robert Ludlum
  by Gina Macdonald
Anne McCaffrey
  by Robin Roberts
Colleen McCullough
  by Mary Jean DeMarr
James A. Michener
  by Marilyn S. Severson
Anne Rice
  by Jennifer Smith
Tom Robbins
  by Catherine E. Hoyser and Lorena Laura Stookey
John Saul
  by Paul Bail
Erich Segal
  by Linda C. Pelzer
Gore Vidal
  by Susan Baker and Curtis S. Gibson